GENERAL WILSON'S JOURNAL

SIR ROBERT WILSON

*Engraving in the National Portrait Gallery by William
Ward, after the painting by H. W. Pickersgill*

GENERAL WILSON'S JOURNAL
1812–1814

Edited by
ANTONY BRETT-JAMES

WILLIAM KIMBER
46 WILTON PLACE, LONDON, S.W.1

This edition published in 1964 by
WILLIAM KIMBER AND CO. LIMITED
46 Wilton Place, London, S.W.1

© William Kimber and Co. Limited 1964

MADE AND PRINTED IN GREAT BRITAIN BY PURNELL AND SONS, LTD.
PAULTON (SOMERSET) AND LONDON

INTRODUCTION

An autobiographical fragment written for his children by Sir Robert Wilson contains this sentence: "I have taken as large a part as any man in the affairs of the world in my time; I have seen more of it, been more acquainted with its rulers and distinguished and remarkable men, had more opportunity of being intimate with every class of society from the highest to the lowest, than perhaps has fallen to the lot of any other individual."

Born in 1777 the son of a well-known portrait painter whose electrical researches led to his election to a Fellowship of the Royal Society, Robert Thomas Wilson was educated at Westminster and Winchester before enrolling as a cornet in the 15th Light Dragoons. He served under the Duke of York in the Flanders campaign of 1794 and took part in several sharp engagements, one of which had a rare and influential outcome. On April 24th Wilson's squadron was part of a force which, by routing a very superior French formation at Villiers-en-Couché, prevented the capture of the Austrian Emperor, Francis II. Wilson and seven other officers received special gold medals for their part in this hazardous and gallant charge, and, some time later, the Cross of the Order of Maria Theresa, with the rank of Baron of the Holy Roman Empire and Knight attached.

He accompanied Abercromby's expedition to the Helder, where, in 1799, the 15th Light Dragoons fought with distinction at Egmont-op-Zee, and two years later went with Hompesch's Hussars to Egypt. Of this latter campaign he wrote a history which became widely known, went through several editions, was translated into French, and earned for Wilson the nickname 'Jaffa,' because in the book he accused Napoleon of cruelty towards prisoners and of murdering the sick and wounded of his own army in that town. During his last voyage, and on St. Helena, the defeated Emperor, who at the time of publication had complained without success to the British Government, frequently enquired about Wilson's standing, in particular from William Warden, surgeon on board H.M.S. *Northumberland*.

5

He was obviously still worried by Wilson's former accusations, and sharply denied them.

In 1805, in command of the 20th Light Dragoons, Wilson sailed with Sir David Baird's force via Brazil to the Cape of Good Hope, which was taken from the Dutch early in the following year. On returning to England he joined Lord Hutchinson on a special mission to the Court of Prussia. They accompanied the King to Memel, and then Wilson transferred to the Russian Headquarters, taking part with gallantry in the great battles of Eylau, in February 1807, and later of Friedland. After the Peace of Tilsit he was sent by Canning on several important missions to St. Petersburg. His zeal and activity, coupled with his skill at stealing a march or a boat journey on rival couriers, earned him many compliments. As early as 1800 Wilson had travelled to Vienna on a special mission to our ambassador there, who had sent him on to communicate with the Austrian army in north Italy before sailing to Egypt to join Abercromby: and such assignments were, with few exceptions, to occupy the greatest part of Sir Robert's subsequent career, usually spent with Allied Headquarters fighting Napoleon across Europe, and to bring him much praise and reward.

The year 1808 saw him with the rank of brigadier-general in the Portuguese Army, raising and commanding the Lusitanian Legion in Oporto. Of his 3,000 recruits he could arm and equip only half before he left Oporto to avoid becoming involved in local factions, feuds and intrigues between the Bishop and the Regency. After the retreat and evacuation of Sir John Moore's army in January 1809, Wilson posted his Legion along the Portuguese-Spanish frontier to observe a French division which had been ordered to capture the fortresses of Almeida and Ciudad Rodrigo and then advance into Portugal—an excessive task for the enemy with the force at their disposal, involving as it did a march of 200 miles through mountainous country. But the French commander, with too much to do, did far too little, and allowed himself to be contained by a force which, though small, was commanded by a man having just the enterprise and energy he lacked. Reinforced by some Spanish troops, by stragglers from Moore's retreat, and by Portuguese volunteers, Wilson and the Lusitanian Legion were almost alone in guarding Portugal's eastern borders. By audacity and resourceful leadership he kept the French at a distance for months on end. He ignored timid advice from the British commander in Lisbon to withdraw, probably for evacuation. He carried on a form of partisan warfare, capturing large enemy convoys,

6

enticing the French to desert, spreading false reports of his strength until the French believed peasants who declared that Wilson had 12,000 men when in fact he had barely 3,000. His example influenced the Spanish generals as well as rousing a spirit of resistance among the inhabitants, whose confidence he quickly gained. One of Wilson's staff officers, Benjamin D'Urban, writes frequently in his diary of Wilson's success. On March 14th, for example: "His activity, his gallantry, and that of the British officers with him have once more done wonders." And a year later he was to write: "The French ramble about more at their ease now in front of the whole British Army, than they either did, or dared to do, last year, when nothing overlooked them but Wilson and 600 men."

His Legion helped in the pursuit of Marshal Soult after the recapture of Oporto, but once the battle of Talavera had been fought and Wellington then found himself obliged to retire to Portugal because of a breakdown in supplies, Wilson was cut off by the French and he and his men had great difficulty in scrambling over the mountains. Even though outnumbered and closely pursued, he fought a running fight for nine hours to hold off Marshal Ney, and had to be driven off three positions in turn—a rash and needless action, no doubt, and he held on too long, but he did make the French fight hard and expensively before he continued his hazardous march across the mountains to safety.

It was perhaps inevitable that, when the Legion was incorporated in the newly organised Portuguese Army, Wilson should quarrel with the organiser, Marshal Beresford, who was in any case a difficult man to deal with. Argument and friction led to sharp disputes, so Wilson went home at the end of 1809 and offered himself for special service. He was kept waiting for an unduly long period, but busied himself in the meanwhile by writing another book entitled *Brief Remarks on the Character and Composition of the Russian Army, and a Sketch of the Campaign in Poland in 1806 and 1807*.

At last his offer of service was accepted, and on March 26th 1812, with the local rank of brigadier-general in the British Army, he travelled to Constantinople with Mr. Robert Liston, the newly appointed ambassador to the Sublime Porte of the Ottoman Empire. The next twenty months of Wilson's career are covered in the present volume.

Wilson was in Paris after the second restoration of Louis XVIII, and on January 10th, 1816, he helped Michael Bruce (Lady Hester Stanhope's lover) and Captain John Hely-Hutchinson of the 1st Foot Guards to get Count Lavallette out of the French capital.

7

Napoleon's former Director of Posts had been condemned to death for high treason, but his wife, not unlike Lady Nithsdale a century before, had entered the Conciergerie Prison and exchanged dress, so enabling the Count to slip away. He went into hiding but had still to escape from Paris. It was Wilson's task to drive Lavallette, now disguised as a British officer and ostensibly on a mission for the Duke of Wellington to Munich and Vienna, past the Clichy barrier and on to Mons. This was accomplished safely in Wilson's cabriolet, with Hutchinson riding beside them. The gendarmes had a description of Lavallette, who was in any case well known, and at several points on the route appeared suspicious. When some grey hairs protruded from under the Count's brown wig, Wilson took a pair of scissors and deftly trimmed them; and at one particularly thorough inspection of passports he acted the part of an indignant British General with helpful effect.

Sir Robert was imprudent enough to send an account of this exploit in knight-errantry to his old friend Earl Grey, and the letter was intercepted by the authorities. The three rescuers were arrested, tried in Paris, and on April 24th sentenced to three months in prison, the shortest allowable term for the offences under the relevant article of the French penal code. At the trial Wilson appeared in full uniform, decorated with all his European orders, and produced a strong impression on all present by his speech, in which he said: "Perhaps we were imprudent, but we would rather incur that reproach than the one we should have merited by basely abandoning him, who, full of confidence, threw himself into our arms."

Wilson and Hely-Hutchinson, being officers, were rebuked in a general order issued by the Duke of York in his capacity as Commander-in-Chief, expressing the Prince Regent's grave displeasure at their conduct. Two years later Wilson entered active politics, was returned as Member of Parliament for Southwark, and held the seat for thirteen years through another three elections. His maiden speech, early in 1819, was a failure—described by Henry Edward Fox, afterwards Lord Holland, as "a bad subject in bad hands." Holland wrote in his journal for December 15th, 1820, when Sir Robert called to see him and told some "incredible stories of his battles with serpents in the East": "It is a pity that Walter Scott does not know him, for with a tartan and claymore he would make an admirable character for one of the novels; though his wild, enthusiastic, romantic, chivalrous notions would be considered as out of real life and exaggerated. There is something about him, especially since the story of Lavallette, that makes it impossible to see and hear him without having an admiration for his high spirit and enterprize, and at the same time great contempt for his understanding and judgment."

Wilson was soon in trouble again, calling down upon himself the displeasure of the Prince Regent, now King George IV. At the death of Queen Caroline in August 1821, Sir Robert, who felt indebted for past kindnesses and whose eldest son was her equerry, accompanied the funeral *cortège*. Near Hyde Park a clash occurred between the Household Cavalry and the crowd, and when shots were fired and two men killed, he intervened to prevent further bloodshed. A month later, without official explanation, without trial or an opportunity for self-defence, even without accusation, though he was alleged to have addressed the troops, not through their officers, and urged them to disobey their orders, Major-General Sir Robert Wilson was dismissed from the Army and deprived of his honours. Admiral Lord Cochrane, who was himself ill-used by the Government, wrote in his autobiography forty years later, as Earl of Dundonald: "The act of his dismissal was one of pure despotism, committed by a ministerial faction"; and he referred to political adversaries and a clique who, with unscrupulous hatred, had persecuted Wilson and himself.

Not until William IV's accession in 1830 was Wilson reinstated, and then granted promotion to lieutenant-general, with seniority back-dated five years. In 1842, by now a full general and colonel of his old regiment—the name had been changed from 15th Light Dragoons to 15th Hussars—Wilson was appointed Governor of Gibraltar, where he remained until 1849. Very shortly after returning to London he died suddenly on May 9th in a Cavendish Square hotel, aged seventy-one. He was buried in Westminster Abbey beside his wife Jemima, whom he had married in 1797 and who had died as early as 1823.

. . . . .

Sir Robert liked a fight as well as most men, so much so, in fact, that the Duke of Cumberland assured a Russian officer: "I will answer for him never being out of an action if within possible reach!" He never held back, believing as he did that "every bullet has its billet." For a man who always wanted to see for himself, and yet was shortsighted,[1] the front line was often the right place, and on

---

[1]As early as December 1806 he had written home: "Do not, I beseech you, forget my telescope. My eyes are not as good as they were, and I should not like to gallop by mistake into the midst of a French troop."

9

more than one occasion his presence had great and salutary effects. Though unwilling to trifle life or liberty on some petty service, he thought it incumbent upon him to acquire information sometimes with a degree of hazard, and his propensity for becoming involved in close-fought encounters was well-known and brought down affectionate reproof, not least from Downing Street. In 1814 a Foreign Office friend wrote to inform Wilson that Lord Castlereagh expected "he shall only hear from you or of you as accompanying or reporting the movements of our Allies; and neither breaking your head against stone walls for an additional riband or a *crachat* [Star, or Grand Cross, of an Order] *de plus*, nor sacrificing your comfort and credit at home by being the *enfant gâté* of Princes and Maréchaux de l'Empire abroad."

There was the rub. Sir Robert Wilson, Knight Commander of the Imperial Military Order of Maria Theresa, Knight Commander of the Imperial Military Order of St. George of Russia, Baron of Austria and of the Holy Roman Empire, Knight Grand Cross of the Order of St. Anne of Russia, Knight Grand Cross of the Order of the Red Eagle of Prussia, Knight Commander of the Royal Military Order of the Tower and Sword of Portugal, Knight Commander of the Order of the Crescent of Turkey, Knight Commander of the Order of Merit of Saxony, never received a British decoration.

Just before he was transferred to northern Italy at the beginning of 1814, Wilson received several high foreign orders, and wrote in his diary: "Government may consider these favours as an additional evidence of my being '*un enfant gâté*,' but all here know that I have not acquired them without connecting the honour of my country. I owe nothing to a crooking knee or a false tongue—nothing to any conduct which can stain hereafter."

Outside England his orders were an open sesame. When he went ashore from the Dardanelles in 1812, the local Aga almost cried to see Sir Robert's Turkish medal with the inscription 'Sultan Selim,' a former ruler. Queen Maria Carolina of the Two Sicilies, when he was received by her near Palermo that same year, observed his Cross of Maria Theresa, at once alluded to her connection with that sovereign, her mother, and then burst into tears, whereupon King Ferdinand came into the room and greeted Wilson with 'flattering cordiality.'

But at home his virtues were far less appreciated, and the defects of his qualities weighed more heavily in high places. It was bad enough being a Whig. Even so eminent and respected a figure as Sir John Moore had been the target of squalid intrigue in military and especially in ministerial circles. Wilson did dabble in Whig politics, long before he entered the House of Commons, and was known to correspond with leaders like Charles, 2nd Earl Grey; but for certain senior and responsible diplomats to assume from this fact that he would, if entrusted with any political business while on a foreign mission, act as 'a spy of the Opposition' and should therefore be allowed no further intercourse with the Foreign Office was a most unfair exaggeration. He was not a favourite of Lord Castlereagh, a circumstance which could not fail to weaken his chances of promotion or reward.

Then his propensity for using his initiative, for disobedience of military orders, for independent action, however justified, however brilliant and successful the outcome, skilful as the planning and execution might be, scarcely commended itself to his superiors in rank, and more than once in the Peninsula Sir Robert found himself in trouble.

Men might dislike his uncompromising outspokenness, which, though most acceptable to the Czar or to the Duke of Gloucester, nephew to George II, could also give offence. That he realised the disadvantages to his own career of such candour is shown by something he wrote for the benefit of his children: "Guile has never been any part of my character. What I have thought right I have always avowed and done, to the great prejudice of my fortune but not to the reproach of my name. . . . I might and must have been richer and more prosperous if I had regulated this innate contempt of worldly prudence by considerations of self-interest: but perhaps under their influence I should have relaxed those energies which obtained for me the regard which I possess."

Men might criticise his vanity. In 1810 Major William Warre wrote home from Portugal: "He can never want a trumpeter while he lives, and no man better knows the *art de se faire valoir*"—a slightly acid comment to which Warre then added more tolerantly: "He is a very good fellow as a companion, and a very able light troop officer, and if he would not attempt to be more than he really is, would be more respected." Wilson was well aware of the risk of being considered vain, not least when it came to writing books; and in his *History of the British Expedition to Egypt* he declared: "Certainly the charge of vanity may be prepared against me for appointing myself to a post of so much difficulty and danger; but my excuse rests with the apathy shown by others, whose talents capacitated them more fully for the duty."

Sir Robert's vanity was, more often than not, a genuine pride in sound achievement, for he relished "the consciousness of having been a disinterested, zealous and useful public servant," and he was gratified and touched alike by the affectionate esteem of a Russian soldier or a Cossack commander, the cordiality and confidence of one Allied general after another, and the personal and written testimonies of emperor, king, prince and duke.

Reviewers of his books might feel impelled, as did an anonymous critic in the *Royal Military Chronicle* of 1811, to add to an otherwise laudatory notice some references to a want of prudence and sobriety, a sometimes florid and turgid style, and "the production of an able but intemperate mind." This reviewer continued with, on the whole, perceptive words: "The book is the exact picture of the man. It is full of vigorous feeling, strong painting, and extravagant combinations—deficient in taste—deficient in correctness (both of assertion and reasoning), but never deficient in vigour, and good and honourable intentions." As if these sentiments sounded too harsh a note, the editor of the same journal hastened to assert that "Sir Robert Wilson has effected for the army what Sir Sidney Smith has effected towards the navy, has introduced into it a chivalrous spirit and a knightly gallantry, and associated with it the character of a scholar and a gentleman."

Men might dislike or reject his sometimes wild and 'exaggerated' talk, though much of it reflected Wilson's sudden enthusiasms, impetuous and ardent partisanship, fiery spirit and exceptional energy. They often questioned his judgment, as, for example, Mr. George Jackson, a diplomat who accompanied Sir Charles Stewart to Germany as Secretary of Legation. He wrote sarcastically on February 1st, 1813: "Sir R. Wilson writes that he hopes, but almost doubts, that the Russians will push on to the Vistula. If *he* doubts, little can be left for more reflecting persons and for cooler thinkers to hope for."

However, his endurance, zeal and industry were not to be denied. He toiled conscientiously at his reports, despatches and memoranda. He worked hard at languages. In July 1807 he was kept awake one night until two a.m. by the Cossack leader Platow giving "comical instructions in the Russian language." He did not neglect the cultivation of friendships, for he soon realised that "private friendships contribute to the execution of my duty." But such was his ease of manner, his spontaneous emotional warmth and sympathy, that his friendships took root and flourished without cultivation. Moreover, his watchful diplomacy often found opportunities for reconciling harmful antagonisms. He realised in 1812 that the English were held in high esteem, and he did his utmost to increase that foreign regard for the English character. "Woe to him who trespasses to the prejudice of his country!" he wrote in the following year. "Shame to him who does not augment the fund upon which he drew when a stranger and unknown!"

Having seen how wealthy Russian noblemen readily exchanged palace luxury for the rigours of campaigning, he would in any case have been prepared to live as hard as he worked at the front or at Headquarters. "I have not slept on a bed or even straw for a hundred and twenty odd nights," he noted in January 1814, but that was nothing unusual for a man of Wilson's mettle.

As for personal courage, we have seen how he made his mark on the battlefields of 1794. But he could also rise undaunted to a challenge far from the sounds of musket and gun. For instance, during the journey back from Egypt in 1801 on board a man-of-war, a naval officer boasted that he could climb to the top-mast-head and down again before Wilson could reach the main-tops. "I reached the main-tops before he had even got to the top-mast-head," wrote Wilson, adding as a proud afterthought: "I had never gone aloft till then."

. . . . .

General Sir Robert Wilson's *Private Diary of Travels, Personal Services, and Public Events, during Mission and Employment with the European Armies in the Campaigns of 1812, 1813, 1814, from the Invasion of Russia to the Capture of Paris*—such is the full title—was first published in two large volumes in 1861. The total length ran to 1,050 pages, though the type face and margins were distinctly larger than is economically possible these days. The editor was Wilson's nephew and son-in-law, the Rev. Herbert Randolph, who in the previous year had been responsible for preparing for publication Sir Robert's *Narrative of Events during the Invasion of Russia by Napoleon Bonaparte*, and who, in 1862, published an unfinished autobiographical sketch written by the General and his diaries dealing with his early career down to the Peace of Tilsit in 1807. The two volumes of 1862 bore the title *Life of General Sir Robert Wilson from Autobiographical Memoirs, Journals, Narratives, Correspondence, &c.* The project was never brought to completion, and the journals covering Wilson's service in the Peninsular War, still less his later life in peacetime, have not appeared.

In editing Wilson's *Private Diary* for a new edition, I have made a number of omissions, which require description and explanation. Each of the two original volumes contains lengthy appendices, comprising nearly one hundred letters of a semi-official nature, written by Sir Robert Wilson to Lord Cathcart and Lord Aberdeen for the most part, with a few addressed *to* Wilson by correspondents like the Duke of Gloucester, Mr. Robert Liston, the British Ambassador in Constantinople, the Duke of Oldenburg, and Prince Metternich. These have been omitted, since much of their information already appears in the diary, but a few important extracts have been quoted as footnotes. At the beginning, the journal for April, May and June 1812, in which Wilson describes the voyage to Turkey by way of Cadiz, Palermo and several of the Greek islands, has been cut out, as have the entries made between February and July 1814, when Sir Robert was at Marshal Bellegarde's headquarters in northern Italy or else, after Napoleon's abdication and arrival in Elba, travelling through Switzerland and France to Paris.

From the body of the journal itself, between August 1812 and January 1814, I have pruned various trivialities, details of letters and dispatches received and written by Wilson, certain less interesting or important social encounters, and several accounts, usually ephemeral and rather tedious, of the deployment or engagement of Allied military formations. Wilson devotes many pages to speculation on, for example, what the French and Russian armies are likely to do next, or on whether Austria or Bavaria will enter the war with the Allies: some of these have been left out, as they were soon overtaken by events, the General being proved either right or wrong, more often the former. Several letters written to the Duke of Gloucester and Lord Cathcart, included by Randolph in chronological order with the diary, have been omitted, and also some detailed but impersonal memoranda on the battles of Lützen, Bautzen and Leipsic, and on the autumn campaign of 1813, and, in quite a different sphere, on the Plain of Troy.

So much for the omissions. As some compensation I have inserted paragraphs about the Russian officers and their men, about Cossacks, and about some of the leading personalities who figure in the diary—all taken from Wilson's earlier writings, in particular *Brief Remarks on the Character and Composition of the Russian Army* and his *Narrative of Events during the Invasion of Russia by Napoleon Bonaparte*. This latter work is largely impersonal, but occasionally Sir Robert gives more detail of an episode than he had time or vigour for in his journal, and in such cases I have included all or part of the longer account. I have also quoted from the works of several other men who were with Wilson in Germany in 1813.

In order to write his diary, a tired Wilson had usually to snatch a few minutes from being on horseback or employed on indispensable business. The journal, described as "the image of my thoughts, unpolished by consideration of phraseology," was sent home in instalments to his wife Jemima and brother Edward, whenever a trusted courier or friend was returning to England. He intended that extracts should be passed to a very few friends like the Duke of Gloucester and Lords Hutchinson and Grey, but on several occasions the Duke, in thanking Wilson for sending accounts which contained "the *real* and *true* state of what has happened and of what we might expect," disclosed that he had received the journals, and family letters, exactly as Sir Robert had written them. Wilson was justifiably annoyed at this, not only because, as he complained to Edward in 1813, "you certainly have exposed me to the imputation of a very vain egotism," but also, and more serious, because he heard that "the publicity of my private letters has been one of the principal causes of the hostility of the Government."

His prime motive in keeping the diary with such exemplary zeal was that it should be "a family memorial for the imitation of my children who, I hope, will always be ready, like myself, to sacrifice their all for the public good." Robert and Jemima Wilson had a family of seven sons and six daughters.

Sandhurst and Sylt   A.B.-J.

HISTORICAL SYNOPSIS

On June 26th 1812 Napoleon's immense army crossed the Niemen, and marched straight on Moscow rather than to St. Petersburg further north. By the time he encountered the Russian army early in August at Smolensk, he had lost 100,000 men and 80,000 horses through hunger, disease and desertion. The fight for the city lasted three days and the place was left in flames. Kutusow replaced Barclay de Tolly as Commander-in-Chief, and on September 7th his troops stood and fought at Borodino. In forcing their opponents off the battlefield the invaders incurred losses which they could ill afford so far from base.

A week later Napoleon entered Moscow, but the city blazed, his peace feelers were spurned, and on October 18th he had to order a retreat. When, on November 10th, he reached Smolensk again, his army numbered barely 40,000, and it was to suffer further loss at the crossing of the Beresina. Indeed, less than 2,000 men survived to cross the Niemen, and although the arrival of other contingents raised that total to around 60,000, Napoleon had left behind in Russia at least half a million soldiers and 160,000 horses. He himself quitted his army on December 5th and set off for Paris to deal with a conspiracy and to raise another army.

At this juncture the position of Prussia became all-important. The first movement there against the French came in spite of King Frederick William. General Yorck, inspired by the news of Napoleon's disasters in Russia, acted on his own responsibility to the extent of abandoning his siege of the Russians in Riga and, on December 30th, of signing the Convention of Tauroggen, by which he declared his Prussian contingent of 18,000 men to be neutral. This act, tantamount to open hostility to France, was applauded by the Prussian people and repudiated by their King; but when East Prussia rose spontaneously to greet the advancing Russian troops—Stein had persuaded the Czar not to be content with expelling the French from Russian soil but to carry the war into central Europe—and when, at Königsberg, the East Prussian Provincial Assembly put its forces at the disposal of Napoleon's enemies, Frederick William could hold back no longer.

The remnants of the *Grande Armée* retreated first behind the Oder and then behind the Elbe, leaving strong garrisons in Stettin, Dantzic and the main fortresses of Prussia. On January 22nd the Prussian King left Potsdam, where he no longer felt safe, and went to Breslau in Silesia. At the end of February he and the Czar Alexander signed the Treaty of Kalisch, both promising not to lay down arms until Prussia had regained the territories she had possessed in 1806. By a subsequent declaration any princes or peoples in Germany who did not join the Allies would lose their independence when a settlement was eventually made. On March 4th the French pulled out of Berlin, on the 15th the Czar joined Frederick William in Breslau, and next day Prussia declared war on France.

Napoleon had gone to Germany to face the new coalition, having raised more conscripts and summoned old soldiers from the garrisons of Holland and northern Germany, and still enjoying the loyal support of contingents from Saxony, Bavaria and Westphalia. At the battle of Möckern, a day's march east of Magdeburg, Yorck and Bülow inflicted serious losses on Napoleon's stepson, Eugène de Beauharnais, Viceroy of Italy, but they could not prevent him from joining the Emperor with 38,000 troops on April 29th. By this time the main Russian army had entered Dresden and on Kutusow's death the command devolved upon Wittgenstein. The end of the month saw the Allied sovereigns setting off from Dresden to seek a decisive battle with Napoleon: he, in his turn, had determined to act on the offensive.

With over 250,000 troops he boldly invaded Saxony. On May 2nd, during eight hours of bitter struggle, Napoleon defeated a Russian and Prussian army at Lützen, also called Grossgorschen. The Allies, defeated but unbroken, ventured a second battle, this time at Bautzen, where on May 20th-21st they had eventually to quit the battlefield. Napoleon set up his headquarters in Dresden, and was joined there by Vandamme's corps which had just recaptured Hamburg. Though he had won two victories, they were so hollow and costly that he agreed to the Armistice of Pleswitz, proposed by the astute and unscrupulous Austrian Chancellor, Metternich. During this armistice, which lasted from June 4th until July 20th and was then extended until mid-August, both sides tried to win over the Austrian Emperor. For his active support each was prepared to pay heavily. Thanks to his marriage to Marie Louise, Napoleon thought himself secure. Surely his father-in-law would not desert him. But in any case he counted on the long-standing antagonism between Austria and Prussia, and even promised to restore to the Emperor the whole of Silesia, which had been taken from Maria Theresa by Frederick the Great. Napoleon hoped that if he guaranteed possession of all Poland to Russia, the Czar would forgive the French invasion of his territory.

In the event, Napoleon failed, because the Austrian Emperor placed patriotism before paternal sentiments, while the Czar, now distrusting Napoleon as heartily as once, in 1807, he had trusted him, refused to betray his new ally, the King of Prussia. Accordingly, on June 17th, 1813, Austria, Russia and Prussia signed the Convention of Reichenbach, by which Austria agreed to declare war on France if Napoleon should reject the terms she was about to offer. In his meeting with Napoleon at Dresden, Metternich proposed, *inter alia*, that France should revert to her natural boundaries of the Rhine and Alps, and should restore independence to Holland and reinstate the Bourbons to Spain. On August 12th Napoleon's refusal caused Austria to range her forces on the Allied side, promising 200,000 men and counting on the British assurance of large subsidies.

As well as depriving Napoleon of an expected ally, Austria's intervention endangered his position in Saxony. The Allied plan of campaign was simple though cumbersome. Four armies would converge on Dresden: from the east, Bennigsen's Russian army; from Silesia a Prussian force under Blücher, together with Wittgenstein's Russians; Prince Schwarzenberg's Austrian army from Bohemia and the main Russian army commanded by Barclay de Tolly; and from the north, Bülow's Prussians, Tchernishew's Russian contingent, and the Swedish troops under Bernadotte. The last-mentioned, having accepted the position of heir to the Swedish throne, had in 1812 tried to bargain, first with the Czar, then with Napoleon, his former master, over possession of Norway; obtaining satisfaction from neither side, the erstwhile Marshal of France had remained neutral. But with the retreat of the French from Moscow and the resurgence of Prussia, the Crown Prince of Sweden openly declared himself in support of the Allies and entered Germany with an army of 12,000 men.

Napoleon struck first, and for a while success deserted him. Marshal Oudinot, ordered to take Berlin, was defeated at the battle of Grossbeeren on August 23rd, and two days later Marshal Macdonald lost to Blücher on the Katzbach, Silesia being thereby cleared of French forces. Schwarzenberg, instead of waiting for

Bernadotte and Blücher, attacked the French centre at Dresden, and after two days of savage fighting, on August 26th-27th, was obliged to retreat into Bohemia. Napoleon had suffered severe and irreparable losses, and his soldiers were further depressed by the news that Vandamme, in trying to cut Schwarzenberg's communications, had been forced to capitulate at Kulm with over 10,000 men.

One of the bitterest fights of the campaign occurred at Dennewitz on September 6th, when Bülow, commanding Prussian troops, defeated Marshal Ney and a force of Bavarians, Saxons and men of Würtemberg. Napoleon withdrew to Leipsic and, with 160,000 shaken soldiers, faced more than double that number. Whereas the Emperor could secure no more reinforcements, the Allies had gained further support by virtue of the Treaty of Töplitz, signed on September 19th. Here it was agreed that the Confederation should be dissolved and independence granted to states in south and west Germany whose rulers had so far feared reprisals for having remained on Napoleon's side. Most important of these was Bavaria, who now promised to help with 36,000 troops in return for complete sovereignty.

The strengthened Allies attacked Napoleon, and the outcome was almost inevitable. At Leipsic was fought the 'Battle of the Nations' for three terrible days, October 16th–19th. The hitherto faithful Saxons deserted Napoleon, but even without this defection the ruin of his army would have occurred. Smashed French divisions escaped through one gap and retreated in disorder across Germany. Bavaria's army under Wrede tried to stop the French at Hanau on October 30th, only to be brushed aside. Early in December the French remnants at last crossed the Rhine and reached safety.

The victory of Leipsic was followed by a general rising against the French. Almost alone in remaining loyal was Denmark, who had allied herself to Napoleon after Britain had, in 1807, seized what she had failed to gain by diplomacy: the Danish fleet. For her pains Denmark was, in 1814, to lose Norway to Sweden. Otherwise, that autumn of 1813 saw the blockade of French garrisons holding Hamburg, Magdeburg, Dantzic, Stettin and other cities. An Austrian army invaded northern Italy and defeated Eugène de Beauharnais, while Lord William Bentinck took a strong British force from Sicily to Genoa and rallied local insurgents. Another British corps was sent to Holland to aid the Dutch, who had rebelled and declared for the House of Orange.

Napoleonic France, weary of war, exhausted in manpower,

commercially weakened, had now to face the invasion she had so often inflicted upon others. However, for some weeks the Allied monarchs remained at Frankfort on the right bank of the Rhine, concentrating their forces and conducting protracted negotiations with Napoleon, who was once again offered terms by which France should preserve her natural frontiers marked by the Pyrenees, Alps and the Rhine, provided that she restored all former rulers in Spain, Italy and Holland. Napoleon did not reply until late in December, and his counter-proposals included demands for several cities on the German bank of the Rhine, for a kingdom in Germany for his brother Jérôme, formerly King of Westphalia, and another for Eugène de Beauharnais in Italy. On the last day of the year Blücher and the main Prussian army crossed the Rhine in three columns, whereas further south the Austrian and Russian forces under the command of Schwarzenberg invaded France.

As Sir Robert Wilson was transferred to the Austrian Head-quarters in Italy, the details of this campaign do not concern us here. Suffice it to say that Napoleon fought one of his most skilful campaigns, took swift advantage of every Allied mistake, and would probably have forced Prussia and Austria to retire and seek an armistice had it not been for the persistence of the Czar and of Lord Castlereagh. Eventually, after numerous battles, anxieties, and treaties, the Allies occupied Paris at the beginning of April, Napoleon was obliged to abdicate and go into exile on Elba, while the Bourbons were restored in the person of Louis XVIII, who returned from an exile in England.

1812

July 17th, Constantinople.

Yesterday evening received advice of the war between Russia and France. The Emperor announces it in a letter to the Duke of Richelieu.[1] He says that he had throughout shown the greatest moderation; but since Buonaparte had determined on war, he would oppose energy and constancy.

I could not sleep a moment; my thoughts were in most vehement action. Until I reach the Imperial headquarters I shall be on tenter-hooks.

18th—The Porte[2] now most cordially agrees to my departure, and charges me with its interests; so I hope to be many miles away in forty-eight hours.

My route is first to Schumla to confer with the Grand Vizir;[3] thence to Bucharest to see the General commanding the Russian Danube army; and ultimately to the Imperial Headquarters. I have transferred all my baggage into a pair of saddle-bags, so that I may go *ventre à terre* [at full speed], if money, spurs, and zeal can produce that pace.

July 21st, Pera.

Having taken leave of the various ministers and others residing at Buiukdereh, who had all received me as a well-known friend, I returned to Pera at once in the hope of finding my passport; but the Grand Signor[4] had, on Friday evening, lost his only male child, eight months old, and had been in such affliction that his ministers could not approach him on business.

I do not know how long the Sultan will devote to sorrow, but I believe that the Capitan Pacha saw him yesterday, and that he came partly on purpose to repeat my conversation. As he has

[1] Armand du Plessis, Duc de Richelieu (1766–1822) spent nearly 20 years in exile as one of Russia's chief administrators, before, in 1815, becoming President of Louis XVIII's Ministry in the Paris of the Second Restoration.
[2] Or Sublime Porte, a name given to the Ottoman court and government.
[3] The Sultan's chief minister.
[4] Mahmoud II, Grand Signior and Sultan of the Ottoman Empire.

four wives already pregnant, the loss of Prince Murad is not irreparable.

The principal Dragoman having stated this fact before Mrs. Liston,[1] she misunderstood him, and repeated "Four wives petulant!" "*Pregnant*, madam!" said the ambassador. "God bless me!" shrieked her Excellency, "who could have thought that? I am sure petulant was a more reasonable supposition."—"Four wives pregnant!" The phenomenon seemed to press upon her mind the whole evening, and I shall expect shortly to hear of a visit to the Seraglio.

23rd—The delay in obtaining my firman drives me crazy. Mr. Liston[2] has been obliged to make a vehement remonstrance to the Porte. They plead the Grand Signor's affliction and inattention to business. The Mufti has been to urge resignation and application for the benefit of the Empire. The principal cause of this inattention, as we believe, is apprehension of French displeasure, since the Austrian and French envoys have been making complaints on the subject of my departure. These are ill-timed compliments to my power of doing mischief to their master. I cannot brook further obstacles to my departure, and if I do not receive my passports in twenty-four hours I will put myself in a boat and go to Odessa; although the season is very unfavourable since the wind daily blows a foul gale.

Yesterday, to dissipate thought a little, I went over to Constantinople, but the bazaars had lost their interest, and my attention was so distrait that I did nothing but run against passengers and fall over dogs and kittens lying in the streets. One of them very nearly inflicted on me a severe punishment for my injurious carelessness.

I returned home very early to be equally restless and I rose this morning without having closed my eyes; since I had heard, before going to bed, that there had been several actions, that the Russians had been obliged to quit Wilna, and that they had lost many prisoners. I am well aware of French exaggerations, but I am not less fretted by my impatience to reach the theatre of war and share in Russian fortunes.

25th—The Grand Signior has consented to my departure. I now only await letters.

July 30th, Schumla.

On Monday morning I left the palace. Mrs. Liston, on taking leave, saying: "Although she loved me, she was delighted at my

[1] Henrietta, *née* Marchand, from Jamaica.
[2] Robert Liston (1742–1836) had been Minister in Madrid, Stockholm, Constantinople (1793–6), Washington and the Batavian Republic. He was later knighted.

going away, for she every day feared that I should bring her home the plague, or be brought home with a dagger through my body for trespassing on Turkish property." I left amidst a scene of comic disorder, occasioned by the bustle of my departure and by the preparations for Mr. Liston's public visit to the Caimacan. His house was filled with Turkish officers of state and couriers; his palace yard with horses equipped for the ceremony of procession and my journey.

The first hundred miles that I rode presented only a flat, naked country; fifty of them ran along the sea-shore. The next two hundred and twenty miles were over a partially wooded country and through the Balkan mountains. I reached Schumla in sixty-eight hours, thus beating the Tartars of the Porte by several hours: but to ride such a distance without any kind of repose, over a line of country that in some parts is all but impracticable, in the heat of July, on lame and frequently tired horses, was an exertion beyond the strength of most men. My dragomen, indeed, executed the same undertaking, but only one of them could pretend to any rivalry with me. Allen was so galled that he rode exactly like the children's figure of a man making the letter C.

Instead of obtaining repose at Schumla, I was sent for immediately after my arrival to hold a conference with the Grand Vizir, which lasted four hours. It was a most interesting conversation and I have one or two extraordinary circumstances to repeat hereafter to private and confidential ears.

The Grand Vizir, after the termination of the conference, sent to my quarters twenty dishes; after which I was enabled to retire for rest, and might have slept for two hours if the fleas had not tormented me to the most irritating degree. I was then desired to come, upon a splendidly caparisoned horse, back to the Vizir, and he received me in state. After some ceremonies he waved his hand, the profane withdrew, and then we travelled for two hours over all the affairs of the world. On going away he gave me a very fine sword and a Persian shawl. I am now about again to mount, to the horror even of my Janissary who calculated on this night's rest.

August 1st, Bucharest.

I quitted Schumla with delight, for it was a very hot-bed of plague; and, connecting its physical and military imperfections, I think it ought to be called the headquarters of barbarism.

As we approached the Danube a most severe storm of lightning and rain suddenly broke upon us: the first effect was gloriously splendid,

Gulf of Finland

ST. P.

Lake Peipus

Gulf of
Riga

W

R U

R. Dwina

Polo

Memel

R. Niemen

Pillau Tilsit   Kovno

Königsberg

Dantzic   Friedland   Wilna

Smorgoni   Boriso

Marienwerder   Minsk

R. Beres

Bialystok

R. Boug

Pinsk

Lowicz   To Zamosz 90 miles

N

A

R. Moskva   ⊙ MOSCOW

Borodino • • Mojaisk
          • Fominskoi
Borowsk• Serpoukow
Wiazma •   Malo-
         Jaroslavets
       Kalouga •

LENSK
• Krasnoi

0   100
Scale of Miles

↙ To Kiew 100 Miles

E.G.M.

but no view compensated for the consequences. I was drenched to the bone before I could dismount, and when I did so, I fell to the ground in the dirtiest soil that could be selected by a man in a state of decadence. I regretted this fall more than the very serious one which occurred to me as I rode down the Balkan hills during the night at full speed. God only knows how I was preserved, for the animal pitched with the most furious velocity and turned completely over. Neither of us, however, were hurt, and amidst all the perils of this expedition, I have only been a temporary sufferer from a blow in the eye with one of the branches of the trees.

As soon as the storm lulled I continued my progress to Rutschuk.

Here I was sheltered in the house of an Aga from a second storm; he kindly gave me warm drinks, and on my resolving to embark, he lent me a cloak of state to go down to the boat, which I might have taken to the other side of the Danube, if I had wished it.

A Russian boat carried me over to Giurgevo in half-an-hour. Colonel Kutusow, the commandant, received me as a brother and lavished on me, as a British officer, every attention and honour.

I was in a comparative elysium; recollections of former scenes and present enjoyments, with the magic aid of military music, huzzas, cheers, &c., soon placed me in a paradise that required not even Mahomet's *sine qua non* for its perfection.

At 12 o'clock at night, after four hours of delightful entertainment, I set out in Colonel Kutusow's own carriage, which he insisted on my taking, although it was to return the same day, that he might have it for his march to Choczim the day after.

Is it possible for me not to love such kind and friendly comrades?

At eight o'clock in the morning, after going at the most furious rate and over the rudest ground, with six horses tackled at each post, I arrived here and waited on Admiral Tchichagow,[1] with whom I remained three hours. He then ordered me a handsome quarter in the late French Consul's house, where I have been passing the day alone, that I might write my despatches to Mr. Liston, &c. But, alas! I have made little progress—Morpheus was an irresistible deity; however, considering that I have ridden four hundred and twenty-five miles, rowed six miles on the Danube, and travelled eighty by carriage, in five hours less than five days, including the nine hours passed at Schumla, I must not be reproached for too feeble resistance to the drowsy spell.

[1] Admiral Pavel Vasilievich Tchichagow, commanding the Army of the Danube, was a seaman and diplomat who, at a time of national crisis, was placed in command of a land force. He was later blamed, rather unfairly, for Napoleon's escape across the Beresina.

This would be a delightful city if the streets were not paved with logs of wood, which unhinge every joint as the carriage proceeds. I was quite racked, and all my saddle wounds re-opened, for it must be remembered that Russian carriages have no springs. The remaining route must be traversed in the same species of vehicle, and I shall probably have to bound upon what they call 'timber roads.'

A Mr. Wyburn, from Yorkshire, has just left me to get a carriage, that I may make some necessary visits to generals, hospodars,[1] &c. He is a very fine young man, greatly accomplished in languages, with good manners.

August 6th, Jassy.

On the 3rd I left Bucharest, which place I think, on the whole, an excellent quarter.

Mr. Wyburn accompanied me. His knowledge of languages chiefly induced me to accept his offer of going as far as Russia in my company; and I have hitherto had no reason to regret the resolution on any account. I had bought a Russian kibitka[2] to hold four, and two of my dragoons at first rode but afterwards got into the litter-cars of the country.

We passed various divisions of the Moldavian army all in the highest order. At Fokchani, the Moldavian frontier town, my kibitka fore-wheel gave way; but the Russian soldiers, under the authority of Count Manteuffel and General Lanskoi, replaced it while I was seeking for another wheel in the town. I was overjoyed to meet these excellent persons again: the cordiality was mutual, and I passed a very agreeable hour or two.

The next morning at daybreak the other fore-wheel, unable to resist the shattering of the night, split into fifty parts, and all but threw the whole party into a large body of water that flowed round a Boyard's[3] domain; but here, happily, we found a little open waggon, which I took *bon-gré mal-gré* [willy-nilly]. But I must add that eventually the Boyard, finding us English, gave every aid, and a little car into the bargain for the soldiers, as being larger than the post cars. Thus re-equipped, we renewed our course over a dreary country; I think that, for a hundred miles, we did not see one village. Towards the evening, a second Danube thunderstorm broke over our heads. If I had not been one of the dramatis personæ, I should have enjoyed the scene; but the harder it poured the faster my postilion galloped, and my voiture soon became a mud-

---

[1] Governors (in Moldavia).
[2] A hooded sledge.
[3] A name given to the nobles in Russia, Transylvania and the Danube provinces.

cart. I never was more wretched except when we came to the next post-shed, and found all flown, so that we were obliged to proceed with the same horses: but who can say that he has attained the extreme of misery? The third post-station was also abandoned, and our cattle could do no more. By bribing we prevailed on the postilions to feed their horses—that is, to let them graze for two hours— we in the interval lay in our waggon with a cloak over us: but the dew from the heavens and the earth soon thoroughly soaked it, and then we steamed throughout; for our hay, which formed the bed, became like manure. I will not, however, dwell on these troubles but announce our arrival at Jassy this morning, where the commandant assigned me a superb quarter in the house of the principal Boyard, and where I have been entertained with hospitality and costly magnificence, as well as with the sight of a very pretty Moldavian girl, the wife of the Boyard's son. She possesses graces that would adorn any capital. I term her a girl because I do not think she is fifteen years old, but she is very nearly the mother of a second child, if appearances may be trusted.

This city is handsome, and contains many palaces. The room in which I dined this day was a hundred and twenty feet long, and the other apartments are in proportion. The master of the house has just been with me to request my acceptance of a handsome Petersburg post landaulet, observing that my departure from his house in a country cart would be a reproach to him and his countrymen.

I of course declined, but with difficulty escaped a boon that would have much distressed me.

This is a trait that honours Moldavia and my own country, for to an Englishman only would such an offer have been made. Almost every moment, from high and from low, some incident occurs to show the world's estimation of the British character.

August 14th, Smolensk.

This morning we reached Smolensk, having performed a very severe journey, but much mitigated in its severity by the universal kindness we experienced, and latterly by the scenes of a most beautiful country. I was greatly surprised in '*la petite Russie*' to see as great a population and as richly cultivated land as almost any province in England can produce. I do not think we saw a barren acre for five hundred miles.

At Smolensk I found General Beningsen,[1] Monseigneur Nowosilt-

[1] Levin August Theophil, Count Bennigsen (1745–1826), was born at Brunswick and in 1773 entered the service of Catherine the Great. Barclay said of him that he was so egoistic and full of envy that, despite his ability, he was 'a veritable pest' to the army.

zoff, Prince Galitzin, and many others. No meeting could be more sincerely affectionate.

I dined with Beningsen and others, and have ever since been writing despatches.

To-morrow I go to the armies of Barclay[1] and Bagrathion.[2] God grant that the Emperor may move up from St. Petersburg, for I abhor the idea of retiring from service, and moreover journeying five hundred miles.

Smolensk is a small, walled, uninteresting town. The country round about is wild; but the spot will ever be memorable for the union of Bagrathion's and Barclay's armies, a union that probably saved Russia. Russia has now more than sufficient means to preserve herself and to save the world. She only requires honest direction.

Before embarking on Wilson's journal of his experiences with the Russian army in 1812, it is worth reading some of the observations he made two years before, as a result of earlier missions and campaigns, in his book entitled Brief Remarks on the Character and Composition of the Russian Army.

The infantry is generally composed of athletic men between the ages of 18 and 40, endowed with great bodily strength, but generally of short stature, with martial countenance and complexion; inured to the extremes of weather and hardship; to the worst and scantiest food; to marches for days and nights, of four hours repose and six hours progress; accustomed to laborious toils, and the carriage of heavy burthens; ferocious, but disciplined; obstinately brave, and susceptible of enthusiastic excitements; devoted to their sovereign, their chief, and their country. Religious without being weakened by superstition; patient, docile, and obedient; possessing all the energetic characteristics of a barbarian people, with the advantages engrafted by civilization.

The Russian soldier in general is extremely subordinate, and attached to his officer, who treats him with peculiar kindness, and not as a machine, but as a reasonable being whose attachment he ought to win, although he has authority to command his service. Punishment is not so frequent as in other armies, nor is it very severe.

The higher officers are particularly considerate of them [their men], and promote every occasion for their solace or encourage-

[1] Michael, Prince Barclay de Tolly (1761–1818), a Russian general of Scottish ancestry.
[2] Peter Ivanovich, Prince Bagration (1765–1812) had fought at Austerlitz, Eylau and Friedland.

ment. They share every hardship with a gallant spirit of example that cheers the soldier, and which would afford a valuable model to other armies. They enjoy pleasures within their reach, but they make no pre-arrangement to secure them, or murmur at a deprivation; and with astonishment foreigners must regard the abstinence, the endurance, the total indifference to accommodation, and even the common decencies of the better order of society, with which the high nobility, accustomed to every luxury, in Petersburg and Moscow, proprietors of palaces and royal revenues, encounter the rudeness of the most severe campaigns.

The Russian officer, although frequently making the greatest physical exertions, is, however, inclined to indolent habits when not on actual duty; loves his sleep after food, and dislikes to walk or ride far. This is one of the defects of education. At Petersburg or Moscow no person of rank moves on foot, and a journey of 50 miles on horseback would be an expedition for the city's talk. The Emperor met one morning at Petersburg an English officer [Wilson], and stopped his padroskin (or vehicle). "Where is your carriage?" "Sire, I am walking about to look at your capital." "Ah!" said his Majesty. "I would give a great deal if my officers would imitate such an example, and appreciate justly the great value and utility of that custom which I hear so much prevails in your country."

Finally a paragraph taken from Sir Robert Wilson's Narrative of Events during the Invasion of Russia by Napoleon Bonaparte. *It refers to July 1812.*

No troops can and do defend ground in retreat better than the Russians. Their artillery is so well horsed, so nimbly and so handily worked, that it bowls over almost all irregularities of surface with an ease, lightness, and velocity that give it great superiority. The vivacity of their cavalry, and the unquailing steadiness of their infantry, make it a pleasure to command them in extremest difficulties; for, like the British soldier, the most unbounded confidence may be reposed, to use a sailor's expression, "in their answer to the helm" in every stress of situation.

August 27th, St. Petersburg.

On the 15th I despatched H. Wyburn with all speed out of Smolensk, as the enemy were supposed to be approaching. By the active exertions of Prince Galitzin, I was myself equipped for the field, and conveyance was secured for my dragoons. He who had been too proud to serve under General Barclay, and had quitted the service rather than do it, became my servant. On myself, accustomed as I am to Russian kindness, such a trait had a powerful effect; on Wyburn, who was a stranger to Russia, it seemed to operate as enchantment.

After having seen all that the day presented for observation, Prince Galitzin and I thought it our duty to join General Barclay, as Commander-in-Chief; and General Beningsen left the town for Wiazma, from considerations which I greatly approved.

The night was dark, and I was very weary, having been up all the preceding night to write despatches, &c., instead of reposing as I had for many nights anticipated; but the road was too bad for confidence in my dragoman coachman, and I was obliged to take the reins. Prince Galitzin was in his own carriage, and trusted to his Russian's skill; but in about half an hour his carriage overturned, and proved a landmark that saved mine.

After proceeding about twenty-five wersts (a werst is three-quarters of an English mile)[1] we met Barclay's advanced guard: we therefore halted, saw the army file before us to Smolensk, and then joined the General, who received me very graciously, invited me to remain with his army, and to live at his headquarters when I was not on visits with friends in detached corps. On the march we dined. In the evening, joined Prince Bagrathion's army on the heights opposite Smolensk, and I flew to the Prince and Woronzow. *Quel moment de bonheur!* when I embraced these friends. I only could have sacrified that pleasure to transfer it to the Count, his father,[2] in London.

I stayed in his tent until the march, at midnight, of the Prince's army to join the left. He then gave me a very fine horse to ride, equipped me with a great coat (for the nights are bitterly cold) and a Russian cap in case of a mêlée in battle, that I might be recognised.

In his Narrative *Wilson wrote:*

Bagration was by birth a Georgian, of short stature, with strong dark features and eyes flashing with Asiatic fire. Gentle, gracious, generous, chivalrously brave, he was beloved by every one and admired by all who witnessed his exploits. No officer ever excelled him in the direction of an advance or rear guard; nor had any officer's capacity in these commands ever been more severely tested; especially in the retreat from Pultusk to Eylau in the former war— a retreat of seventeen days and of as many furious combats in which

---

[1] Rather less: about 1,166 yards.
[2] Count Simon Woronzov was for many years Russian Ambassador in London.

his skill, unwearying energy, and daring courage were incessantly exemplified. They were indeed so many days of triumph for his fame (p. 156).

As soon as day dawned I accompanied the General into Smolensk. The action on the right soon commenced. Rode round all the posts with the General; but stopping to have a shoe fixed on at one of the advances, I was by another picquet deemed a French parlementaire[1] and conducted, notwithstanding my remonstrance, to Count Siewers, who for a moment was under the same mistake.

The action soon became more serious. I was here, there, and everywhere.

Towards the evening, however, I had opportunity of being useful by inducing the General to put four battalions in reserve into the streets of the town and by clearing the bridge, as I once had done before in the Polish campaign at Wehlau. My horse was almost knocked up, but nevertheless he went till night proved a friend to man and beast, when he reposed a couple of hours. In order to counteract the intention of General Barclay to quit Smolensk, I was, about ten o'clock at night, obliged to mount again and re-enter the town to take the opinions of General Doctorow and Prince Eugène of Wüitemberg, as to the capability of longer defence. The former said we had done '*trop ou trop peu*'; the latter engaged, with eight thousand men, to defend the city ten days, and begged of me to assure the General of the necessity of further defence. I had at least a dozen letters from officers of rank on the subject, as they thought I had access to and influence with the Commander-in-chief that no one else had. Woronzow also, from Bagrathion's camp, urged me, and declared that every officer and soldier was ambitious to join the garrison.

The Duke Alexander of Würtemberg,[2] an excellent officer and most friendly man, with myself, endeavoured to change the General's resolution. I cited Eylau, the preservation of Königsberg, &c. I proposed a sally with ten thousand men, whilst the Cossacks passed the Dnieper on the right and attacked the enemy's baggage and depôts, greatly exposed: but in vain; the order to retire was given. The sacred image of the Virgin was removed, and before daybreak the town was completely evacuated.

I cannot express the indignation that prevailed. The sacrifice of so many brave men; the destruction of an important town unneces-

[1] Bearer of a flag of truce.
[2] Uncle to the Russian Emperor.

sarily; the suspicion that Buonaparte directed Russian counsels; the sight of the holy city in flames, &c., &c., worked strongly on the feelings of the Russians. I even, in this moment of disappointment and wrath, regretted the exertions I had made and the hazards I had run (for I had had my 'hair-breadth 'scapes') for objects which the General seemed to determine should be unattainable.

This day was made memorable to me for my first interview with Platow.[1] Brave brother! Those who have the joy of embracing a father after a long chace may experience what I felt—but no others. He presented me to his people, my old comrades, in terms too flattering for my record. He gave me two Cossacks, horses, &c., and entreated me, on my return from St. Petersburg, to be more with him than even heretofore, as he would make my residence more agreeable by putting all that he commanded at my disposition.

At night, after seeing the fires of Smolensk augmented by the conflagration of about seven hundred houses, after having ourselves bombarded the town to incommode the enemy, an 'order' of the General which the army executed with reluctance, "as the image of the Holy Virgin had so long abode there" (a superstition probably originated by a warrior king, who knew the value of this position), I proceeded with the General on march: but finding that the column halted, I rode on to see the cause; when I found, at the distance of four wersts, a driver asleep at the top of the hill, which he had feared to descend. He had paused here for two hours, and the men behind him had sunk also into repose, so that the cause of detention was not investigated until my arrival. Baron Brinken,[2] a Courland nobleman, who afterwards became my aide-de-camp, was with me. He will bear witness to my toil for three hours, on account of the difficulty of descent, occasioned by causes stated in my despatches.

In his Narrative *Wilson comments:*
I found that the first four ammunition waggons, with two pieces of cannon, twelve-pounders, had overpowered the horses in the descent of the nearest hill, and that they lay at the bottom, with wheels or limbers broken, and all the horses killed or maimed; every succeeding gun and ammunition waggon had therefore to be held back by the soldiers fixing ropes on them, and that could not be done

[1] Matvei Ivanovich Platow (1757–1818) had in 1801 been nominated by the Czar as Hetman of the Cossacks of the Don. In 1807 Platow told the King of Prussia that Wilson "was not only his adjutant but his brother, and that he had no other name for me but Boatt Wilson, which in the Russian language signifies brother."
[2] An officer of the Czar's Hussar Guards.

till daylight; and moreover, as too frequently occurs in night marches, most of the drivers fell asleep (p. 107).

I verily believe that my vigilance saved a great misfortune to the world. A longer delay would have infallibly enabled the enemy afterwards to execute what he proposed; but in consequence of our onward movement he could not effect it in time. This is an anecdote, however, that I give solely for private notice; for I would not on any account, not for any rank or wealth, ever bring any exertions of my own forward that tended to censure friends and gallant comrades.

To my despatches I must again refer for the proceedings of the day; but as those who are interested about me would wish to know my personal share in this most important action, I must repeat that I was 'here, there, and everywhere' until sunset, when I must particularize my being with General Barclay, going forward with him, and at last charging with the column that saved the day, and with it the independence of Europe.

Sir Robert's Narrative *contains additional detail of his part in the battle.*

It was about sunset when the enemy on the main road upon the left bank, flattering themselves that their right was gaining ground, made a desperate effort to force the hill, on which several Russian guns were placed, and which commanded the whole position and also in reverse the outlet of the cross road, beyond which a boggy rivulet ran intersecting the route; over this only one bridge with loose planks afforded passage for the artillery and infantry until night, when two others were thrown across by Duke Alexander of Würtemberg. For an instant the Russian guns and troops supporting, overwhelmed with shells, shot and musketry, flew back to seek shelter behind the crest of the hill; but General Barclay, who had been superintending the action with his rearguard, admonished by the cannonade at Loubino and Waloutina Gora of the new danger to his advanced guard, opportunely arrived at this moment and seeing the extent of the danger to his column galloped forward, sword in hand, at the head of his staff (including myself, with two Russian officers attached to me as aides-de-camp), orderlies, and rallying fugitives, and crying out: "Victory or death! We must preserve this post or perish!" by his energy and example reanimating all, recovered possession of the height, and thus, under God's favour, the army was preserved! (108–9).

The storm of fire was heavy; but, so help me God and my sword hereafter, I would rather have died with Barclay than have quitted the ground: and I was resolved with him not to quit it in flight.

After the action I went to Strogonow, who commanded the rear-guard of the proposed march:—a little before daybreak we moved.

Headquarters were in a miserable village; but I found good fare with the Duke of Oldenburg, and enjoyed the luxury of a toilette under the shelter of a pig-stye.

As I did not think there would be a general battle, for reasons stated in my despatch, and as I had urgent motives to communicate with the Emperor, for reasons there also assigned, I took my corporal with me, my dragoon being very ill with fatigue, and, accompanied by Baron Brinken, set out for St. Petersburg. I carried with me a letter of recommendation from General Barclay, and the earnest entreaty of the whole army to expose the truth to the Emperor.

28th—We rode to Dorogobouche. Here we found Prince Bagrathion, Woronzow, &c.; and here we parted with them, under the same injunctions. With Woronzow I left two dragoons, my horses and cart.

We travelled in the carriages of the post telagas, little four-wheeled carts without any springs. The distance we had then to traverse exceeded eight hundred wersts—six hundred miles.

At Wiazma we were entertained at breakfast by Mr. Birt, an English doctor, who is greatly esteemed by the Russians, and who has, on the present occasion, assisted the wounded with a liberality that will long be recorded in Russia.

When we had gained the high Moscow road, about three hundred wersts from St. Petersburg, the Grand Duke Constantine[1] overtook me from the army, entered my room just as I had washed and changed, and made me sit down by him to talk for an hour.

I had not been honoured since the peace of Tilsit [1807] with His Royal Highness's friendship, but at the rising on this occasion we were a little more intimate.

In the midst of our discourse he spoke of *Napoleon*. I called him *Buonaparte* in my answer. "Whom do you speak of?" he asked. "Why, sir," I answered, "Buonaparte, Buonaparte!" "I thought," he said, "you meant *Lucien*, not *Napoleon Emperor of France, King of Italy*," &c. "I know, sir," I replied again, "that you have made his acquaintance under these titles, and I am sure, sir, you repent it: thank God! I am not in that situation and I cannot, even *en étiquette*, address him with any term of respect."

[1] Brother of the Emperor Alexander I.

The Duke was not offended with my freedom, but, on going away, he whispered something in my ear which proved to me that his attachment to Buonaparte is not much stronger than was Bellingham's to Mr. Perceval.[1]

About a hundred wersts further I met Prince Kutusow,[2] on his way to command the armies, and employ Beningsen, &c. The Prince alighted from his carriage, and we talked under a shed for about an hour. I was much flattered by his cordial invitation to rejoin the army. Taking me by the hand, he said: "Lose no time to return; I have great need of such a comrade as yourself in the cabinet and in the field."

Wilson wrote in his Narrative:

Marshal Prince Kutusov was born noble and was still more nobly allied by marriage. In his youth he was regarded as a very gallant officer, and had served with distinction. Wounded several times, on one occasion he lost an eye, but the expression of his countenance was still engagingly intellectual. . . .

A *bon vivant*—polished, courteous, shrewd as a Greek, naturally intelligent as an Asiatic and well instructed as an European—he was more disposed to trust to diplomacy for his success than to martial prowess, for which by his age and the state of his constitution he was no longer qualified.

When he rejoined the army he was seventy-four years old, and though hale, so very corpulent and unwieldy that he was obliged to move about, even when in the field, in a little four-wheeled carriage with a head, called a droska (pp. 130–1).

Brinken, who was with me, accustomed to see these high personages treat all others with dignified reserve, if not with offensive hauteur, could scarcely believe all that he saw on my travels, and is still in a trance of surprise from what has occurred here. On the 27th, in the evening, I reached St. Petersburg, very much fagged when in my telaga, but not in the least when I got out.

I drove to the Hôtel de l'Europe, where I found my good friend Lord Tyrconnel.[3]

The same evening I wrote despatches, and called on one or two friendly ministers.

[1] Spencer Perceval, the Prime Minister, had been assassinated by John Bellingham, a Liverpool merchant, as he was entering the House of Commons on May 11th.

[2] Mikhail Hilarionovich Golenischev-Kutusov (1745-1813), Russian Commander-in-Chief.

[3] The young Earl of Tyrconnel, formerly A.D.C. to the Duke of York, was an attaché at the St. Petersburg embassy, but carried away by enthusiasm and adventure, he joined Admiral Tchichagow as a volunteer and died of excessive cold and fatigue. See October 9th and December 26th.

Sept 3rd—I have been playing a bold and high part on this stage. I have been the organ of the Russian army and nation, and I hope one of the best friends that a sovereign ever had in a foreigner. But supposing that all I now propose succeeds, I shall ever have to regret that the irresolution of British counsels so long kept me in a state of inactivity. Not on my own account do I grieve for this, but as a friend to my country and an Anti-Buonapartist.

Our objects would have been earlier attained, and many painful sacrifices would have been avoided. But destiny, perhaps, forbad that ministers should be sooner delethargized, that the world's aspiring despot should be sooner destroyed. It may appear presumptuous to attach so much importance to my arrival on the Continent, but I can verify my opinion hereafter.

6th—On the 4th Lord Cathcart[1] arrived, just as I was going to the Emperor, who had come the evening before. After some conversation with him rather remarkable and somewhat unexpected, I went to Kaminienstroff, where I had detained the Emperor[2] half an hour; the second *faux-pas* in decorum that I have committed, for my servant, two days before, stopped the Empress in her carriage, that I might give her a letter which he knew I was going to the palace to deliver, and I was obliged to descend from my own to make an apology, which, however, was most graciously received.

The Emperor, on my being introduced into his cabinet, would not suffer me to kiss his hand, but took me in his arms and kissed me repeatedly.

A most important and very delicate conversation for two hours and a half then followed, and I went away in high admiration of the Emperor's good sense and love of sincerity.[3]

The next morning I received a note to dine with the Emperor. Before I went I had a long conference with Lord Cathcart, which

[1] William Schaw Cathcart, 1st Viscount (1755–1843), had studied law in Dresden, served in the American War of Independence, in two expeditions to Hanover, and had commanded at the bombardment of Copenhagen in 1807. Like his father before him, he was appointed Ambassador at the Court of St. Petersburg, and on campaign was to accompany the Czar in both his civil and military capacities. He continued as ambassador until 1821. Mr. George Jackson wrote of "*le vieux Général diplomate*": "the old man's deep faith in his great talents as a negotiator and in the expertness with which he wields alike the pen and the sword makes the grossest flattery seem to him but as the language of sincerity and a tribute due to his surpassing abilities."

[2] Alexander I (1777–1825) came to the throne after the murder of his father, Paul, in 1801. He married Elizabeth, daughter of the Prince of Baden.

[3] After an earlier meeting with the Czar, Wilson had written, on August 20th, 1807: "Alexander has a good, and affectionate heart . . . He wants only good counsellors. But if he had less virtue he would still command my services, for has not his conduct to me been one series of honouring friendship? Was ever individual more distinguished or more warmly cherished by a sovereign, when there was neither high desert nor secret service?"

was so far satisfactory that he assured me he should write to England and report that in every transaction I have acquitted myself with the zeal and propriety to which I lay my pretensions, and that he embraces all the views which I entertain. He had before told me he had written to England that he "thought it fortunate that I had expressed a wish to reside with the army, as no other man but myself could be there with the same prestige"; and he has more reason now to be satisfied of my power with that army, since the Emperor has expressed himself on that subject in the most decisive manner, and has authorized me to repeat to him and to my Government whatever opinions or statements I may deem it expedient to communicate. I thought it best to tell the Emperor that I could not serve without such permission, for that I would not act clandestinely. His answer was worthy of a wise Prince and honourable to myself.

The dinner was magnificent. The Empress-mother, the Empress, the Grand Duchessestrina, the Duchess of Würtemberg, the Princess Amelia, &c., were present. The party seemed to be made for a particular distinction, as such a meeting is very rare. Before dinner the Emperor and Empress especially addressed themselves to me; and after dinner in the adjoining room the Empress first spoke with me for a quarter of an hour, and then the Emperor for a full half-hour. The compliment was so marked—since neither conversed with any other person above a few moments and even so much only with two or three grandees—that every one of my friends noticed it to me afterwards; and if they had known all circumstances they would have been still more surprised.

From the Emperor's I went for a short time to Count Strogonow's, where Princess Galitzin told me a very 'flattering tale' about the Dowager Empress. It must not, however, be supposed that I notice these honours and compliments from any vain motives. I mark them to contrast what occurred on my second visit here,[1] and as a proof of the position in which I now stand, and from which I may be useful to my country and the cause of Europe.

At night I went to several parties. With Countess Potoski I passed a most agreeable hour, as she is one of the most accomplished women I ever met with: and as Madame de Staël[2] is going away, I joined

[1] In October 1807, owing to a misunderstanding, Wilson's letter to the Czar was returned unopened.

[2] Germaine de Staël (1766–1817), author of *Corinne*, *Delphine* and *De l'Allemagne*, was in flight from Napoleon and hoping to reach England, but had to travel via Vienna and in July 1812 entered Russia with her children and her lover. She spent two months there, stayed with Miloradovich in Kiev and Count Rostopchin at his country estate. On the morrow of Borodino she set off for Sweden and reached England in the summer of 1813.

her party for another hour, and adventured in the presence of such a *bel esprit* to discuss several topics very vehemently. 'Fortune favours the bold'; and I retired in full possession of her favour, and loaded with her encomiums, which I appreciate highly, as she is certainly a very clever woman and I strongly recommend her to the attentions of my friends in England when she goes there.

This morning I have received a request from the English gentlemen here to preside as chairman at a dinner to be given in commemoration of the battle of Salamanca.[1] I am selected in preference to Lord Cathcart as having served under Lord Wellington's orders, and although I am not ambitious of a president's duty, I felt that I could not decline; and really my admiration of the talent displayed on that occasion by Lord W. makes me desirous of an opportunity to render my homage to it. The day is not named, but I hope it may be early, as I am most impatient to rejoin the army.

9th—On the 7th I dined with the Dowager Empress to meet the Emperor and Imperial family. I experienced the same flattering attentions as had marked my former receptions, and as I sat immediately opposite the Empresses, at a very narrow table, I had opportunity for an unremitting conversation.

Yesterday was incessantly occupied with business until dinner time, when I made myself chaperon to Captain [William] Bowles of the Navy, Macdonald, and several of Lord Cathcart's staff. We nearly mustered a regiment in the several houses to which we went, but all were delighted at the sight of the '*masse en rouge*.'

Captain Dawson,[2] a brother of Lord Portarlington's, in Lord Cathcart's staff, is likely, in my opinion, to be the favourite, but the group is very respectable, and I make no doubt will continue popular.

Lord Cathcart's two sons[3] are excellent specimens, but they will not have the same opportunity as the others of going about, as Lord Cathcart employs them on his diplomatic business, in which he is most secret and most mysterious to the profane.

This morning I received a message from Princess Amelia to attend her at eight o'clock this evening; a flattering courtesy which has peculiar interest in these times.

To obtain Lord Cathcart's powers for a week, I think that I would, from love to the common interest, consent to lead the rest of my life in a solitude, and feast on the pleasure of knowing and seeing

[1] Wellington defeated the French under Marshal Marmont there on July 22nd, 1812.
[2] Hon. George Lionel Dawson, 1st Dragoon Guards, brother of the 2nd Earl.
[3] Frederick and George. The latter, as a Lieutenant in 6th Dragoon Guards, served as extra A.D.C. to Wellington at Waterloo. In 1850 he published "Commentaries on the war in Russia and Germany in 1812 and 1813", and in 1854 was killed at the battle of Inkerman, while commanding the 4th Division.

the effects of my interference in the State, as they generalised for the advantage of the world.

Every hour endears Russia more and more to me.

I do not know, however, that my popularity may not receive a shock. My Russian work[1] is being translated into Russian, French, and German, so it will be universally read, and no man could ever yet please all the world with a picture. Still, if any are offended, I shall say: *"Amicus Plato, amicus Socrates, sed magis amica veritas."* What is an Englishman without sincerity? The most despicable abortion in nature.

12th—I have just returned from one of the most interesting and magnificent scenes in the world—the ceremony in the church of Alexander Neufsky[2] on the baptism day of the Emperor. So splendid a sight I never beheld, and the Empress adorned the spectacle with a grace that even Lord Cathcart admitted was unparalleled in his recollection. After the service, Prince Gortschakow read a despatch from Marshal Kutusow, announcing the defeat of Buonaparte in a great battle [Borodino]. The effect was glorious. The recompences of the Emperor were then proclaimed. Two hundred thousand roubles (two shillings each) to Prince Kutusow, with the rank of Marshal: twenty-five roubles to each private soldier. My dear friend Woronzow is wounded, but did not quit the field. I am more than ever impatient to return, that I may be of use to him, as well as pursue the career of true glory. I am happy to think that I left two of my dragoons with him; they will, I am sure, attend well to him.

September 27th, Woronowo.

On the 15th of September, after having dined on the preceding day with the Emperor, and had a long private conference with him subsequently, from which I returned full of proofs of his favour and confidence; having taken leave of the Empress-mother and the gracious and graceful Empress, &c., the Grand Duke with whom I had a public battle to fight for two hours, Lord Cathcart from whom I parted on the most friendly terms, and all my numerous associates, &c., &c., Lord Tyrconnel and I, my corporal, Lord T.'s servant and a field-jäger left St. Petersburg.

Baron Brinken, of the Hussar Guards, whom the Emperor gave me as an aide-de-camp, could not be equipped by his tailor in time, and remained to follow me.

[1] *Brief Remarks on the Character and Composition of the Russian Army*, published in 1810.
[2] A national hero and revered saint in Russia (1220–63). He beat Sweden on the banks of the Neva (hence the name Nevsky), and defeated the Knights of the Teutonic Order at Lake Peipus in 1242.

My mode of conveyance was improved, for I now had a carriage with hind springs, which broke in some degree the violence of the action upon the wooden roads; but still I was far from personal ease. My mind was, however, quite comfortable, for I felt that my residence had been eminently useful at St. Petersburg, and that every succeeding day would more and more exemplify that fact. We travelled unremittingly night and day, without any remarkable incident, until we reached Twer, a hundred and twenty wersts from Moscow, where we heard of the fall and the firing of that city.

We then proceeded within fifty wersts from Moscow, rounded the burning city, whose flames fired the whole sky, keeping about that distance until we reached the road to Wladimir, when we bore upon Kolomna, Kaszira, and Serpoukow, and reached, on the seventh day, the headquarters at Krasnoi Pakra, thirty-two wersts distant from Moscow, on the Kalouga road. The distance from St. Petersburg, by the road we took, exceeded eleven hundred wersts, and the latter part of the route being cross country, we had great difficulty in procuring horses. The weather added to our inconvenience, as the rain poured for the last three days, but the kindness and zeal of all sorts of people greatly solaced us, and the bearing of the fugitive nobility and commonalty from Moscow, who covered the country, was a noble specimen of patriotism, that made us forget our own disappointments and vexations.

There was not one who did not disdain to mourn over his own particular afflictions, and when I told them of the Emperor's resolution to continue the war without remission whilst a Frenchman remained in arms on Russian territory, many wept for joy, many kissed me (young and fair as well as old), and they cheered as others might have done when their losses were repaired and their wanderings had ceased.

The same sentiment animates all classes in this illustrious army. It was their first question, and I was almost suffocated with caresses when I pledged the Emperor's perseverance.

I found Prince Kutusow in the very noble mansion of Count Soltikow,[1] where I obtained an apartment rather more calculated for summer than for autumn, but as good as those of my friends. It would be tedious to recapitulate the personal attentions and kindness which we received; it was a series of the most liberal and flattering services. Prince Kutusow gave me two of the Emperor's horses to ride, as Count Woronzow had taken mine with him for their

---

[1] President of the Imperial Russian Council and of the Council of Ministers, Soltikow had been in charge of the education of the Czar and Grand Duke Constantine.

protection. And Colonel Keating gave me four others to draw my britzska.[1] Lord Tyrconnel had the good fortune to buy a bargain and at once arrange his establishment, but he had the same offers to supply his needs.

Yesterday morning, Platow gave me a beautiful Cossack horse, which was very acceptable, but having written to the Emperor that I should ride his horse in the first battle, I have not restored him to his *écuyer* as yet.

Last night, as it was found that the provisions for the army came in slowly on account of the roads being spoilt by the incessant rain, Prince Kutusow resolved to march his army on the Kalouga road, whence his supplies come, nine wersts in the course of the day. I therefore resolved to come on with General Beningsen, Count [Feodor Vasilievich] Rostopchin the Governor of Moscow, and Platow, who is a little unwell. Last night General Beningsen stopped in a village one werst from hence and we proceeded to the Count's house, which is one of the most superb edifices I ever saw. There are two groups of figures from the antique—grooms holding rampant horses—placed upon the Saracen towers at the extremity of his stables, which, for gigantic mould and skilful execution, are worthy of the original Roman design. They are modelled from the Monte Cavallo horses. The whole suite is in the best style of building, and the grounds equal in scenery, from eminence and distribution of wood and water, any residence in the British dominions.

I could not help feeling great pain at seeing this noble establishment wrecked and ruined by the necessity of the times, or refrain from bowing in homage to the superior public virtue and magnanimous philosophy of a man who beholds this additional scene of devastation of his fortune (after having lost at Moscow, in the firing of the city, a mansion worth more than a hundred thousand pounds, including the second library in the empire and a collection of valuables endeared by their possession for ages in his family) without expressing any other regret than that he was not allowed, as he himself proposed to the Emperor and the Marshals, to put the torch to his own house and then blaze the city systematically. Moscow has, happily for Russia and the world, been consumed by fire; but it was the act of individuals, and not the regulated measure of the grandees of the kingdom, which these illustrious patriots (for the city is their own) desired as a proud monument of their resolution to sacrifice everything to honour and allegiance.

It is now time that I should note some of the military events that

[1] An open carriage with hood.

occurred after my departure from the army, for the satisfaction of my friends, who may rely on the impartiality and accuracy of my statements.

The Russian army, having changed commanders, continued its retreat on the village of Borodino, between Mojaisk and Gjatsk, on the high Moscow road. It was here reinforced by eighteen thousand effective men under General Milaradowitch,[1] and twenty-one thousand militia, chiefly armed with pikes, under General Markow. The total number of the Russian army, exclusive of militia, amounted to a hundred and five thousand effective men.

The French army amounted to a hundred and thirty thousand, reinforcements having been drawn to it from the military posts occupied by the enemy.

Buonaparte, contrary to all expectation, as he had omitted the favourable moment for attacking the Russians on the march from Smolensk to repass the Dnieper, presented his army in order of battle on the 24th. It is possible that the appointment of Prince Kutusow had baffled his hopes of peace, and that he felt himself now obliged to effect that by force which he expected to obtain by the influence of fear in the Russian Cabinet.

Prince Bagrathion's army sustained the Russian left, but it was very much advanced in front of the centre and right. A battery of seven guns on a hill covered the advance of Prince Bagrathion's army, which I shall in future call the 'second army.'

The action began about two o'clock in the afternoon of the 24th and was furiously fought on both sides until near dusk, when the enemy possessed himself of the hill and battery, and obliged the second army to retire and take up its position in alignment with the first army, keeping some hills in its front on which batteries were erected. On the morning of the 25th, the French with all their forces fell again upon Prince Bagrathion and, after a desperate resistance, compelled him to retreat.

The reserves of the first army were then under the necessity of moving to the left and front to oppose the enemy, whilst the Russian line threw back its left, so as to form an angle with a part of the centre and right: at the salient point of this angle was a battery which commanded the position, and which, after the most obstinate conflicts, the enemy carried.

The Russians had more than six hundred guns in the field, but

[1] General Mikhail Andreivich Miloradovich commanded the rearguard during the retreat to Moscow, negotiated a short armistice for the evacuation of the city, and, later on, led the Russian advance-guard pressing the French retreat.

the principal fire was sustained by about two hundred and sixty-eight pieces.

The Russians lost in the battle of Borodino thirty-six thousand killed and wounded: three generals killed, nine wounded; fifteen hundred officers killed and wounded.

Bagration was gravely wounded at Borodino and in his Narrative *Wilson later wrote, in the third person:*

On the evacuation of Moscow, he was borne towards the interior in a litter by relays of grenadiers, and to the last was as anxious for all the details of what was passing as if he had been still at the head of his army.

When Sir Robert Wilson told him what the Emperor had declared with regard to the rejection of all treaty with Napoleon "whilst an armed Frenchman should be in Russia," he pressed his hand convulsively, and said: "Dear General, you have made me die happy, for then Russia will assuredly not be disgraced."

Mortification coming on, he breathed his last on the 24th of September at Sima, on the road to Wladimir (pp. 156–7).

The loss of the French could not but be far greater. Calculations so far could not err; but it now appears from their own correspondence that they estimate their loss at twenty-six generals *hors-de-combat* (of whom seven were killed) and thirty-five thousand men.

Prince Kutusow was recommended to attack the enemy the day after the battle, or the next morning; but, by a fatality always attending Russian operations, he determined on retreat and the enemy was sufficiently active to lose no time in profiting by that intention.

Prince Kutusow, to the last day but one, however, always declared that he would fight for 'Moscow' before and in the city. He then called a council of war, which resolved: that the position proposed (five wersts from Moscow), having an inclined plane from its crest to the town, could not be occupied without the assurance of the army being lost in case of the enemy's succeeding in dislodging the Russian line; that the best defence of Moscow was an offensive operation, but, as the enemy had now time to collect his forces, that this measure was not so advisable as it might have been a few hours after the battle of Borodino; that—the greater part of the inhabitants having left Moscow, the greater part of the property having been removed—by firing the city the enemy would only gain a town which, by the unanimous consent of the Sovereign and the people, had no longer any consideration in the Empire; that the Russian grand army ought not to be shattered so much as to be unable to resume offensive operations when the other armies of Russia, destined to act upon the flank and rear communications of the enemy, were at their posts, since the plan of campaign might not only fail, but those armies, calculating upon central aid, might be sacrificed; that the French would be obliged to weaken their army of operation by the occupation of Moscow, whereas the Russian army would daily be acquiring strength; that, in short, the contest was for the Russian Empire, not for Moscow or any other city.

Such arrangements were made as the time admitted. The troops passed through the city; the multitude who had any means of conveyance left the town; and Count Rostopchin, the Governor, assures me that not less than sixty-three thousand carriages of every description passed the barriers, exclusive of the army carriages.

On the 14th of September the Russian rearguard commenced its movement through the city, but as the enemy seemed inclined to press, he sent word to Buonaparte, through Murat, that he would defend the streets to the last extremity and fire the town if he was incommoded. Murat sent a civil answer and the rearguard filed through, but a thousand workmen of the garrison battalion, employed at the arsenal, having remained too long, were made prisoners.

When Murat entered, the Crown magazines of forage, of wine (not less than thirteen millions of quarts), of brandy, of military stores and of powder were blazing. As he approached the arsenal, the populace, frantic, rushed upon him and his troops.

The enemy, victorious, hoped and expected to repose in an emporium of riches and luxuriant abundance until that peace was made which Buonaparte promised to his army at Smolensk. But the Russians resolved on inflicting a species of vengeance more disastrous in its consequences than the slaughter of the sword. All the houses of the nobility, all the warehouses of the merchants, all the shops, &c., were fired and, notwithstanding every effort of the enemy, the conflagration raged and rendered Moscow one flaming pile, so that, as the enemy stated themselves, they occupied only the site where the city stood, and their embarrassments were increased by an erroneous calculation that their needs would be supplied by the resources of Moscow. They invariably represent their difficulties to be such as to render a stay at Moscow impossible. Some speculate upon a march to the Ukraine which Buonaparte, as a captain, ought to have occupied after he left Smolensk, and this I thought he would have done; but they seem in utter ignorance of the state of the Russian army and of the Moldavian army being on march to join

General Tormanssow. Yet I hardly think that Buonaparte will now, for military or political reasons, draw off to his right. The success of the operation must be doubtful to him and it must commence by sacrificing every hope of possessing himself by political influence of his great desideratum—Peace. It must commence by removing every apprehension for St. Petersburg, by evacuating Courland, &c., or by his sacrificing the corps stationed at present on the left of his line.

The calculation of reinforcement to the Russian army by the Council of War has been fully answered. I myself have seen a hundred and forty-four pieces of cannon refused, and eight thousand as fine troops as any in the regular army arrive, with several thousand militia. To-morrow and on the ensuing days of next week fifteen thousand regular infantry, under Prince Labanow, are expected; four thousand Cossacks will be here in eight days; and four thousand five hundred, under Colonel de Witt, from Kiew, have joined General Tormanssow. Two thousand horse given by the province of Toula, and two thousand horses for the remnant of the artillery and cavalry of this army, also given by that province exclusive of its militia contingent, are in our camp; while eighty-four thousand militia are on their march from the neighbouring provinces to be fused into the ranks of the regular army and will successively arrive in the month of October.

Exclusively of these supplies, an immense army is forming in the province of Kasan, under the command of General Tolstoy.[1]

With the means of such an empire, with the spirit of such a people, with the base of such an army, can I doubt of Russia's triumph and the establishment of at least one independent State in the North of Europe?

I could express stronger hopes and assign more indisputable reasons for their realization, but I would not risk by indiscretion the chances of their successful issue.

Every day since we have been here, prisoners in parties of fifty, and even of a hundred, have been brought in, chiefly wounded. During the five days that we remained at Krasnoi Pakra, thirteen hundred and forty-two were delivered to the commandant at headquarters. Of course many more are killed, for such is the inveteracy of the peasants that they buy prisoners of the Cossacks for several roubles to put them to death. Two guns have been taken by the peasants; vast quantities of baggage, &c., both going to and from

---

[1] Alexander Ivanovich Ostermann-Tolstoy.

Moscow; much melted silver, which I myself have seen: and some of the guards—of whom two squadrons were taken—told me that they had been obliged to blow up a convoy of sixty powder-waggons, rather than suffer them to be made a prize. In brief, the Spanish guerrilla warfare never was more successful, and certainly was not so formidable to the enemy.

The prisoners, not French, but foreigners, all hold but one language: they all describe themselves as victims to an insatiable ambition and say that privations of every kind have been the prelude to their loss of liberty.

I am not painting these things *en couleur de rose*. They are most sacredly true; I have not made one exaggerated representation. The truth is sufficient: it wants no garnish.

I do not mean to say that I have nothing to wish for to render success more rapid; but whatever imperfections may still exist in this army, whatever changes it may be necessary to make, whatever new regulations it may be necessary to enforce, thank God! Buonaparte is in such case that he cannot prevent a signal overthrow. When fate presides, and Russian courage is its instrument, chiefs may wrangle or may err, due precautions may be neglected, but he must fall. Nor am I inclined to think that he has more capacity to secure his safety than other men, for the whole of his campaign has been a series of faults with want of sufficient enterprise.

My headquarters are with Prince Kutusow, but as he is very unequal to much exertion in society and likes to be retired, I generally take my seat at Beningsen's table, where I have a regular cover at all times; but yesterday I had a very pleasant dinner with the Duke of Würtemberg: this day I dined with Count Rostopchin and Platow.

As the day was very bitter and raw, and I had still much to write, I contented myself with a walk to the Prince of Oldenburg after dinner, to talk over German affairs and fight battles over again which it would have been well for Europe if they had never been fought.

29th—Yesterday I rode to the advanced posts, which remained on the river Pakra. The enemy had lodged themselves opposite, but without any disposition to inconvenience our parties.

The Cossacks continue to obtain great success. Five hundred Frenchmen have been taken by them as the enemy's column retrograded from the Kolomna road; and yesterday fourteen carts, two of which contained gold and silver to the amount of fifteen thousand ducats, were taken on the Podolsk road. All the prisoners concur in stating that the French army is in the state we desire and it appears that Buonaparte is in some danger in Moscow. Eighty Russians, concealed in the Kremlin, where he is lodged, attempted to fire the building while he was asleep and he was obliged to fly from the palace at night.

From an intercepted letter, it appears that the French call the battle of Borodino, '*La bataille des généraux,*' thirty-two, whose names we have, being killed and wounded. Davoust[1] was struck three times.

October 1st, Woronowo.

The day before yesterday, General Milaradowitch attacked and drove back the enemy with some loss. Count Potoski was made prisoner and, in the night, General Ferrier, with two aides-de-camp, was taken by the Cossacks. The non-commissioned officer who made him prisoner gallantly refused the offer of his purse and watch. He seems to be a person of some consideration for Murat sent immediately to have him exchanged, which was refused.

Yesterday I was almost all day on horseback, with one advanced guard or other. The enemy had pushed a corps forward which I saw was a parade corps, but Prince Kutusow differed in opinion. The position of the mutual outposts was the most extraordinary I had ever seen in war, for they were so interwoven as to present fronts on all points of the compass, and I do not think I ever got so close to an enemy's corps for the purpose of reconnoitring as I did to Prince Poniatowsky's.[2] It was almost the same as being in his camp.

At night the Cossacks attacked and killed two hundred Cuirassiers on a foraging party, and made eighty-five prisoners. I was a friend to three poor brutes (horses), which had been dreadfully wounded, and had been in torture for some hours: at my entreaty General Milaradowitch ordered them to be shot.

This morning the army marched ten wersts. I waited, with Count Rostopchin, to see him fire his palace and all surrounding premises. It was a magnificent act, executed with feeling, dignity, and philosophy. The motive was pure patriotism.

On the preceding day, seventeen hundred and twenty of his peasants (all on this property) came in a body to request permission to leave their houses, effects, and the bones of their fathers, and retire to the Count's estates in the interior of Russia, which leave was granted. Never was a more affecting procession. But what a

---

[1] Marshal Louis Nicholas Davout, Prince of Eckmühl, in command of the 1st Corps.
[2] Josef Anton Poniatowsky (1763–1813), nephew of the last King of Poland, commanded the 5th (Polish) Corps under Napoleon.

country is this Russia! What patriotic virtue! What nobility of spirit! Shame! for shame on Dr. Clarke[1] who has calumniated such a nation. The flames had raged about two hours, when we received advice that the enemy had retreated, but the Count expressed no regret; on the contrary, he conversed quite calmly with me, and waited until we saw some colossal statues of men and horses fall.

Certainly the property destroyed could not be replaced for a hundred thousand pounds. The house and premises rivalled any that we have in England.

The firing of Ephesus[2] won a dishonourable immortality; the firing of Woronowo ought to ensure, and will ensure, a lasting record of Russian patriotism.

In his Narrative *Sir Robert describes this dramatic episode at greater length.*

The very stabling was of rare grandeur, surmounted over the gateways by colossal casts of the Monte Cavallo horses and figures which he had brought from Rome, with costly models of all the principal Roman and Grecian buildings and statues that filled a large gallery in the palace, the interior of which was most splendidly and tastefully furnished with every article of luxurious use and ornament that foreign countries could supply.

. . . Rostopchin, on hearing the picquets commence skirmishing, and seeing the enemy in movement, entered his palace, begging his friends to accompany him. On arriving at the porch, burning torches were distributed to every one. Mounting the stairs, and reaching his state bedroom, Rostopchin paused a moment, and then said to the English General [Wilson], "That is my marriage bed; I have not the heart to set it on fire; you must spare me this pain." When Rostopchin had himself set on fire all the rest of the apartment then, and not before, his wish was executed. Each apartment was ignited as the party proceeded, and in a quarter of an hour the whole was one blazing mass. Rostopchin then proceeded to the stables which were quickly in flames, and afterwards stood in front contemplating the progress of the fire and the falling fragments.

When the last of the Cavallo group was precipitated, he said, "I am at ease"; and as the enemy's shots were now whistling around,

---

[1] Edward Daniel Clarke (1769–1822), a well-known traveller, visited Russia in 1800. In 1808 he became Professor of Mineralogy at Cambridge, and two years later began the publication of his *Travels in Various Countries of Europe, Asia and Africa*. He and Wilson had met in Egypt.

[2] The great temple was fired in 356 B.C., on the night Alexander the Great was born, by an Ephesian wishing to perpetuate his own memory.

he and all retired, leaving the enemy the following alarming and instructive lesson affixed to a conspicuous pillar:

"I have ornamented during eight years this mansion-seat, where I have lived happy in the bosom of my family.

"The inhabitants of this property, to the number of seventeen hundred and twenty, quit it at your approach, and I voluntarily set the house on fire, that it may not be polluted by your presence.

"Frenchmen, I abandoned to you my two houses at Moscow, with their furniture and contents worth half a million roubles. *Here* you will find only *ashes*" (pp. 178–80).

At this place I found Allen[1] and my dragoons, who had just come. It appears that since I left him in Turkey he has experienced all the kindness, all the hospitality that I myself have ever received; and in all places he has been served by the master of the house from his own table. He is full of gratitude, and astonishment at such predilection for the English.

This is but a sorry village, although the houses are warm and weatherproof; but the best peasant's cot is a great contrast to the palace of Woronowo.

General Milaradowitch has just sent me a French horse as a present, with saddle, bridle, &c. He seems as generous and as brave as his friend, the ever-to-be-lamented Bagrathion. I now more than ever prize the Circassian dagger he gave me, and which I sent to Hopkinson's with my fine sword and a favourite pistol, by Captain Wyburn.

October 3rd, Tarouza.

The army has continued its movements behind the Pakra. The enemy followed cautiously, and only maintained a distant artillery fire. At night the Cossacks attacked a convoy, made eighty-four prisoners, and possessed themselves of many waggons laden with bread.

Dined with the Duke of Würtemberg, to whom I more and more attach myself, as he is full of goodness and military knowledge.

4th—A great but accidental fire dislodged us all yesterday. The Duke of Oldenburg, however, preserved his kitchen and I fêted with him.

The cannonade recommenced about noon, and the French cavalry fell into a Cossack ambuscade—five hundred were killed and a hundred and eighty made prisoners. It was a very gallant affair, most ably conducted. We are now in a commanding position, strongly reinforced, and all wears the face of successful promise.

[1] Wilson's orderly.

Our main army is as numerous as that of the enemy—I believe, indeed, stronger. He is environed by numerous difficulties, and very superior forces are pressing upon his flanks and rear. We have our supplies; he wants them. We are habituated to climate; he has everything to fear from it.

It is a great moment—an awful epoch! The operations of the last seventeen years, the victories of France, the errors of the continental Powers, are all now gathered together, and await the decision of the fate of ninety thousand men plunged above five hundred miles into the heart of a warlike and powerful nation, whose army has never yet, during this war, suffered actual defeat.

I fear that the enemy will not attack us; but if he attempts to manœuvre on our left, he will find that we can counteract his plans by offensive operations more congenial to the feelings of the army, although not so advantageous to the common cause—for a little longer.

Platow is about to vault again into the saddle. There was a little *més-entendu*, which I have arranged. Twenty-one regiments from the Don will encamp in fifteen days; four are already arrived. Of these twelve thousand he will take four thousand, his own regiment now here, with some artillery and chasseurs, and then Murat will be, within six weeks, without one squadron in the field. I propose to accompany his first enterprise, as it is one of great interest.

Lord Tyrconnel will go the day after to-morrow to Admiral Tchichagow to remain with him. I then shall be left again without an Englishman, but I have asked Lord Cathcart to lend me Captain Dawson, Lord Portarlington's brother and Lord Rosslyn's aide-de-camp. The weather has been very cold for the last two days, but fine, which is a variety. I already begin to regret my departure from Constantinople without my pelisses.

The cannonade recommences, and I must go and see my fine fellows and comrades, the Cossacks, work. I am happy to say that from services rendered to their Hetman, I am more popular than ever with them. With regard to the army at large, I remain, as heretofore, the object of every attention.

As Wilson had a good deal to do, and a particular affinity, with the Cossacks from the Don and Volga, it is worth quoting some of his paragraphs about them in Brief Remarks on the Character and Composition of the Russian Army.

Mounted on a very little, ill-conditioned, but well-bred horse, which can walk at the rate of five miles an hour with ease, or, in his speed, dispute the race with the swiftest—with a short whip on his wrist (as he wears no spur)—armed with the lance, a pistol in his girdle, and a sword, he never fears a competitor in single combat; but in the late war he irresistibly attacked every opposing squadron in the field.

They act in dispersion, and when they do re-unite to charge, it is not with a systematic formation, but *en masse*, or what in Germany is called the swarm attack.

Dexterous in the management of a horse that is guided only by the snaffle, they can twist and bend their course through the most intricate country at full speed. They have only a snaffle bridle on their horses for the convenience of feeding at all times, and even in the presence of an enemy. If their horses had bits, they could not take advantage of every opportunity to graze and they would be ruined; for their activity is too incessant to admit of long stops for regular feeding.

His dress is simple; a blue jacket (with a white frog on the cuff or cape) fastened with hooks; a pair of loose trowsers, plaited so as to cover and conceal the opening in front; a pair of short boots; a black cap made of the unborn lamb, from which depends a red pandour sack, a plume on the side of the cap, or, what is more common, except in the Attaman's regiment, merely a cloth cap with a kind of sack hanging behind, in which he stuffs his provisions or other articles; and a white or black hair Circassian short cloak— is the costume of the Cossaque on service of his country.

As I propose to make an experiment during the winter, I want the best pocket portable thermometer sent out. I wish it to be got at Dollond's.[1]

General Barclay quits the army. We lose a brave executive officer, who greatly distinguished himself at Borodino; but his departure will do good by removing a spirit of dissension that was injurious to the general interests.

White bread is six shillings a loaf; sugar, ten shillings a pound; butter not to be had; and very little of anything in camp but meat and black biscuit; yet all are well and gay, and, by some means or another, we have daily a comparative banquet.

For want of my people from Woronzow and my canteens from Constantinople, I cannot yet boast of a good breakfast or tea establishment; but I mean to be *fort* in both, and Prince Galitzin yesterday gave me a cow to assist my good intentions.

I wish Keate[2] to be told, that the day before yesterday I saw a

---

[1] Peter Dollond (1730–1820) was a distinguished optician in the Strand, London.
[2] Thomas Keate (1745–1821), the celebrated surgeon at St. George's Hospital, London, who was three times Master of the College of Surgeons.

Cossack have his arm extracted from the shoulder joint, who had ridden twenty miles after having been struck by a cannon shot. He never spoke during the operation, which was performed by Dr. Wiley[1] in less than four minutes; but he talked afterwards quite composedly. The next morning he drank tea, walked about his room, and then got into a cart, which carried him fourteen miles. He is now proceeding several hundred miles to the Don, and is, according to the last report, doing very well. This operation of extracting the arm is a frequent operation here, and seldom fails of cure.

October 9th, Tarouza. Imperial Headquarters.

Soon after I had sent away my last letter, I mounted my horse to see an action at the advanced posts. Buonaparte, it was said, had just arrived, and Murat commanded in person; but, notwithstanding various attempts of resolute character on every point of the line, the Russians not only maintained their ground but drove the enemy back three wersts.

Had I been able to procure two guns at the instant I wanted them I should have greatly aided the carnage, but they came too late. As I rode up amongst the chasseurs, to reconnoitre the spot for this artillery, a chasseur of the Russians, mistaking me for a French General, levelled at me; but General Ouwarrow and Count Osterman, who were in the rear, saw it, and called out to him to save the shot: the enemy's, however, passed thick enough, but respected man and horse. It was a most interesting, and in its consequences will prove a most important, combat.

The loss of the enemy was very considerable: they left four caissons on the ground, and a wood and plain covered with dead. As I have said in my official despatch, artillery, cavalry, and infantry all proved that they possessed a warrantable confidence of superiority.

The next morning Buonaparte sent a letter to request permission for an aide-de-camp-general to come to headquarters, and speak on important matters with Marshal Kutusow. The Marshal had answered that he himself would meet him beyond the advanced posts, before I knew of his flag of truce.

However, upon my strong representations against the intercourse and my statement of the mischievous consequences of such a pro-

[1] James Wylie (1768–1854) entered Russian service as a regimental surgeon in 1790 and later became physician to the imperial court in St. Petersburg. For thirty years he was president of the Medical Academy which he founded in 1804. In 1812 Wylie was appointed Director of the Medical Department of the Russian Ministry of War. Two years later, when he accompanied the Czar to London, he was knighted by the Prince Regent.

ceeding—such an *empressement* to enter into negotiations with the enemy—in which representations I was supported by the Duke of Würtemberg and Prince Oldenburg whom I brought to the Marshal for that purpose, the Marshal consented to send Prince Wolkonsky to the advanced posts.

The Prince went as aide-de-camp-general of the Emperor, and met General Lauriston,[1] who told him that he had important matters to communicate to the Marshal in person: it was then settled that General Lauriston should at night see the Marshal in his own headquarters.

The strictest forms of etiquette were preserved, and everything would have proved a dignified sense of superiority if General Beningsen had not indiscreetly gone the same day to the advanced posts and held a conversation with Murat, who came when he was told that General Beningsen was there. The conversation was very insignificant, the principal remark of Murat being, "*Ce n'est pas un climat pour un Roi de Naples*":[2] but the appearance was pernicious, and any unnecessary address of these invaders *en Souverain, une bassesse volontaire,* which I think will be marked by the Emperor's displeasure.

At night Marshal Kutusow wished the Duke of Würtemberg and myself to be present when Lauriston entered, that he might let him see how he was *entouré en conseil.*

After mutual salutations from the Marshal, that Lauriston might not be ignorant who we were, we retired, but waited very near and saw that the conversation was very animated on the part of the Marshal by his gestures.

In half an hour Prince Wolkonsky was called in, and in a quarter of an hour afterwards, General Lauriston came out with a very discontented air, and spoke in such a manner that every person was satisfied that he had been disappointed. The Marshal, on our entering, told us what had passed.

General Lauriston had complained, first, of the barbarity of the Russians towards the French. The Marshal answered, that he could not civilize a nation in three months who regarded the enemy as a marauding force of Tartars under a Ginghis Khan.

Lauriston said: "But at least there is some difference." "In fact," said the Marshal, "there may be, but none in the eyes of the people: I can only answer for my own troops." General Lauriston had no

[1] Jacques-Alexandre-Bernard Law, Marquis de Lauriston (1768–1828) had been French ambassador in St. Petersburg before the outbreak of war.
[2] Marshal Murat was King of Naples.

complaint to make against them. He then adverted to an armistice, saying that "Nature herself would, in a short time, oblige it." The Marshal said he had no authority on that head.

General Lauriston soon again returned to the subject of an armistice, and said: "You must not think we wish it because our affairs are desperate. *Nos deux armées sont à peu près égales.* You are nearer your supplies and reinforcements than we are, but we also have reinforcements. Perhaps you have heard that our affairs are disastrous in Spain?" "I have," said the Marshal, "from Sir Robert Wilson, whom you saw near me, and with whom I have daily interviews." "Oh!" said the General, "Wilson may have reasons to exaggerate his statements." "None," said the Marshal; "he tells me things as they are, with all the naïveté of candour." Lauriston resumed: "We have, indeed, received a check by the *bêtise* of Marshal Marmont, and Madrid, *en attendant*, is occupied by the English;[1] but they will soon be driven out, and everything will be restored in that country by the numerous forces marching there." He then denied the burning of Moscow by the French, observing: "It is so inconsistent with the French character, that if we take London we shall not fire that city."

As I was returning home at midnight, with the Duke of Oldenburg, in a droska,[2] we were overset. The droska fell upon my right leg, and remained some minutes, until the Duke, who was unhurt, extricated himself, and raised it, with the help of Captain Fanshaw his aide-de-camp. I could not get up alone, and when I did rise I was in great pain and very sick; but I proceeded in the droska to my village, and remained the rest of the night in darkness and in misery, as we had no candles, and no means of relief. The next morning Prince Wolkonsky came to my quarters soon after daybreak, and we gave him some hot tea, and my letters for Lord Cathcart and the Emperor.

The surgeon soon after arrived and dressed my leg, which was greatly scraped in the skin, and cut on the right and left of the ankle pretty deep, and very much swollen.

In the evening, understanding that Murat complained of being fired at as a breach of convention, I went to the Marshal to ask an explanation officially. The Marshal gave me his honour that there was no convention, and he then denied also the report of any negotiation with the enemy, admitting that he had no power whatever to

---

[1] After Marmont's defeat at the battle of Salamanca, Wellington's troops entered Madrid on August 12th.
[2] A low, four-wheeled carriage.

enter into it, or to make an armistice. At night I went over to another quarter, a werst off, and lodged in an unfinished house, with the Duke of Würtemberg. The Duke of Oldenburg took the next apartment. We changed for the worse in regard to warmth, but for the better as to light and cleanliness.

The next day I went over to the headquarters, which had fallen back a little. Thence I went in a droska to General Milaradowitch, when I heard various amusing anecdotes.

Murat had come to the advanced posts originally to meet General Beningsen, who had the indiscretion to court an interview. From that time he had occasionally presented himself to General Milaradowitch who commands our advanced posts, and who is an *élève* of Suwarrow[1] and brother soldier of the ever-to-be-lamented Bagrathion.

Milaradowitch in one interview said: "I wish that I could see a real charge of cavalry: our officers and men wish it much, especially in such a fine plain; but whenever we move on your squadrons seek support from their infantry or artillery." Murat was silent.

Again Milaradowitch said: "It is really an outrage to let so many of your dead remain unburied, and your wounded lie in that wood. I will give you permission to come within my posts and remove them."

Murat owned that on the 4th the Russians had an indisputable pretension to the honour of the day.

There never was a man better qualified to treat with Murat than Milaradowitch. His manner, the tone of his voice, his gestures, &c., render him superior to Murat in fanfaronade, while his singular courage, and the unbounded confidence of his soldiers, secure him every respect from the enemy.

General Korf,[2] who is a most excellent man, with a fund of dry humour, on the same day met General Amande at the advanced posts. The conversation soon turned on peace. General Amande observed: "We are really quite tired of this war: give us passports and we will depart." "Oh! no, General," said Korf, "you came without being invited; when you go away you must take French leave." "Ah!" said General Amande, "but it is really a pity that two nations who esteem each other should be carrying on a war of extermination: we will make our excuses for having intruded, and shake hands upon our respective frontiers." "Yes," replied the Russian, "we believe that you have lately learnt to esteem us, but would you continue to do so if we suffered you to escape with arms

[1] Alexander Suwarow (1729–1800) drove the French out of North Italy in 1799.
[2] Feodor Karlovich, Baron Korff.

in your hands?" "*Parbleu!*" sighed Monsieur Amande, "I see that there is no talking to you about peace now and that we shall not be able to make it."

The language of Murat and General Amande is the universal language of all who communicate with us, or who are taken. It is the content of every letter found in the pockets of the enemy and I sent one this day to the Spanish Ambassador, addressed to the Prince of Eckmühl,[1] from an officer in the Spanish corps, in which he requests permission to go into the 57th regiment, as he is satisfied that his honour will be ruined by the desertion of his men on the first occasion. Discontent and need and apprehension are hourly augmenting the difficulties of Buonaparte; these, added to the daily multiplying forces of the Russians, and the approaching rudeness of the climate, will, I think, very soon render his case desperate. We wish he would attack our camp, but fear that he will not. His army entered Moscow eighty-two thousand effective men; since then he has lost several thousand killed, and I have seen several thousand prisoners.

Yesterday two hundred French cuirassier foragers were made prisoners. A general came with a flag of truce to remonstrate against the cruelty of the Cossacks in falling upon "poor men only going in search of a little hay!" Sweet innocents! How tender! how humane! how considerate these myrmidons have become!

I am sorry to say that my second expedition in droska was almost as grievous as my first. I lost, by some negligence of an abstract cogitation *en chemin*, my bourka, that was the pride of my wardrobe, the envy of the army, which I calculated upon for a dry skin in autumn rains, for comfort in the severest frost. I have, however, offered a hundred roubles (£10 English) to recover it and hope to succeed, as the loss and offer are announced in General Orders, which is a very unusual compliment in Russian service.

This day, in obedience to Dr. Wiley's strict commands, who was very angry at my going out yesterday and the day before, and in compliance (to own the real truth) with necessity, I remained at home, and wrote despatches to Mr. Liston and Admiral Tchichagow, the latter of which Lord Tyrconnel is to carry.

My leg is so swollen and the wound so angry, that I cannot put my foot to the ground. I fear it will be long before the ankle will recover its strength. However I *must* and *will* ride, if there is anything to do. The pain is acute, but I am more anxious about the final restoration of the limb to its power than any immediate relief.

[1] Marshal Davout.

My despatches to Mr. Liston will have an important effect at Constantinople and in the Mediterranean. This communication alone renders my position here of the greatest value to the British interests; but I may, without presumption, say that I have every day since my arrival rendered essential service to my country, to the Emperor and to the common cause.

My interference with respect to the proposed degradation of the Marshal by his visit to the advanced posts has received general approbation; and, with just confidence, I am considered as one who will guard the Emperor's honour and interests as well as those with which I am charged as a British envoy, from insult or duplicity.

9th—Lord Tyrconnel left me this morning for Admiral Tchichagow. He is a great personal loss, but public duty obliged me to send him.

My leg improved a little and therefore I thought I might venture to get as far as General Milaradowitch. The general had, the day before, seen Murat, who asked him personally to let his cavalry forage to the right and left. Milaradowitch answered: "Why, would you wish to deprive us of the pleasure of taking your finest cavaliers of France *comme des poules*?" "Oh! then I shall take my measures: I shall march my foraging columns with infantry and artillery on the flanks." "It is exactly what I wish, that I may order my regiments to give them the *rencontre*."

Murat galloped off and instead of his marching the columns to protect his foragers, the Cossacks took last night forty-three cuirassiers and carabineers, and fifty-three this morning.

The Marshal, on my return, wished me to dine with him, but I was afraid of his luxuries; I therefore went to the Duke of Oldenburg, as he lives more simply and allows my vinegar bottle to be on table, although a mistake now and then gives him a wry face and a pain in his stomach.

At my quarters I found one of my dragoons and one of my Cossacks; the others are marching under escort with my horses from Woronzow. They had been taken up about a hundred wersts off upon suspicion of being French who had seduced two Cossacks. Some general, known to me, released them. There is no rambling about now; all the peasantry are armed and they are most terrible inquisitors.

My calculation was erroneous about my leg. It swelled considerably in consequence of my ride, but the swelling is now going down fast. The wounds are just as they ought to be, thanks to the vinegar-and-water system.

October 13th, Tarouza.

Since the departure of Lord Tyrconnel more than a thousand prisoners have been sent in, chiefly cavalry with their horses, but these are too bad for the Emperor's service.

The bearded warriors of the Don (being chiefly veterans and fathers of families, who are distinguished by bearded honours) continue to arrive, and 'General Winter', who is our most powerful ally, has already presented the torrents of his advanced guard.

Yesterday I rode to dine with Strogonow. The camp, which is a glorious spectacle, being now arranged in order of battle, was particularly cheerful, as the capture of Madrid was being universally celebrated.

On my return Platow loaded me with pears, Don wine better in my opinion than Champagne and a fine dried sturgeon to eat like smoked salmon. I value this present the more as it enables me to distribute 'the goods the gods provide'.

My leg is still a little pillar, with three wounds in it; but notwithstanding doctor's orders and anger and a little pain, I go about in droska and occasionally mount a horse for half an hour, confiding in the vinegar-and-water system and an assurance that I only double the time of cure by motion. My cavalier appearance is, indeed, not very military—a leg without a boot, and a foot without a stirrup.

I was yesterday acting the part of a pacificator between the Marshal and General Beningsen, but peace can only be temporary. This army has not yet moved, but I hope we shall march a little to our left to menace the Smolensk road. Borowsk is our proper point to bear upon.

While I was dining with Platow and a great party of general officers the day before yesterday, Platow received a letter from one of the Tartar regiments informing him that they had made prize of a considerable sum of gold and silver which had been melted by the enemy from church ornaments; but that they placed their prize at his disposal, as they thought it a sacrilege to take it from their country.

'*Le beau sentiment*' is not extinguished here, however rare in these times, and I could write a many-paged book of verified anecdotes that would shame the niggardliness of other more civilized countries.

It is true the light troops have no want of unrighteous gold; they have taken so many horses, watches, Louis-d'ors, &c., that one Cossack regiment has divided booty that gives every man eighty-four pounds sterling.

There is now a noble prize awaiting them. Three hundred and fifty waggons, laden with Buonaparte's plunder, was proceeding under the escort of four regiments of cavalry and two battalions of infantry on the Mojaisk road.

Three hundred Cossacks charged at night, killed all the horses of the waggons, rendered the column immovable and have given advice to three thousand men under the command of General Dorokow,[1] who has marched to profit by the occasion.

The Don regiments continue to pour in. Such a reinforcement of cavalry was perhaps never equalled, and Tyrconnel writes me word that there are nineteen regiments at Pultawa only waiting orders to march.

The Don regiments are welcome guests *sous tous les rapports*. They bring us the most agreeable wines, sturgeon, caviare, and large barrels of red and white grapes, of which Platow has given me a superabundant share.

At three o'clock I remount my horse. General Beningsen is already gone to the advanced guard; but I am now prudent enough to give my leg all the repose I can, and unremittingly to mortify the appetite that I may indulge necessary activity.

17th—Until yesterday I was combating momentarily against very severe pain. My wounds in the leg burned like the effect of hot sealing wax, but the goodness of system triumphed and the bad flesh having sloughed off, I am in rapid progress towards recovery.

I passed, notwithstanding, a delightful night. The Cossack chiefs fêted me with all their luxuries, amusements, honours, &c. The enemy were not distant more than six hundred yards, and grouped to hear the music. The singers gave me their famous boat song, and the enemy having recognized my vessel, the answer to the hail was: "She is charged with Spanish victories."

Soon after daybreak I rode along the line of videttes, and Murat made his appearance. We looked at each other for a quarter of an hour and both dismounted to have a fairer gaze. He then sent an officer forward, but I desired Captain Fanshaw, who was with me, to request that he would return to his line.

Two days before I had sent one of my dragoons to a circle of French and Austrian officers, whilst I passed slowly by with the Prince of Oldenburg, that they might see and communicate to others that we were here. They were very much struck with his appearance and made many inquiries, which were suitably answered. The dragoon was very well mounted, is an excellent horseman and a good-looking man, so that the *tout-ensemble* was favourable.

[1] Major-General Ivan Semenovich Dorokow was killed on October 24th at the battle of Malo-Jaroslavets. Being rather deaf, he misjudged the distance of musketry fire.

18th—Yesterday, soon after daybreak, the action commenced as was proposed; the enemy were completely surprised; Murat had but just time to mount his horse. All his silver, equipage, bed, &c., even his plume, were taken.

Only one Russian corps, General Bagawouth's, was in fact seriously engaged; and with that and the Cossacks I happened to be at the most critical moment of their service, especially when the latter charged the enemy's cuirassiers and carabineers, which was done in the most able and gallant manner.

Had the Marshal but seconded General Beningsen's attack with the vigour that suited the occasion far greater advantage might have been obtained, but the result has militarily, politically, and morally, been very favourable to the Russian interests.

The French camps were quite disgusting. They were full of dead horses, many of which were prepared as butchers' meat. Elliott, General Clarke's[1] nephew, assures me that for the last twelve days he has been living with the rest of Murat's army on horseflesh, without salt, and without any bread. He says that Buonaparte was to have been in camp the same day and that it was believed he meant again to offer peace, and if peace was refused to force his way to the Ukraine, as retreat by the road by which he entered was impracticable, all the provisions having been consumed.

The event of yesterday will probably influence him to change his plan and to seek safety rather by flight than by force. He may, perhaps, by the sacrifice of all his artillery, baggage, &c., reach the Dwina by the route of Witepsk or Polotsk, but he ought not to attempt it, and I think he will not, since a new arrangement must be made for the command of this army which will probably place it in more activity.

As Elliott was plundered of all his money, &c., I gave him a hundred roubles, had his wounds dressed, and filled his vacant interior with a good dinner, breakfast, &c.

I knew General Clarke had been very civil to many English prisoners, and perceive that he is a friend of Lord Hutchinson's.[2] I was therefore moved to show kindness to Elliott, as well on public as on private grounds.

It was singular that he was with Murat when we reconnoitred each other the day before and that the officer who came forward to speak should have been killed. He tells me that Murat was very anxious for a conversation.

[1] Henri-Jacques-Guillaume Clarke, Duc de Feltre (1765–1818) was Minister of War.
[2] General John Hely-Hutchinson, Baron Hutchinson, afterwards 2nd Earl of Donoughmore (1757–1832) was one of Wilson's closest friends. They had served together in Holland and Egypt and again on the mission to Prussia and Russia in 1806–7.

The Cossacks are so rich that they now sell the most valuable articles for a little gold, as that alone is portable in addition to their stock. They must have gained yesterday an immense booty. I only could pick up a few amusing letters, chiefly from the frail fair.

Having been eighteen hours on horseback, I was considerably uneasy in my leg; but this morning the swelling has subsided, and the wounds are so rapidly healing that I hope in another week to wear a boot.

My correspondence with various quarters will keep me quiet for another day, and that repose will quite establish recovery, without further subjection to incidental use or *abuse* by exercise.

I am not, however, so totally to blame, as I am without any assistance here and must be everywhere myself to see with my own eyes, for I can only trust my credit to them. Since I left St. Petersburg I have not had one line from Lord Cathcart, or any other person. This is a species of banishment that diminishes very much the pleasure of my employment, and is very prejudicial to the service.

More prisoners are momentarily brought in. Above fifteen hundred arc now before our eyes, in wretched condition, with teeth chattering, &c. The peasants have bought numbers from the Cossacks, at two silver roubles a head, to kill them.

General Baltier is taken. He was chief of Poniatowski's artillery. Another general is killed. Five guns and two standards are among the trophies, but the most consolatory is the rescue of three hundred wounded Russians, in a church which the enemy had just fired.

This town is a complete heap of ruins. It is impossible to see such devastation and not find some excuse for the vengeance of the Russians.

October 27th, Kougy, 40 wersts from Kaluga.

On the 22nd, I marched with a corps of General Doctorow's,[1] comprised of twelve thousand infantry, three thousand cavalry, and eighty cannon, to effect a coup-de-main against a corps of ten thousand French, supposed to be at Fominskoi, distant thirty wersts.

When we came within seven wersts, I saw that the attempt was madly rash: the enemy's corps was not posted in any town, consequently could resist and retreat; the grand army was known to be at Woronowo, distant only twenty wersts, the day before; all reasonable conjecture induced the assurance that Buonaparte was on the alert, and moving to his right that he might gain our left.

I believe all were of my opinion who had any judgment; but the

---

[1] General Dmitri Sergeivich Dokhturov commanded the 6th Army Corps.

fear of a clamour from the thoughtless would have induced perseverance, had I not, without any phrase, at the council of war expressed my conviction that success was impracticable, and disaster probable. I prevailed so far as to obtain a delay for better information.

At dusk we received full assurance that Buonaparte, having evacuated Moscow, was with his guards and Davoust's corps only four wersts from Fominskoi, and that Borowsk, a town ten wersts in rear of our left, was in the possession of his advanced guard.

I had now the credit of forethought and prudence; and many admitted to me that they had seen the same dangers, but that I was the only man who could have prevented the misfortune; for no man could insinuate anything against my inclination to engage the enemy. They said, too, that my interference was considered as a greater proof of the honest attachment which I felt to the Russians; whereas any expression of doubt on their part was liable to, and did indeed incur, misrepresentation.

Doctorow sent to the Marshal for further reinforcements, and immediately began his march on Malo-Jaroslavets, distant thirty wersts. We made every possible effort, but the enemy from Borowsk had lodged themselves before our arrival.

As my despatches to Lord Cathcart—which will, I presume, be published—contain all the military narrative of the transactions, I shall only say that I had the honour to open the ball and plant the first guns that saved the town, for the enemy were pouring in. Our corps was in the greatest confusion, ignorant of the Kalouga road, and having to defile with all our incumbrances round the town to gain it. It was a most critical moment and the hour so saved enabled the resistance which was afterwards so obstinately made. I pushed the guns into short grape distance. After the first four rounds the enemy's columns broke, and *sauve qui peut* was the general effort up and down the hill. The slaughter must have been considerable. This, in some measure, indemnified me for the disappointment I had experienced in the first combat, when, after my return from St. Petersburg, the occasion was as fine but lost from want of cannon being at hand. The Russians and the enemy fought desperately.

Wilson provides further details of this exploit in his Narrative:
Doctorow ordered two regiments of chasseurs, supported by two more, to dash into the town, and drive the enemy (whom some fugitive inhabitants reported to have reached and entered it) out of the

place, and over the river Lougea, which ran immediately below, and destroy his bridge.

The chasseurs charged forward and quickly dislodged the enemy in the town; but at the bottom of the hill on which it is built ran a deep ravine, the opposite side of which covered the bridge, and behind this ravine the enemy found inassailable shelter.

The English General [Wilson] having gone upon the right flank of the town to reconnoitre this embankment and the position of the bridge, perceived, as day dawned, a large body of the enemy descending the lofty hill on the left bank of the river to pass the bridge and enter the town: this dense body was flocking forward as if quite at ease and unconscious of any serious opposition being designed to the passage and occupation.

The English General, having reported this incident to Doctorow, galloped with a battery of light artillery placed under his directions to an elevation which he had selected for its site, and opened its fire almost within grape shot of the mass. At the first discharge there was a general halt, on the second a wavering, on the third a total dispersion, and every one flew forward or scrambled up the hill to get out of reach of this unexpected cannonade.

The movement of the advanced guard was thus checked, and nearly an hour gained before the Viceroy [Eugène de Beauharnais] (who afterwards told the English General at Mantua "that the first shot made him start with more alarm than he had ever felt in his life, as he foresaw at once the fatal consequences") could arrive in person, bring up his artillery, and re-establish order: an essential hour for the Russians (pp. 223–5).

The town of Aspern[1] was not more heroically contended for. But whenever the enemy appeared out of the town the Russians gained an easy victory, even over the Guards, who latterly were engaged and whom Buonaparte was seen to be addressing as they descended the hill to pass the river.

The shot, shell and balls fell in showers from time to time in all parts of the field, but there was no time at that moment for consideration of peril. Every man present was obliged to do his duty, for the need demanded every exertion.

The Russians only accuse *one person* of being deficient in example; in addition to the heavy charges which can be brought against him for ignorance in the conduct of the troops, for sloth, for indecision

[1] May 21–22, 1809, on the Danube, fought between the Austrians under the Archduke Charles and Masséna's French troops.

of counsels, for panic operations and for "a desire to let the enemy pass unmolested." Marshal Kutusow affords a memorable instance of incapacity in a chief, of an absence of any quality that ought to distinguish a commander. Although within five wersts of the action from daybreak, he never had even the curiosity to appear in the field until five o'clock in the evening; and when he did come he never went forward, but, like Canute[1] on the sea-shore, took his station and said to the balls: "Come no further than three hundred paces from me."—and they, unlike the rebel waves, obeyed.[2]

Beningsen, on the other hand, was everywhere; and I accompanied him alone into the town when he arrived, for he would not allow any suite to follow. I have done my duty and put those in possession of the facts who can prevent their pernicious repetition.

The firing of the town was a terrible expedient. All the wounded who could not move were burnt, but I have seen this so often that I cease to feel the same horror that I felt at first. At Moscow officers and men alike perished.

The night was anxious, and I was very hungry, but morning came and I was more frightened and more famished. The weak old Marshal took alarm. He ordered a movement to the rear as soon as day dawned when the enemy began to fire. The columns clashed, the horses could not draw through the mud, the bridges over the marsh were broken, the wounded crawling away were crying for aid, and such a scene of confusion ensued as determined me to take my part with the rearguard as the least evil.

The good countenance, however, of this rearguard checked the advance of the enemy. Gradually the difficulties diminished, the army collected three wersts from the town, order was re-established and there was not a man but the Marshal who would not have thanked Providence for a general battle at that very moment. The transitions from confidence to fear, from joy to despair, are as frequent as the movements of this army and its occupation of positions, for courage is our only shield.

I had just time to write a note to the Emperor and one to Lord Cathcart, from the drum-head of one of the battalions of Guards, before the courier went off.

The next morning we moved here, as it was proper to cover the Medynsk road after having uncovered the position of Malo-

[1] King Canute, son of the Danish King, landed in England in 1015.
[2] In a footnote in his *Narrative*, Wilson relates that after Kutusow's arrival on the field, the Prince of Oldenburg rode up and asked Wilson if he had seen the Marshal. The English General, pointing to a distant tree, said: "He may be in that direction." "No," replied the Prince tartly, "that cannot be, for I have just seen a shell pass beyond."

Jaroslavets; where we might have destroyed any enemy who attempted to debouch from the town, for we had seven hundred guns within grape distance and above a hundred thousand men: while Platow and ten thousand of his brave Cossacks are hanging on the rear of the enemy, and have already presented us with sixteen cannon and all the printing press, depôt of maps, &c., belonging to him, besides securing for themselves an immense booty.

This morning the enemy was retreating, probably to gain the Smolensk road. The Marshal will sing *Te Deum*, but the rest of the army 'hymns of lamentation.'

If the French army is not wrecked before it reaches the frontier, the Marshal, old and infirm as he is, ought to be shot.

I rely, however, on the Cossacks and light troops, whom I shall certainly join if I find that the main army is thrown out.

Our news from Admiral Tchichagow is excellent, and from every quarter; but there is on this account more reason to prevent the re-appearance of Buonaparte with an army, lest the embryo of good be crushed.

Baron Brinken, my Russian aide-de-camp, arrived, charged with various kind letters from Lord Cathcart, &c., many honourable proofs of Imperial favour, but unfortunately no letters from England.

I have been profiting by my few hours' leisure to send a courier to Constantinople, one to Lord Tyrconnel, and one to St. Petersburg, but this constant writing furrows my face fast; at least so I am *told*, for I have not seen it myself since I left St. Petersburg.

My leg is not yet quite well. It also has had its transitions, but I think it past relapse, and sure of restoration to form.

General Clarke's nephew remained with my people (who really are the admiration of the army for their gallantry and courtesy) three days. I then despatched him, with a very strong letter of recommendation to all the Russians, a good cloak and two hundred roubles. I offered to procure his exchange, but he declined until the French were out of their embarrassments, as he had "had enough of horse-flesh and Cossack iron."

October 30th, Medinsk.

Yesterday we marched to Poloianameya, a great cloth-manu-factory. There is not in England a more extensive establishment or a mercantile residence more magnificent. I was lodged in some of the best apartments, but I would gladly have exchanged for any ordinary hovel, as the day was bitterly cold, and the stoves smoked so much that they could not be used.

This morning we marched to Medinsk, where the Cossacks

defeated the advanced guard of Prince Poniatowski, taking General Cassewitch, killing Colonel Chevers—married to Princess Czartory-sky—wounding another Colonel, destroying a great many men and capturing five pieces of cannon. The ground is still covered with dead horses and men. In the prison are also about a hundred prisoners, who, on General Beningsen's entrance, asked for some horseflesh, as they had seen a horse die before their windows.

The captives pay dear for their master's crimes; those are the happiest, indeed, who quit their chains and their lives together.

The massacre at Moscow seems to have been very terrible: not less than four thousand, the greater part convalescent sick and wounded—but the Russians have great wrongs to avenge. Buona-parte was very cruel in the capital, executing many without proof of guilt, for offences which he had no right to punish with death.

The French also have habitually shot all the Russian soldiers who from wounds, &c., could not keep up with the line of march.

We are now in pursuit of the enemy, who is flying with all expedition: he has already destroyed above a thousand waggons. The army is highly indignant with the Marshal for his conduct of the operations: by a false movement, occasioned by his personal terror rather than by an error of judgment, he has made a circuit of near eighty wersts and has lost sight of the enemy, whom he ought to have daily brought to action and never to have quitted with his main army while ten thousand remained together.

I can scarcely behave with common decency in his presence. His feebleness outrages me to such a degree that I have declared, if he remains Commander-in-chief, that I must retire from this army.

November 1st, Selino.

This day we marched here and had the agreeable news of Platow's capture of twenty cannon and two standards, and the destruction of two battalions at the convent of Kollodiy, near Borodino.

The whole road to Mojaisk was enveloped in smoke; we saw various explosions of powder waggons, and heard a cannonade in the line forward with this village; but we have fifty wersts to reach Wiasma and I fear much that we shall not arrive in time. Had we moved on Joukhnow after we quitted Malo-Jaroslavets, as we all besought the Marshal to do, we should have been now in an impregnable position facing Wiasma, and the golden glorious opportunity lost at Malo-Jaroslavets might have been retrieved.

The army has been without food the whole of this day and I fear we must march to-morrow without any, as the provision-waggons are left far behind; but the troops support every privation with wonderful spirit. How lamentable that they should have been so commanded! that they should have been deprived of the recompense their courage merited! that their toils should have been so unnecessarily continued! and that so much more blood must be shed to effect partial success when the whole prize was in their hands!

The peasants of the village in which we now are have wreaked dreadful vengeance on many of the enemy. Fifty were seized here and buried alive. A dog, belonging to one of the unfortunate men, daily went to the French camp and returned to his master's grave. The peasants were afraid of discovery, but they were a fortnight before they could kill the faithful animal.

According to intercepted letters from Buonaparte to Savary,[1] he is retiring on Wilna, but I hope the Admiral [Tchichagow] will intercept his progress on that route. All the peasants, and the few prisoners who escape death, declare that famine makes great havoc. Their only nourishment is horse-flesh, which many cannot eat as it produces dysentery.

When the poor fellows are taken, they place the fusees of the peasants at their own heads or hearts that they may be sooner destroyed; but this indulgence is not always allowed them. The peasant who grants this grace thinks himself almost guilty of a sin. All the letters, and all the French men with whom I have conversed, state that four things have greatly surprised them in Russia:

1. The population and cultivation.
2. The goodness of the roads.
3. The sacrifices made by the nobility.
4. The obedience and attachment of the peasantry to their masters.

Had they waited a little longer, the French would have been astonished by the cold, but they chose a most auspicious moment to retire: a season unknown to Russia. However, it has favoured us also; for we could not in ordinary times have passed the cross-roads, as we have done, to remedy the Marshal's ignorance, to use the lightest term.

November 5th, Wiasma.

We marched on the 2nd again. Another forced march. Saw the enemy's line of retreat by the uninterrupted train of flames and smoke, that extended many wersts.

On the third every one was ignorant where General Milaradowitch was with his advanced guard, as he had been separated from us

---

[1] Anne Jean Marie René Savary, Duc de Rovigo (1774-1833) had been Minister of Police since 1810.

several days. I determined to wait no longer with the main army, which had wearied itself with wanderings; I therefore took three Cossacks and my dragoons, with Brinken: the cannonade which we soon heard directed our course; after twenty-five wersts' march we saw the mutual combatants. Anxious to get as quickly as possible to the scene, I endeavoured to pass a *marais* [swamp]; my led horse first plunged in and I and my own horse shared the same fate immediately afterwards: I was in a hole, many feet deep, but supported myself by my arms; with some difficulty I was extricated, but wet to my breast: the horses required more exertion and time, but they were saved. Opposed thus unexpectedly by water impediments we were obliged to make a detour round a wood, but we arrived in time to witness a very glorious spectacle.

General Milaradowitch had engaged the enemy soon after daybreak, driving before him, with his powerful artillery and heavy bodies of cavalry and infantry, Marshals Murat, Davoust, and Beauharnais'[1] *corps d'armée*; while Platow in rear of his left, and Orloff in rear of his right, menaced his communications.

The French manœuvred steadily, but the Russian cavalry charged and cut down to a man several detached columns of infantry. The cannon swept their lines and the infantry pressed them in every direction. The enemy, obliged to give way incessantly for twelve wersts, blew up numbers of powder-waggons, and abandoned carriages, cars and baggage of every description and all his wounded that could not walk. The route and the fields were covered with their ruins, and for many years the French have not seen such an unhappy day: they could not have lost less than six thousand men. Amongst the prisoners is the chief of Davoust's corps.

Quoad the future?

The Cossacks had entered the town of Wiasma, but retired again, as the enemy's whole body fell upon it. The enemy, however, only entered to fire the town and abandon it, being charged through with great carnage. Favoured by night, they continued their march with the greatest precipitation to rejoin Buonaparte, who, with his guards, had preceded three days in forced march.

We hope, however, again to reach the enemy—at least their rearguard—and it is natural to expect that snow will check their whole line of march.

The Cossacks are most active, and the booty made is immense: what is yet to be made is so tempting that they venture on very daring

---

[1] Prince Eugène de Beauharnais, son of the ex-Empress Josephine, was Viceroy of Italy and commanded the 4th Corps.

incursions. The day before yesterday they took several hundred carts and two twelve-pounders out of the main road. I saw the guns, and the artillerymen confessed that the attack was most audacious.

Had our army been well directed, we should have been at Wiasma two days before the enemy, and the whole fifty thousand men that engaged us yesterday must have surrendered, for they could not have forced the position that we should have occupied with seventy thousand, whilst above thirty thousand were thundering in their rear; nor could they have awaited forty-eight hours any succours, if succours had been near, as they were without food.

The misconduct of the Marshal quite makes me wild. However, much has been done and much more will be done, for the enemy has a long gauntlet yet to run. It is certain that so much distress and so much dishonour have never tarnished the French arms since Buonaparte was the leader; his military prestige is quite ruined.

We had our escapes again, but I am too familiarised to hazard ever to note them, or even to observe them at the time, if surrounding friends did not remonstrate. I am too happy and too eager to be useful to heed personal considerations in great moments.

I have thought the matters I had to communicate so important for the Emperor and Lord Cathcart and also for General Wittgenstein, that I have dispatched Baron Brinken by the short route to St. Petersburg, and hope he will arrive there in four days. I have now completed my tour round Moscow, Wiasma being the point I started from. Our main army is come within five wersts, but the enemy must be more than twenty ahead. I am mounting, with General Milaradowitch, to pursue with the advanced guard. We shall reach him about midday.

In a letter dated from St. Petersburg on November 10, F. P. Werry wrote to William Hamilton, Under Secretary of State for Foreign Affairs:
Wilson, the Russians tell me, is in the hottest part of every action; he charges with the Cossacks, who call him brother. He gets into *mêlées*, scours the country; and, at night, I verily believe, never sleeps, for he writes folios of despatches, in which he introduces all kinds of matter. He is an astonishing fellow. The parties, jealousies and intrigues in the army are too numerous for him to escape their vortices; he reconciles the Russian generals, but gets himself into hot water. (133)

November 13th, Lobkovo.
After I had dispatched Baron Brinken on the fifth of November to St. Petersburg, I returned to Wiasma. The shells that the enemy had

buried in the different houses then burning were continually exploding, and the passage through the streets was very dangerous. This thoughtless conduct of the enemy was the death-warrant of many an unfortunate wretch. I had the satisfaction, however, of seeing a very interesting Swiss family saved. The two daughters were as beautiful young women as I ever saw in my life. The first day I proceeded forty wersts, the next seventeen, the next twenty-five, when we entered Dorogobouche by force, the enemy having two divisions in the town who attempted some resistance. The marches were very severe, as the weather was of the most desperate character; but the scene for the whole route presented such a spectacle that every personal consideration was absorbed by the feelings that the sight of so much woe excited.

The naked masses of dead and dying men; the mangled carcases of ten thousand horses, which had, in some cases, been cut for food before life had ceased, the craving of famine at other points forming groups of cannibals; the air enveloped in flame and smoke; the prayers of hundreds of naked wretches, flying from the peasantry whose shouts of vengeance echoed incessantly through the woods; the wrecks of cannon, powder-waggons, military stores of all descriptions, and every ordinary as well as extraordinary ill of war combined with the asperity of the climate, formed such a scene as probably was never witnessed to such an extent in the history of the world.

At Wiasma, fifty French, by a savage order, were burned alive. In another village fifty men had been buried alive; but these terrible acts of ferocity were minor features,—they ended in death with comparatively little protracted suffering. Here, death so much invited, so solicited as a friend, came with dilatory step; but still he came without interval of torturing pause.

I will cite three or four of the most painful incidents that I witnessed.

1. A number of naked men, whose backs had been frozen while they warmed the front of their bodies, sat round the burning embers of a hut. Sensible at last to the chill of the air, they had succeeded in turning themselves, when the fire caught the congealed flesh, and a hard burnt crust covered the whole of their backs. The wretches were still living as I passed.

2. Sixty dying naked men, whose necks were laid upon a felled tree, while Russian men and women with large faggot-sticks, singing in chorus and hopping round, with repeated blows struck out their brains in succession.

71

3. A group of wounded men, at the ashes of another cottage, sitting and lying over the body of a comrade which they had roasted, and the flesh of which they had begun to eat.

4. A French woman, naked to her chemise, with black, long, dishevelled hair, sitting on the snow, where she had remained the whole day and in that situation had been delivered of a child, which had afterwards been stolen from her. This was the extreme of mental anguish and bodily suffering.

I could cite a variety of other sad and sorry calamities, but the very recollection is loathsome.

As a man and as an Englishman, I did all in my power to mitigate their griefs. I saved the woman; I gave what little bread I had to the famished; but my all was a mite, and my aid to the afflicted was, from a combination of controlling circumstances, but very inadequate to my desire. Even lives that I preserved were probably but prolonged for a very short date. One anecdote of a veteran French grenadier I, however, must notice. I was just putting a bit of biscuit into my own mouth, when I turned my eye upon his gaze. It was too expressive to be resisted; I gave him what I designed for myself. The tears burst from his eyes, he seemed to bless the morsel, and then, amidst sobs of gratitude, expressed his hope that an Englishman might never want a benefactor in his need. He lived but a few moments afterwards.

Wilson's account of these scenes in the Narrative, *though repetitive in part, gives additional sidelights.*

On coming to the first enemy's bivouac on the morning of the 5th, some Cossacks accompanying the English General, seeing a gun and several tumbrils at the bottom of a ravine, with the horses lying on the ground, dismounted, and taking up the feet of several, hallooed, ran, and kissed the English General's knees and horse, danced, and made fantastic gestures like crazy men. When the delirium had somewhat subsided, they pointed to the horses' shoes and said—"God has made Napoleon forget that there was a winter in our country. In spite of Kutusow the enemy's bones shall remain in Russia."

It was soon ascertained that all horses of the enemy's army were in the same improperly-shod state, except those of the Polish corps, and the Emperor's own, which the Duke de Vicenza[1], with due foresight, had kept always roughshod, as is the usage of the Russians.

[1] Armand de Caulaincourt was Napoleon's Grand Equerry and later Foreign Minister.

From that time the road was strewed with guns, tumbrils, equipages, men, and horses; for no foraging parties could quit the high-road in search of provisions, and consequently the debility hourly increased.

Thousands of horses soon lay groaning on the route, with great pieces of flesh cut off their necks and most fleshy parts by the passing soldiery for food; whilst thousands of naked wretches were wandering like spectres, who seemed to have no sight or sense, and who only kept reeling on till frost, famine, or the Cossack lance put an end to their power of motion. In that wretched state no nourishment could have saved them. There were continual instances, even amongst the Russians, of their lying down, dozing, and dying within a quarter of an hour after a little bread had been supplied.

All prisoners, however, were immediately and invariably stripped stark naked and marched in columns in that state, or turned adrift to be the sport and the victims of the peasantry, who would not always let them, as they sought to do, point and hold the muzzles of the guns against their own heads or hearts to terminate their suffering in the most certain and expeditious manner; for the peasantry thought that this mitigation of torture "would be an offence against the avenging God of Russia, and deprive them of His further protection."

A remarkable instance of this cruel spirit of retaliation was exhibited on the pursuit to Wiazma.

Milaradowitch, Beningsen, Korf, and the English General, with various others, were proceeding on the high-road, about a mile from the town, where they found a crowd of peasant-women, with sticks in their hands, hopping round a felled pine-tree, on each side of which lay about sixty naked prisoners, prostrate, but with their heads on the tree, which those furies were striking in accompaniment to a national air or song which they were yelling in concert; while several hundred armed peasants were quietly looking on as guardians of the direful orgies. When the cavalcade approached, the sufferers uttered piercing shrieks, and kept incessantly crying: '*La mort, la mort, la mort!*"

Near Dorogobouche a young and handsome Frenchwoman lay naked, writhing in the snow, which was ensanguined all around her. On hearing the sound of voices she raised her head, from which extremely long black, shining hair flowed over the whole person. Tossing her arms about with wildest expression of agony, she kept frantically crying: '*Rendez moi mon enfant*'—Restore me my babe. When soothed sufficiently to explain her story, she related: "that on sinking from weakness, a child newly born had been snatched away from her; that she had been stripped by her associates, and then stabbed to prevent her falling alive into the hands of their pursuers."

Even amongst the Russians there were also instances—and those not rare—of benevolently disposed and highly-educated men adopting measures of equally unjustifiable character to terminate protracted sufferings.

When General Beningsen and the English General, with their staffs, were one afternoon on the march, they fell in with a column of seven hundred naked prisoners under a Cossack escort; this column, according to the certificate given on starting, had consisted of twelve hundred and fifty men, and the commandant stated "that he had twice renewed it, as the original party dropped off, from the prisoners he collected en route, and that he was then about completing his number again."

Amongst this wretched convoy was a young man who attracted notice by his appearance, and by his keeping a little aloof from the main group. One of General Beningsen's staff, of high titular rank,[1] after entering into some conversation with him about his country, rank, and capture, asked him 'if he did not under present circumstances wish for death?' 'Yes,' said the unhappy man, 'I do, if I cannot be rescued, for I know I must in a few hours perish by inanition, or by the Cossack lance, as I have seen so many hundred comrades do, on being unable from cold, hunger, and fatigue to keep up. There are those in France who will lament my fate—for their sake I should wish to return; but if that be impossible, the sooner this ignominy and suffering are over the better." The questioner then said that "from the bottom of his heart he pitied his fate, but that aid for his preservation was impossible: if, however, he really wished to die at once, and would lie down on his back, to give proof of the interest he took in him, he himself would inflict the death blow on his throat."

General Beningsen was some little distance in advance, but the English General, who had stopped to hear the conversation, on finding that such a cruel issue was proposed, remonstrated against the idea, urging the necessity "of saving the unfortunate officer,"— for so he proved to be—'*coûte que coûte*,' after having excited hopes by engaging in a discourse with him.

Finding that there was no inclination to abandon the intention, the English General spurred forward to overtake and bring back

[1] The Grand Duke Constantine.

General Beningsen; but happening to turn round before he could reach him, he saw the Russian officer, who had dismounted, strike with his sabre the fatal blow that severed the head nearly from the body! nor could this officer afterwards be made to think that he had done a reprehensible act. He defended it "by the motive, and the relief afforded to the sufferer, there being no means to save him, and if there had been, no one daring to employ them."

The slaughter of the prisoners with every imaginable previous mode of torture by the peasantry still continuing, the English General sent off a despatch to the Emperor Alexander "to represent the horrors of these outrages and propose a check." The Emperor by an express courier instantly transmitted an order "to prohibit the parties under the severest menaces of his displeasure and punishment"; at the same time he directed "a ducat in gold to be paid for any prisoner delivered up by peasant or soldier to any civil authority for safe custody." The order was beneficial as well as creditable, but still the conductors were offered a higher price for their charge, and frequently were prevailed on to surrender their trust, for they doubted the justifiable validity of the order.

Famine also ruthlessly decimated the enemy's ranks. Groups were frequently overtaken, gathered round the burning or burnt embers of buildings which had afforded cover for some wounded or frozen; many in these groups were employed in peeling off with their fingers and making a repast of the charred flesh of their comrades' remains.

The English General having asked one soldier of most martial expression, so occupied, "if this food was not loathsome to him?" "Yes," he said, "it was; but he did not eat it to preserve life—*that* he had sought in vain to lose—only to lull gnawing agonies." On giving the grenadier a piece of food, which happened to be at command, he seized it with voracity, as if he would devour it whole; but suddenly checking himself, he appeared suffocating with emotion: looking at the bread, then at the donor, tears rolled down his cheeks; endeavouring to rise, and making an effort as if he would catch at the hand which administered to his want, he fell back and had expired before he could be reached.

Innumerable dogs crouched on the bodies of their former masters, looking in their faces, and howling their hunger and their loss; whilst others were tearing the still living flesh from the feet, hands, and limbs of moaning wretches who could not defend themselves, and whose torment was still greater, as in many cases their consciousness and senses remained unimpaired.

The clinging of the dogs to their masters' corpses was most remarkable and interesting. At the commencement of the retreat, at a village near Selino, a detachment of fifty of the enemy had been surprised. The peasants resolved to bury them alive in a pit: a drummer boy bravely led the devoted party and sprang into the grave. A dog belonging to one of the victims could not be secured; every day, however, the dog went to the neighbouring camp, and came back with a bit of food in his mouth to sit and moan over the newly-turned earth. It was a fortnight before he could be killed by the peasants, afraid of discovery (pp. 255-60).

When we approached Dorogobouche everyone was convinced that the enemy had abandoned the town; but, being in the front, I conjured the general to take the same precautions as if he was sure that the town was to be defended, and I prevailed upon him to send some chasseurs to gain the heights. The counsel was useful: he lost, as it was, a hundred men unnecessarily. We were very near being killed ourselves, and entirely missed the opportunity of taking the two divisions. I dread presumption and its consequence—negligence —in war. Honour is a worse forfeit than life.

Just before the town was cleared two Würtembergers were taken, nearly famished: I was very much struck with the appearance and answers of one, and from a respect for our Princess Royal[1] I took them under special protection, having them well fed, &c., and I have asked their liberty, that one or the other may get to Würtemberg and relate the tale of what has befallen their comrades.

The strongest company of the Würtemberg troops now consists of four men; and of the six guns they brought with them, four were thrown into the river the same day, and I believe the two others were taken on the day following.

The town of Dorogobouche had not suffered so much as Wiasma. We obtained a tolerable quarter. The next day I put myself in a sledge with Count Osterman, as General Milaradowitch had orders to join the main army. We were overturned twice in the snow, which proved a disagreeable cold bath, but, after a journey of forty-five wersts, reached Jelnia where we received the news of Platow's success and of the surrender of two thousand men of a depôt under the command of General Augereau, who, it seems, had been neglected by the enemy.

Platow's success was a great pleasure to me. I had guaranteed his

[1] On May 18, 1797, Charlotte, Princess Royal of England, 4th child of George III, had married Friedrich Karl Wilhelm, King and Elector of Würtemberg.

good service to the Emperor, for when I came to the army I found him without command and nearly at death's door with chagrin and indignation. Since then he very nearly was removed, as calumny and jealousy have free access to the Marshal. I wrote on this occasion to the Emperor that "General Platow had given the best answer to his enemies."

Since the evacuation of Moscow I reckon that the enemy has lost in dead, killed, and wounded, twenty-five thousand men, exclusive of many wounded moving with him, and not less than twelve hundred powder-waggons fully charged, taken or blown up.

After such success it may be thought unreasonable to be dissatisfied; but I make these very successes so obtained a charge against the Marshal's conduct of the army.

Our detachments, climate, and the bad arrangements of the enemy have effected all that has been done: but our main army has kept aloof; has suffered an enemy so situated, so distressed, so feeble, to gain his communications and resources. Nay, the Russian main army fled, or rather was made to fly, from this enemy at Malo-Jaroslavets, and purposely avoided traversing his route at Wiasma. The three corps there engaged must have laid down their arms, and would have laid down their arms, if but one corps had occupied the town while the corps of Milaradowitch attacked in front. Our marches were studiously made to avoid the enemy, and a preconcerted system deprived Russia of the glory, and the common cause of a success that would have terminated the war.

Buonaparte has experienced great losses, but he has not been crushed; he has lost a specific number of cannon and of men, and much reputation; he has greatly discontented his army and injured his popularity: but if he passes the Dnieper he can command and combine the concentrated movements of a hundred thousand men in a friendly country, awe Austria and Prussia, and greatly incommode Russia before he is dislodged from the Vistula.

If ever a vigorous measure was necessary, if ever battle was justifiable, it was on the late occasions.

Marmont at Salamanca did not offer so fair an opportunity, nor would the consequences have been so important.

We are now in ancient Poland. The enemy here have all the peasants as friends. The Russian peasantry were hostile to the invader from his plunder of the churches, &c.; time will show whether they were adverse to his revolutionary principles. I am glad, however, to be in Poland, notwithstanding the public enmity.

77

The mode of life, &c., is more European, or rather more generally European: "Of comfort let no man speak."

Yesterday we marched here. This day we have halted. As a soldier, I regret this fatal delay: as an envoy, I rejoice in the opportunity of completing my correspondence.

We ought to have moved on Krasnoi on the road from Smolensk to Orsza, without a moment's loss of time. Expedition might have recovered some of the advantages which we abandoned at Wiasma by our pusillanimity, or tenderness for the enemy.

To-morrow, however, I go to the advanced guard, which is again under the orders of Milaradowitch, and it shall not be my fault if we do not oblige the Marshal to a trespass upon his friend's interests. He is a sad old rogue, hating English connection, and basely preferring to independent alliance with us a servitude to the *canaille* crew who govern France and her fiefs.

I have experienced that 'out of sight' is not 'out of mind' in a certain great family.

November 15th, Tchelkanovo.

Thirteen hundred men, a thousand artillery horses left in these environs to refresh, three hundred waggons, two hundred oxen, great magazines, and other booty became the prize of the Cossacks the day before yesterday.

Four hundred and eighty men yesterday fell into the hands of the Chasseurs of the Guard, and a thousand this day into the hands of General Milaradowitch.

Had the army not halted yesterday Poniatowski and his corps must have been taken; he passed last night ten wersts from hence. Why we halted the Marshal only knows. This same halt enabled Buonaparte with his Guards to reach Krasnoi, and finally escape us at the single point at which we could intercept him. Why had Buonaparte this *pont d'or*[1]? The Marshal and the devil only can tell.

Buonaparte did not let his people in this neighbourhood know of his retreat from Moscow. The prisoners taken, including General Augereau's party, were reposing in perfect security. I fear his rear-guard, on evacuating Smolensk, will retire by the road that the Dnieper covers, and join Buonaparte a little beyond Orsza: the distance is only forty wersts. We may then put on ass's ears. Europe will deck us with them, at all events, in the records of these times.

All the French columns are bearing upon Borisow in the first instance, but the Moscow army is too *délabré* [in too bad a state] to remain in the first line; and therefore, as Buonaparte is too weak to

---

[1] Facility for escape.

maintain a position without it, he must *bon-gré mal-gré* fall back behind the Memel.

I have asked for twelve hundred British dragoons, six hundred chasseurs, and a brigade of horse artillery for next campaign. If the English Government grants my request, I shall erect on that basis a force of some consideration. Platow alone will give me six regiments of Cossacks. Of Germans I may have any number and such additional Russian regular forces as my objects may require. Once in the field, such a force will be no insignificant feature.

I extend my view, it will be said, where others dare not lift their sight; but ambition has an eagle eye and can shoot its beams in the sun's blaze.

I have just heard that an English officer has reached Wiasma to join me. I presume and hope it is Dawson, Lord Portarlington's brother and Lord Rosslyn's aide-de-camp. He will save me the loss of many a night's rest by being an amanuensis.

I have, in my former Diary[1], approved of Poland as offering more comfort in its cottages and habits of life; but alas! I find more dirt, more children, and more cats than in Russia.

November 19th, Droubino.

The action of the 17th occasioned me great pain. I was mortified to see Buonaparte retire when his escape was impossible if the order for intercepting the Orsza road had been given but two hours earlier. I was on the road with General Keating; the enemy passed like flocks of sheep without even offering to fire on us. It was then that the Cossacks came to us and said: "What a shame to let these spectres walk from their graves!"

With twenty guns and a thousand horse to protect them I would have engaged for the capture, surrender, or destruction of twenty thousand men; with a little infantry and a short time to have posted it behind the ravines, for the possession of the whole.

The enemy were famished, weary, weak and cold, and terrified by surrounding perils. Many had no muskets; more had no ammunition. Not one circumstance favoured them, but all conspired against them. Can there be a stronger or clearer proof than the sacrifice of Ney and his corps?

If Buonaparte had not thought safety impossible in case of the Russians gaining the Orsza road, would he have abandoned ten thousand men with more than a hundred and forty cannon; and his best men, chiefly fresh troops, as far as eight thousand? The rest

---

[1] See *The Life of General Sir Robert Wilson.*

were a collection of what had formed the garrison of Smolensk, and the stragglers of the corps.

Adversity has truly poured on Buonaparte's head; he has lost his fortunes, and with his fortunes his reputation, for never was a retreat so wretchedly conducted.

Marshal Ney's[1] march on the left bank of the Dnieper, when he had a good and safe route on the right, is a prodigy of destiny.

I arrived just in time to see the magnificent attacks and repulse of the enemy. As I have written to the Emperor, "It was a conflict of heroes, and even the vanquished have acquired honour."

The carnage was tremendous; the ground was covered with the dead and dying; the Russian bayonets were dripping with the crimson torrents; the poor wounded wretches lay shivering in the snow, imploring death, which many are destined to experience with more suffering; for famine awaits them, and cold—indeed, it awaits all the prisoners for many days to come. The pike also points at their lives, when they proceed fainting from mutilation and exposure.

Happy are those who are slain in the field. Thousands have only lived a few days to perish with accumulated misery.

I have written strongly on this subject. It is time to terminate these injurious and revolting barbarities.

Fate is truly inevitable. We halted two days in five. We marched only fifteen and seventeen wersts a day, and yet we found the enemy at Krasnoi. The Marshal certainly was more surprised than pleased. He succeeded, however, in saving Buonaparte a second time. More he could not do. The fortune of Russia prevailed after the Marshal had effected that service for his friend.

The Marshal, however, is like 'the Vicar' when Buonaparte is 'the distressed hare.' He begins to think him more faulty and to aim at his person, which is no longer deemed sacred. I think he would now permit a gun to be fired at Majesty: at least his language this day authorises such an opinion. Dead bodies, moving 'ghosts,' mangled carcases, standards, artillery and powder-waggons, carriages, and all species of wrecks, cover the roads and fill every wood.

The baggage taken is enormous, and its value immense. One waggon was full of gold and silver ingots. Another military chest had two hundred thousand pounds in specie. Davoust's carriage had his Marshal's staff, all his insignia, private correspondence, the French cyphers, manuscript maps, &c. Others had all Beauharnais' property and effects.

[1] Michel Ney (1769–1815), 'the bravest of the brave,' showed superb courage and tenacity in the French retreat as well as distinguishing himself at Smolensk and Borodino, for which battle he was given the title 'Prince de la Moskova'.

Buonaparte has now lost, since the commencement of the campaign, two hundred thousand men, of whom eighty-two thousand are actually prisoners; seventeen generals are captives; above four hundred cannon are in the Russian parks; more than forty standards are in, or on their way to, the Palace of St. Petersburg; and a vast variety of trophies will deck the hall of victory.

The ruin is gigantic in the aggregate. It might have been complete, and the column of Russian glory might now have been fixed on the tomb of the world's enemy.

November 25th, Staroselie, right bank of the Dnieper, ten wersts from Kopis.

The enemy continued his retreat, abandoning Orsza with five hundred sick men and twenty-five cannon, and losing to Count Augerausky several hundred men and four cannon, and to Colonel Sislavin several hundred dismounted dragoons. The day before yesterday we entered Kopis, a tolerably good town by comparison and filled with Jews, who for exorbitant payment provided some white bread and wine. A column of the French had passed two days before, but had not destroyed the place—they were grateful for not having been destroyed themselves, which might and ought to have been done.

December 1st, Usza.

After leaving the station at which I dated my last letter, we marched to Kroughloé, an estate of Marshal Woronzow's which he inherited from Princess Danskow in preference to her daughter. There are three thousand peasants upon it. The site is very picturesque, but the house is in a ruinous state. At the end of its garden runs the river which formed the ancient boundary of Poland.

In the middle of the night I saw two peasants creep into my room, and lie down by the stove to thaw themselves on one of the bitterest nights I ever knew. Their presumption was great, but they seemed to plead 'Poor Tom's a-cold,' and I let them remain.

The next morning General Beningsen was, by an order of the Marshal, sent from the army. The dissensions had long been very injurious to the service, but the Marshal took this step at the time when General Beningsen had for the good of the service taken pains to prove his wish for reconciliation.

The Emperor must now express his opinion as to the merits of the rivals.

I do not pretend to say that Beningsen, as *Commander-in-chief*, would have followed his own counsels offered as *Second-in-command*; but this I know, that if he had directed the Marshal's decisions,

Buonaparte would be now out of all sphere of mischievous action in this world.

I remained the whole day with Beningsen at Kroughloé. The next morning we parted with mutual regrets.

Having sent on my horses, I proceeded in a traineau. It occupied twenty-four hours to regain the headquarters, as we lost our road and enjoyed all the comforts of eighteen degrees of frost with a heavy snow falling.

We marched to Arckova on *glass*. I wrote there long despatches to the Emperor and Lord Cathcart, and received many letters from Tyrconnel and other persons, but, alas! none from England. At night I was tormented by a multiplicity of ills—aged sick, squalling brats, cockroaches and earwigs in millions.

We are truly living with paupers of the lowest class: no English workhouse would receive such a set. In England I would not, for ten thousand a year, inhabit such dwellings and keep such society; and in a Polish hovel, to tell the truth, glory shines dimly.

I have, however, resolved to repel all infants in future. They may go to the bears in the woods, but 'I'll none of them.'

This morning I crossed the Beresina, not yet frozen, which I thought a favourable circumstance, but it was of no importance. Shared quarters with General Tormanssow this day. General Dombrowsky occupied them ten days since.

I now proceed to military details of greater interest than those which have previously occurred, because they close the tale of Buonaparte's perilous retreat.

Lord Tyrconnel had informed me of Admiral Tchichagow's having left General Sacken[1] with twenty thousand men to watch the Austrians, and of his having marched in the direction of Minsk himself with thirty thousand men, giving orders to General Ertel to join with fifteen thousand, who by some mismanagement never moved from Mozyr.

On the 28th I received advice that Admiral Tchichagow's advanced guard, under General Lambert, had surprised the troops at Minsk sufficiently to prevent the conflagration of great magazines and to secure a hospital with three thousand men. The Jews, who knew of the Admiral's approach, concealed the intelligence from the enemy, as they prefer Russian toleration and moderation in the rule of their nation to the heavy imposts and military conscriptions of the French and Poles.

A further account brought advice of General Cassewitch having

---

[1] General Baron Fabien von der Osten Sacken, a German in Russian service.

surrendered to General Lambert with two thousand six hundred men; of General Dombrowski having lost seven hundred men in the environs of the village in which I am writing; and that a considerable number of prisoners were made by the detached parties in various directions, and a great quantity of baggage taken.

A courier brought advice from Count Wittgenstein[1] that he had reached Baran, driving Victor and St. Cyr before him. It was also stated that General Tchaplitz had occupied the Vileika route to Wilna by a post at Zembin and, as we were now moving on Igumen, Buonaparte's retreat was deemed impracticable.

Joy and exultation were general. Perhaps I was the only man in the army who feared that the toil was neither perfect nor strong enough to retain the prey. I had always represented the necessity of pressing upon the enemy with an army; of keeping him in view and under our fire.

If it was necessary to watch the Igumen road, I wished it to be done with two corps, and not by our whole force.

I had described our delays at Krasnoi as fatal, and our marches by cross-roads in a false direction as ruinous to our army.

I will not, however, weary others by a *raisonnement* which is now of little use. I shall, on the contrary, write narrative connectedly and not note the statements particularly as they were from time to time received.

It appears, then, that Admiral Tchichagow's advanced guard, under General Lambert, on the 20th pursued General Dombrowski to the entrenchments of the *tête-du-pont* of Borisow, stormed them, although the Russians were greatly outnumbered, and carried them, with a loss to the enemy of two thousand killed and three thousand prisoners.

On the 23rd the advanced guard of the French army, retiring from us, reached Borisow, surprised the Russians, took seven hundred chasseurs and a great part of the equipages of the Admiral's head-quarters, with the Admiral's correspondence; but did not reach the bridge in time to save it from being effectually fired.

The Admiral took up a position opposite Borisow, anxiously expecting tidings from us and the sight of our advanced guard. On the 25th the Admiral, conceiving from the same report which deceived us that the enemy would attempt to pass the Beresina River at Beresino, and thus scour the Igumen road, and not knowing our movement in this direction, left General Langeron in front of Borisow, recalled General Tchaplitz from Zembin, and proceeded

---

[1] Lieut.-General Count Peter Wittgenstein, German commander of the 1st Army Corps.

thirty wersts on the road to Beresino and to a village called Shouli-faka.

The enemy had, however, found the piles of the old bridge leading to Zembin perfect, and therefore they had only to relay planks: this was quickly done, and two divisions were pushed across to occupy Zembin. General Langeron, who was at Borisow, hearing of this passage, which took place on the 26th, sent back Tchaplitz to Zembin, but he arrived too late and could not dislodge the enemy.

The Admiral returned on the 27th to Borisow, but had thirteen wersts further to march to reach the *tête-du-pont* of the enemy, which was defended by thirty cannon.

The same day Count Wittgenstein reached the enemy's rearguard and intercepted its junction with the main body. In the morning of the 28th, General Camus, several other generals, and seven thousand men laid down their arms, and three thousand men whom Platow surrounded at Borisow also surrendered.

The Admiral, on the morning of the 28th, had commenced his attack on the corps of troops that covered the filing of the enemy's army. This corps, commanded by Oudinot, was strongly posted in a wood with a surrounding *marais* partially frozen. The Russians, consequently, could only use their tirailleurs and lost four thousand men in the action. The French had not so many men killed or wounded; but General Legrand was killed and Marshal Oudinot, General Merle and another general wounded.

Towards dusk the advanced guard of General Wittgenstein reached the heights that commanded the original bridge and a new foot-bridge on the Beresina over which the enemy was passing. Three batteries were immediately established. When the bridge was ordered to be burnt the next morning, a scene of confusion and terror ensued that by every account must have been horrible.

Carriages, guns, infantry, cavalry, women and children, all rushed to the flaming piles. The mass was chiefly composed of persons whom Buonaparte would not save in the first instance to the hazard of his best troops.

Many were drowned, many burnt, many crushed; and very many killed or mangled by the shot that ploughed this fatal ground.

All the remaining equipages of the French army, including the plunder of the churches of Moscow and immense treasure, much of which was in French gold coin, fell into the hands of Count Wittgenstein's army. But the great prize had escaped; as I embrace the whole view and do not confine myself to partial incidents, I lamented, and could not joy in the intelligence.

On the 29th, as the enemy had broken down several small but necessary bridges, for the passage of the marsh, the armies of Admiral Tchichagow and Count Wittgenstein were obliged to remain inactive; but on the 30th the enemy's small rearguard of his grand rearguard was driven by General Tchaplitz from Zembin with the loss of three guns, several officers and three hundred men; and General Lanskoi, who had preceded the enemy, reported his capture of General Kamenskoi, thirty officers, the commandant o Buonaparte's headquarters and four hundred men.

I suppose, from every account, and from my own calculation s, that the enemy cleared himself with forty-five thousand effective men. To this number must be added twenty-five thousand under Macdonald; the Austro-French army which has been checked at Roudnia by Sacken with the loss of two thousand prisoners; one Saxon standard; one eagle and much equipage; Augereau's corps; small garrisons; and the Polish reserves.

I estimate the whole thus:

Buonaparte	..	..	..	45,000
Macdonald	..	..	..	25,000
Austro-French	..	..	..	40,000
Detached	..	..	..	5,000
				115,000
Augereau	..	..	..	30,000
Polish Reserve	..	..	..	8,000
Grand Total	..		..	153,000

The remains of three hundred thousand which passed the Russian frontier.

It is now that all will regret opportunities lost. It is now that the crowns of complete victory disdained at Malo-Jaroslavets, Wiazma and Krasnoi will flit before the eyes of those most blinded by ignorance.

When will fortune again woo us to achieve without peril or loss in one day what so many years, so much treasure, so many brave armies had in vain attempted heretofore?

How many toilsome marches, how many doubtful conflicts, how many anxious days and nights, how much life, how much property would have been saved merely by an attitude of resistance!

I give to the Russians all due, and that is high honour, for their patriotism and courage; but the escape of Buonaparte with a train carrying arms is a stain upon their escutcheon. I have so often recapitulated Buonaparte's difficulties while he was at Moscow, I have so frequently represented the impediments opposed to his retreat, that I shall not again press the subject. The whole must be familiar to every one who speaks of famine, climate, distance and doubly superior force at the outset and knows that every day augmented the disproportion and added to the inefficiency of the enemy.

Buonaparte, however, has lost his military credit altogether with his army. He has committed faults of which the most ignorant would not have been guilty, if they had acquired command; they are unparalleled in magnitude and in mischief to his own interests; and if France does remain true to him, he has made himself dependent on Austria and Prussia. It is to be hoped that both powers will remember national wrongs and personal injuries, and that they will not be so false to themselves, as with their own means now to contend that France may preserve Germanic influence and Italian dominion.

Whatever may be their dislike or fear of Russia, at least I will hope that they are wise enough to see that this is the moment to acquire their own independence, to recover their losses and to strengthen themselves, so as to be superior to enmity or ambition.

December 6th, Dobrieka, 35 Wersts from Minsk.

The weather is severe in the extreme, above eighteen degrees of cold this day; and there is not a bottle of wine with the army. If one accidentally appears, the price given for the worst quality is twenty-four shillings English currency; a pound of white bread costs three shillings; and everything else is in proportion. These prices, with the misery of our habitations, certainly make Newgate at once a preferable residence.[1]

In eight days we shall all concentrate about Wilna; but if the enemy does evacuate, or we force it, I fear there will be little additional supply in our markets.

Nine o'clock.—I have just returned from dinner with General Tormanssow, and we had one bottle of wine. This is really such an agreeable surprise that I cannot help noticing it.

'It never rains but it pours.' My Cossacks have also brought six

---

[1] Wilson's *Narrative* contains additional details about the intense cold: "The thermometer was twenty-seven and thirty degrees below freezing point, with sky generally clear, and a subtle, keen, razor-cutting, creeping wind that penetrated skin, muscle, and bone to the very marrow, rendering the surface as white and the whole limb affected as fragile as alabaster. . . . These ravages were terrifically destructive. A general recklessness confounded all ranks, command ceased, and it became a '*sauve qui peut*' at a funeral pace" (pp. 342–3).

ducks, a bull calf, and six loaves of white bread. This enables me
to be very generous to friends, who like myself will ask no questions
but 'take the goods the gods provide.'

Minsk.

Yesterday, in a dreadfully cold day, I came here on horseback
without any accident, though my horses were not rough-shod.
Many persons were less fortunate, and various accidents, as I hear,
occurred in the different columns, some of a serious nature.

I was much pleased to find Minsk an excellent town, which had
not been plundered, and which afforded various supplies, at a dear
rate, but still supplies. The commandant was an old friend. The
Duke of Würtemberg came about four hours afterwards, with Dawson, &c. They travelled in carriages and were more frozen than
myself.

Met an old servant of General Gardiner's who had been head
groom to General Radziwil. Established him as my 'maître d'hôtel'
for the occasion. But, although I got a tolerably good quarter, alas!
I could find no wood for the stoves and that night and this morning
I was in splendid misery, and longed for my cabins with cockroaches, earwigs, children, scents, &c. It was near ten o'clock before
I could get a fire lighted in a chimney and the air was afterwards so
severe that water froze at the distance of three feet from a wood
blaze that in England would have scorched intolerably at twelve
feet.

My dragoons are all chilled to the bones and I am obliged to
procure them here sheep-skin coats. However, when in the air I
defied the cold, for I even took off the great coat that I had been
accustomed to wear in order that it might be repaired, and walked
about, with the thermometer at 19 degrees, in my jacket without any
waistcoat. The vanity of the act, I believe, kept me warm, for I was
not so cold as I had frequently been before in less frost and with more
covering.

Wilson has this to say in his Narrative:

During these last marches, the Russian troops who were moving
through a country devastated by the enemy, suffered nearly as
much as they did from want of food, fuel, and clothing.

The soldier had no additional covering for the night bivouacs
on the frozen snow; and to sleep longer than half an hour at a time
was probable death. Officers and men, therefore, were obliged to
relieve each other in their snatches of sleep, and to force up the
reluctant and frequently resisting slumberers.

Firing could scarcely ever be obtained; and when obtained the fire could only be approached with great caution, as it caused gangrene of the frozen parts; but as water itself froze at only three feet from the largest bivouac fires, it was almost necessary to burn before the sensation of heat could be felt.

Above ninety thousand perished; and out of ten thousand recruits who afterwards marched on Wilna as a reinforcement, only fifteen hundred reached that city: the greater part of these were conveyed to the hospitals as sick or mutilated. One of the chief causes of their losses was that the trowsers becoming worn by the continued marches in the inner part of the thighs exposed the flesh, so that the frost struck into it when chafed, and irritated it with virulent activity (pp. 352-3).

Passed a very pleasant day. Met many friends, and was in agreeable society which I did not expect, for I supposed that at least all the noblesse of the place would have fled.

The variety of interests that are felt and operating here present a curious tableau. I think, however, all men concur in abhorring Buonaparte.

Among the prisoners I found a fine young man, the nephew of Talleyrand. He had his leg broken at Polotzk by a ball, and in the affair of the Beresina he was wounded in three places while attempting to save Oudinot then wounded by a ball in the loins, and who was withdrawing on horseback from the fire.

The Commandant Colonel Knoring had been kind to him, but still he was in great need. To the nephew of Talleyrand, in disgrace now for opposition to the Spanish and Russian wars, I felt disposed to do that which I would not have done if the family had been prospering in Buonaparte's smiles. I gave him two shirts out of the small stock left me, two waistcoats that I never wore, and two hundred and fifty roubles, which, in English currency, is near £25. Hammersley may note this young man's being taken care of, and his going to Kiew where he will be well treated; but on no account the loan—or gift as it may be. I have particular reasons that this act should not be accompanied by any incident that may detract from its liberality, but I have no objection to let Bosville know that one of my motives was his ancient friendship with the uncle.

I have, in many instances, done other acts of kindness to other officers; but truly the whole revenue of many a sovereign prince would not suffice to clothe the naked and relieve all the wretchedness that forcibly claims aid.

Minsk was a hospital for the French and eight thousand died here; four hundred and fifty were lying unburied when the Russians entered; and there were above three thousand sick in hospital of French, and two thousand Russians.

There were great magazines here, many of which were hastily disposed of, under the apprehension of the Austrians' approach. Six thousand muskets were also taken here in depôt. Buonaparte had proposed to fall back by this route. The operations at Borisow threw him upon Wilna.

Minsk contains four thousand Christian inhabitants, and four hundred Jews. The wealth that this town possesses is therefore considerable, but the country round has been much distressed by requisitions.

I acquired here the intelligence that the Austrians have taken Pinsk, with great magazines, and that they push their posts to Stolpitz, and about fifty wersts from hence. Their force, with the Saxons, &c., is estimated at forty thousand strong, and they have their very best regiments with them. Sacken's action was against Regnier and the Saxons, not against Schwartzenberg and the Austrians.

There is no communication with Sacken, and his present position is therefore uncertain. I have, however, no fear for his safety, as he can draw back upon Jitomir, where he will find the Little Russia militia forty thousand strong.

At Wilna, it appears, Buonaparte has a reserve of twenty thousand at least; and I suspect, from every account, that he has retired stronger than was supposed and that, notwithstanding his daily losses, he will still have considerable means; but his military and political influence, his claim of invincibility, his moral authority—all are shattered, and beyond his own power of recovery. What may be done for him time will show, but the Cabinets of Europe have always been so foolish that I do not expect wisdom on this occasion, however propitious.

I have learnt many curious anecdotes of Buonaparte: those relating to his inquietudes are not the least interesting.

When he saw Ney enter, after his escape with a handful of men, he could scarcely speak to welcome the Marshal, who, it is said, was loud in his reproaches against Davoust, and indirectly against the Emperor.

December 13th, Vishnev.

On the 11th we quitted Minsk, after the Duke had given a breakfast, and his officers a dance which was attended by about twenty

Polish ladies, two or three of them very pretty. It was a frost of twenty degrees, and a very cutting wind. I went in a traineau for the first ten wersts, and my nose froze once, but not to a serious degree: timely observation of General Rolt restored circulation. The coachman's cheek was more severely nipped, but he quickly regained its colour by sharp rubbing.

After the first ten wersts, I attempted to ride; but I had scarcely gone a werst before a Russian carter roared out to me to stop, and made the most anxious signs to me to dismount. I had no sooner done so, than he filled his hands with snow, and rubbed my face violently. I followed his efforts, but the frost had so deadened the nose and right cheek that very little effect was perceptible for some time and the carter actually moaned over me as if I was his own child. At length I felt the blood return, and with much pain. It was impossible for me to brave the inclement air any more for that day, and I got into a calash that was passing. In five wersts the calash broke down. I then put myself into a one-horse traineau, carrying wine and provisions in boxes to General Tormassnow. In four wersts the traineau overset, and I hurt myself sensibly for the time by falling on a pocket pistol which I carry in my over-dress. For fifteen wersts I went on again very wretched, but carefully rubbing my nose from time to time, and covering it from the wind as much as I could: but it was more exposed than other noses, as I wear only a general's cap without any shade.

During my progress the carter's nose twice froze in splotches as big as half-a-crown and we made a compact to regard each other every five minutes. At the end of twenty wersts, I got into a better traineau, in which a stranger was passing, and in five wersts more reached Volojin, where our headquarters were; but on ascending the hill on foot a grenadier stopped me to tell me that my nose was again frozen. I really was quite miserable; rough destiny had resolved to make me a martyr, for there would be no living without a nose. I hastened to General Tormanssow; as soon as I entered he told me that my cheek was frozen and congratulated me on the preservation of my nose which showed the effects of its congelation.

A warm room soon broke the skin, and inflammation succeeded morbidity. This morning one side was scaled as if I had been burnt and the rigidity of the skin was so great that it felt as if it was a piece of dried and distended flesh. This uncomfortable sensation has somewhat passed, but it will be several days before I can show my face again with any satisfaction. I had not myself seen it for many weeks until this morning, and I was quite frightened and disgusted. Bosville's distorting glass never presented such outré proportions.

The accident has made me think very seriously, and I am of opinion that glory, without a nose, can never be 'a gay seducer,' so war in this climate is too perilous for voluntary service. Truly the service is rude beyond all parallel and certainly no money can indemnify for the injury that health must sustain from such a season, such privations and such endurance.

At Minsk, a horse that cost £50, English currency, with an English saddle, was lost. My *porte-feuille*, with several papers of great importance, has shared the same fate, and this day Dawson's servant has lost a new pair of pistols of his master's and a cloak that is worth its weight in gold in nights that average 25 degrees of frost. God give us a good deliverance! but this campaign has sadly shattered me hitherto. I shall return, if no other mishap occurs, with an unshaped leg, and the wrinkles of a grand climacterism.

The Marshal having ordered the guards, the grenadiers and the cuirassiers to Wilna, I am going there with the Duke of Würtemberg to-morrow; but I go with regret, as I am sure the movement is false and that we ought to push the Austrians at Novogrodek, so that we may reach the Vistula this year.

The weather was not so very severe this day, but I rode with speed to get my nose out of the open air as quickly as possible.

A good monastery received us, General Tormanssow fed us, and the Duke 'tea'd'; so the day passed well. The Grand Duke, before I mounted, came to our quarters and received me most cordially.

December 17th, Wilna.

I had scarcely concluded, when Brinken made his appearance, bringing me a letter from the Emperor in his own hand, and of a most gracious content,[1] and I had a further proof of the Emperor's regard in finding that Brinken, in consequence of going with my letters, had been made a captain: this, considering that he had only six weeks before been appointed to the guards, is an unprecedented favour and mark of goodwill.

I also received letters from Lord Cathcart of a very satisfactory nature; one from Lord Castlereagh, or rather an extract, not quite so liberal in its spirit, but my revenge will be to force his acknowledgment of my good services to the country without any party spirit influencing that duty. He ought to know that I should be

[1] The Czar thanked Wilson for keeping him so exactly informed on what was happening in the army.

unacceptable to the estimable portion of the party if I permitted any feeling to operate that was detrimental to the public good.

I also received a letter from Lord Grey, which I value more than all the favours of His Royal Highness's Government to favourites; one from the Duke of Gloucester truly kind; a variety from different friends; and—the last-mentioned not the least valued—several from my family, in one of which a *thirteenth* offspring is announced. I also got a packet full of useful clothes, &c., and I was altogether rendered very happy. I was, however, sorry to find that Wyburn was laid up with a fever at Stockholm.

The next morning the Duke of Würtemberg and myself resolved to go to Wilna, and we went that day thirty-five wersts. I rode on horseback. Twenty-eight degrees of cold. A separate quarter was assigned me, which Dawson and I at nine at night endeavoured to find; but after wandering about to all the villages round for two hours, we were obliged to retrace our steps, and take a bench at the Duke's.

At five in the morning I again started, and with more success, as a peasant was with me. The cold had increased, and I was almost frozen when I arrived two wersts' distance. The fear of the wolves even, now in their raging season, had not warmed my blood.

I rode that day thirty-five more wersts, and missed my road; so, instead of being with the Duke, I found myself with General Milaradowitch. As soon as I entered the room I found various hands pointing to my face which was generally frozen, but, by the application of snow immediately, after some time the blood returned.

General Milaradowitch was himself laid up with a frozen eye, and almost every one present was a sufferer from the inclement weather.

I passed a very agreeable day, and this morning came into Wilna along a road covered with human carcases, frozen in the contortions of expiring agonies. The entrance of the town was literally choked with dead bodies of men and horses, tumbrils, guns, carts, &c., and the streets were filled with traineaus carrying off the dead that still crowded the way.

Painters and sculptors would be benefited by the specimens. Accustomed as I am to scenes of carnage and distress, it is a repeated picture that I loathe the more that I see of it. For the last two months I have seen very nearly as many dead and dying as living beings. The enemy have a disease internally, occasioned by eating horse-flesh without bread and salt, that carries off nine-tenths even of those who survive the field and epidemic sickness. Change of diet causes almost instant death, unless very carefully regulated. I have seen comparatively hale men, after a little food, lie down, doze, and die in half an hour. The dead, however, are to be envied. With frost to twenty-eight and thirty degrees, naked bodies and infirm health offer but subjects for terrible torments: imagination cannot conceive the reality. One incident I must, however, note. Yesterday I saw four men grouped together, hands and legs frozen, minds yet vigorous, and two dogs tearing their feet.

I arrived at Wilna just as the Marshal was going to dine. From the plains of misery I passed to the banquet.

After dinner I found my quarters—a magnificent summer palace, but a winter ice-house; no fireplace, and only one stove, so that there are eighteen degrees of frost in the room in which I am obliged to sit and to rest at night.

Here I heard of Lord Tyrconnel's being sick in the house of an English Professor in the University of Wilna. I immediately went to see him and found that he had been very ill, but was recovering. He will not, however, be able to quit Wilna for some time. Soon afterwards I heard of Woronzow's arrival, and dined with him this day. He is in excellent health, and scarcely limps. Admiral Tchichagow had only gone away half an hour before I called upon him. We both wish much to meet, but I shall soon follow him if he passes the Niemen, which is yet doubtful.

This evening I went to the play and was almost frozen. As it was a state occasion I was obliged to remain till the conclusion, but my teeth chattered again and when I rose to go I could scarcely use my limbs. There was not one lady in the house, which added to the wretchedness.

I now come to my quarters and although sitting close to the stove my feet are as ice, and my hand can scarcely hold the pen. I have, however, much to write, and must write the greater part of this night again to be ready for the courier. It is a critical moment and want of energy may be very injurious yet to Russia.

December 26th, Wilna.

On the 20th died George, Earl of Tyrconnel, aged twenty-five years. Few persons ever enjoyed so good a reputation without exciting envy. None will ever have been more sincerely regretted. Commonly men without enemies are automatons, without independent thought or energy of action. Lord Tyrconnel had a vigour of mind which was polished with so much urbanity, that the exertion of it never alarmed the pride of others. His conduct at St. Petersburg, in several very delicate transactions, proved his power of executing with decision the conclusions of his judgment. His public correspondence will show that he was more highly qualified for public employment than was generally presumed; and converse with him certified that he must have devoted many an hour to reading, which might have been supposed, from his love of society, to have passed less profitably.

On the 22nd the corpse was carried to the grave, escorted by two companies of the Imperial Guards, and interred with every honour that could be shown. I was, of course, chief mourner. The scene was solemn, and the tones of the music were irresistibly affecting. The human mind is strangely organized; existing misery is seldom participated with deep sympathy, but fanciful woe melts the obduracy of habit and philosophy.

"It is a strange world!" Adam is reported to have said when he entered into it; and so the last man will say.

I had the mournful occupation afterwards of making the necessary arrangements for disposal of property, &c.

I did in all things as I would be done by, when there was no sufficient rule to guide me and I hope the family will be satisfied that all has been done not only for the best, but, under the circumstances, in the best way.

In the evening the Emperor glided into the town. The next morning there was a great levée. The Emperor made a speech, thanked the officers for their services, and reproved the University for its disloyalty. His Majesty also alluded to the future, and encouraged the hope of a continued campaign to the Vistula.

Yesterday was the Emperor's birthday.

Parade, a confidential conference with the Emperor, mess, and twenty-five degrees of frost, were the incidents of the morning. The Marshal gave a great state dinner to the Emperor afterwards, on the occasion of his receiving the Order of St. George of the First Class.

"It is a strange world" quoth Adam again; and so will his posterity again say.

Glory for me has lost all her charms. I shall become a Timon from contempt of the world's puppets. Happy are they who know not the arcana of the mechanism that conducts the world's affairs. Happy are they who never reason on causes or effects.

Some details of this 'confidential conference' appear in Wilson's Narrative:
On the morning of the 26th December Alexander sent for the English General, and after a few appropriations to the festival, said:

"General, I have called you into my cabinet to make a painful confession; but I rely on your honour and prudence. I wished to have avoided it, but I could not bear to appear inconsistent in your estimate of my proceedings; which I must be thought if my motives were not explained. . . .

"You have always told me the *truth*—truth I could not obtain through any other channel.

"I know that the Marshal has done nothing he ought to have done—nothing against the enemy that he could avoid; all his successes have been *forced* upon him. He has been playing some of his old Turkish tricks, but the nobility of Moscow support him, and insist on his presiding over the national glory of this war. In half an hour I must therefore (and he paused for a minute) decorate this man with the great Order of St. George, and by so doing commit a trespass on its institution; for it is the highest honour, and hitherto the purest, of the empire. But I will not ask you to be present—I should feel too much humiliated if you were; but I have no choice—I must submit to a controlling necessity. I will, however, not again leave my army, and there shall be no opportunity given for additional misdirection by the Marshal.

"He is an old man, and therefore I would have you show him suitable courtesies, and not refuse them when offered on his part.

"I wish to put an end to every appearance of ill will, and to take from this day a new departure, which I mean to make one of gratitude to Providence and of grace to all" (pp. 356–7).

The entertainment was splendid and the coup-d'œil rare. Thought was my chief banquet on this occasion and I feasted sumptuously. The knife and fork, however, occasionally took advantage of a vacuum.

In the evening there was a ball, which was attended by about thirty ladies, several very handsome; and those who were not so had all the attractions of their country—variety, figure, taste in dress, and grace of movement.

I did not dance at first, for reasons, as I thought, of propriety, when the Emperor came up twice to me and noticed my forbearance, in a manner that admitted of no longer non-compliance with his expectations. It was, indeed, a particular day, and the Marshal's ball; so I ought to have considered the feelings of others rather than my own—to have remembered that I was a public, not a private person on that occasion.

I danced the Polonaise, Parade, Promenade, and one country

dance. After the Emperor retired I was obliged to remain a little while, from a continuation of the same policy.

I had the satisfaction of finding old England high in favour with the Polish ladies. Dr. Clarke has roused up ancient charges against our general national habits, and the French agents have been busy in all quarters to give them credit. The Polish ladies, however, are adamant to the calumny; they admire the spirit of England. They think us, indeed, the indirect cause of their misfortunes, but they reverence the national pride which sustains the conflict. Our originalities are no defects in their eyes, but proofs of independence, and envy with them is not deepened by hatred. There are very few among them who have not been at Vienna, very few who have not there known Englishmen whom they esteemed. It must not be supposed that I write this from a casual observation, or that it is a superficial and solitary opinion. I have far stronger grounds and very solid reasons for my opinion. I cannot, however, explain them.

30th—Sickness has made very serious progress in this city. In fifteen days nine thousand prisoners have died, and in one eighteen hours seven hundred. The mortality has extended of course to the inhabitants. The physicians have ordered straw to be burnt before every house, but the pestilential atmosphere is not to be corrected by such lenitives; and as if fate resolved to spread the contagion to the utmost, there has been a thaw for the last twenty-four hours.

In the spring Wilna must be a complete charnel-house. All the carcases which are removed from the streets and hospitals are laid at a short distance from the town in great masses; and then such parts as the wolves have not devoured during the winter will throw pestiferous miasmata back upon the city, which, from its position, is always shrouded in vapour. I rode yesterday round the town to look at the camp which the enemy proposed to trace, and in all directions I saw mountains of human bodies, and carcases of beasts. Disgusting as the sight was, I could not help occasionally stopping to contemplate the attitudes in which those who had been frozen had died. The greater part happened to have been writhing with some agony at the instant their hearts' blood congealed; some were raised upon their hands with their heads bent back and their eyes uplifted, as if still imploring aid from the passers-by.

Desgenettes[1] tells me that the loss of the enemy to Wilna amounted to two hundred thousand men, and he thus confirmed my calculation.

[1] René-Nicolas Dufriche, Baron Desgenettes, chief physician to the Grand Army.

In his Narrative *Wilson wrote of Wilna in December 1812:*

The hospital of St. Bazile presented the most awful and hideous sight: seven thousand five hundred bodies were piled like pigs of lead over one another in the corridors; carcases were strewn about in every part; and all the broken windows and walls were stuffed with feet, legs, arms, hands, trunks and heads to fit the apertures, and keep out the air from the yet living.

The putrefaction of the thawing flesh, where the parts touched and the process of decomposition was in action, emitted the most cadaverous smell.

Nevertheless in each of these pestilential and icy répertoires three or four grenadiers of the Guard were posted, inhaling the pestilential effluvia.

On the English General [Wilson] making the Emperor acquainted with this inconsiderate 'employment of his finest troops,' he went himself to the convent and inspected the chambers, speaking the kindest words to the unfortunate inmates, and giving the requisite directions for their treatment. The Grand Duke followed his example, but caught the epidemy, from which he with difficulty recovered (p. 354).

Every day some property belonging to the enemy is discovered, or we have proofs of its destruction.

At Wilna Buonaparte burnt his state tent lined with shawls, &c., all his table-linen, his state bed, &c. Here also were buried or destroyed all the trophies that he took from Moscow. Desgenettes, however, tells me that he had previously ordered drawings to be taken of them, and that he intends to re-make them at Paris. Even the cross which he took from the great church at Moscow, and which broke in its descent, was here partly abandoned. Had he carried it away entire and set it up at Paris, when the whole truth, as I have written to Mr. Liston, blazed upon its story, the people of France would have regarded it as a memorial of their misfortunes and their disgrace: a fraud will but add to the reproach.

The news of the day is that Beningsen and Tolly are both coming back to the army, and that Tchichagow, whose pursuit of the enemy to Wilna after the passage of the Beresina was a lesson to us of energy, is to take place of Romanzow, whose 'state-health' does not admit of his further continuation in office—*Forsan et hæc olim meminisse juvabit.*[1]

[1]Virgil's *Aeneid*, i, 203. "The day may dawn when this plight shall be sweet to remember."

1813

Jan. 5th, 1813—In a private audience which I had of the Emperor the day before yesterday, I had good reason to admire him, and to be proud of the conduct which I have pursued.

It is impossible for me to record the conversation, but I had the satisfaction of knowing that he accorded with my opinion on every subject.

The defection of the Prussians is a most important event. It is not only the diminution of the enemy's strength by fifteen thousand men and fifty cannon, but it opens a great field, and unhinges Buonaparte's system.

If my suggestions thereupon are adopted we shall have clear ground to the Elbe very soon.

The troops are on march from every point. This morning I attended the Emperor to see eight thousand guards inspected. I never saw men in higher order, and perhaps never such a fine body of men. After such a campaign their appearance was perfectly marvellous, and the martial character of the scene was augmented by the number of dead that covered the ground.

I find the Polish women the greatest patriots. But they are chiefly resolved on having a Court, and they do not much care who presides if that object be obtained. The French counterfeit royalty is here of as much value as the old coinage.

January 10th, Merecz.

In the evening of the 8th—after having visited my Spaniards in the hospitals; after having passed masses of dead, dying, and filth that horrify me by recollection; after having given two hundred ducats to Colonel O'Donnell for a detachment of three hundred Spaniards, and one hundred ducats to twenty Piedmontese officers for their clothing and maintenance to Memel, whither the Emperor, at my request, has ordered them, when they can move there; after having made arrangements for the protection of a nephew of Mrs. Robert Adair (the ambassador's wife)[1] who was here in extreme

---

[1] Sir Robert Adair (1763–1855) married Angélique Gabrielle, daughter of the Marquis d'Hazincourt.

misery; after having saved him and clothed him, and done the same by an English sailor, whom the French marched from Königsberg with five others; after having obtained Desgenettes' release, and advanced to him two hundred ducats, part of which was to be appropriated to the use of young Fontanges[1] and the two sons of the Minister of Holland; after having taken leave of my Polish friends, with whom I hope not to have diminished opinion previously entertained of the English; after having adjusted a mass of public business, and cleared all official correspondence to the day of departure; after having had a long conversation with the Prussian general, [Emilius Friedrich] Kleist, who had made the convention[2] with General Yorck;[3] after having again looked at the spot where my long-to-be-regretted friend reposes in peace—I mounted my horse, very near dusk, in company with Dawson. My Russian aide-de-camp, still ill of his fever, was immovable in his bed.

We rode forty wersts, and, conducted by a favouring star that guided us a little out of our road, we reached a major of dragoons, who hospitably received us. The next morning, at day-break, we rode the same distance, and arrived several hours before the Emperor. All other generals and almost all other officers perform their journeys in traineaux or carriages, covered with furs and furbelows, but since Moscow I have always ridden without a rag of additional covering other than my blue greatcoat, except in heavy snow, when I have put on my Cossack bourka [cloak].

I confess that there is some vanity in this deviation from general practice, but it is in its effect beneficial.

General Tormanssow being obliged to give up his quarters in consequence of some bad arrangement which excluded the Marshal from a habitation, I shared mine with him, and was very happy to pay this attention to a very respectable and agreeable old man— old in years but in constitution a youth.

The next day I proceeded to this place, memorable for the death of John Sobieski.[4] But I could not find one inhabitant who had ever heard of this heroic king. So fleeting is fame and so limited!

[1] Captain Amable-Hugues de Fontanges, a former officer in the service of Holland, had been captured at Wilna.
[2] The Convention of Tauroggen, signed on December 30th, 1812, between Prussia and Russia.
[3] Hans David Ludwig Yorck (1759–1830), son of a Pomeranian captain claiming English descent. He entered the army in 1772, was cashiered for insubordination, and served in the Dutch East Indies. He later rejoined the Prussian service. In 1812, on his own responsibility, he gave up besieging the Russians in Riga when he heard of Napoleon's retreat, and declared his corps neutral.
[4] John III, King of Poland (1624–96). When the Turks besieged Vienna in 1683 he saved the city and perhaps Christendom by winning a great victory.

January 17th, Sukleva.

At night Charles arrived and brought me a great packet of letters from all quarters. I was very glad to see him and to have his despatches, public and private. There was a variety of the agreeable and the unsatisfactory, but the agreeable prevailed. I was particularly pleased to receive my family correspondence, as I had long been a stranger to all communication with England.

From Merecz we have been proceeding by regular marches to this place, where we are halting for one day. The main army is proceeding on Wittenberg. Wittgenstein is at Königsberg checking the French at Pillau and at Marienwerder. Tchichagow is moving across an old theatre to approach us at Wittenberg; and Sacken and Doctorow's, late Ertel's, corps, are moving between the Narew and the Boug. The total force makes about a hundred thousand men. The wreck is powerful from moral energy, but it is only a wreck. How many thousands would have been saved by the opportune sacrifice of a few hundreds at Wiazma and Krasnoi.

Had I commanded ten thousand, or I might almost say five thousand men, Buonaparte would never again have sat on the throne of France.

This is not a fanfaronade. I do not mean by the monosyllable, *I*, to place myself in undue prominence, but to exemplify the frequent and facile power of concluding the revolutionary war, which was offered to any one who should have been authorised to act. There was only one Russian officer who did not feel ambitious to accomplish the achievement. There were various ways of attaining this successful issue—there was only one way of avoiding it—and that one was selected by the Agamemnon of the host.

We have now doubtful enterprises to undertake. We have now formidable impediments to overcome; and if Austria does not join us, in my opinion, these impediments are invincible to the Russians *alone*, even under able direction. Already the enemy outnumbers us; already we need plans of strategy and all the energy of our means. The truncheon, however, remains in the hands of an unsubstantial phantom, who has neither principle, military talent, nor personal resolution. The genius of Russia is powerful and prodigal of protection; but the genius of Russia must have tractable and efficient engines successfully to conduct a campaign against skill and force.

The day before yesterday, at six o'clock, as I was rising from my bench, for I have not slept on a bed or even straw for a hundred and twenty odd nights, I saw a flame in an oven, which I thought was too ardent. I, however, undressed to put on clean linen, and, when without clothes, I heard from the outside a cry of 'fire.' I wa obliged to sally out from the hut without anything on my feet and without *inexpressibles* [trousers] in a cold of twenty degrees. The fire had already gained the roof. We cleared all our goods and chattels out as fast as possible, and had the good fortune to save the hut also by throwing snow into the flames. We had just re-entered, miserably cold with wet on all sides from melted snow that momentarily iced, when a second alarm occasioned a second removal; but it was not so necessary and we again possessed ourselves of what might be called still a dark dungeon.

Charles, who had been accustomed to some hardships, confessed that he had never seen such inconvenience in war as we are now enduring from vile lodging, filth and cold, but if he had been in Russia with us, he would have thought himself here in a comparative paradise. I wish some of His Majesty's ministers could but pass a night with us. They would learn a lesson useful to those they employ in these countries.

January 20th, Lyk.

Another chimney was on fire in my house on the 18th; I, fortunately, however, put it out myself. The people of the house were in fault. To keep the room warm they had perforated the board which stops up the chimney, thinking that the smoke would pass through and the flame would not reach. The night was a miserable one. Several Jew children *croaked* from sunset to daybreak; I have now declared permanent war—and I feel Herodian[1]—whatever may be the cruelty in removing them.

We have now entered Prussia. The country is much improved and the people far cleaner and better clothed and lodged. A Prussian officer, in his zeal for the service and in gratitude for a kindness which I proposed to show him and his wife about a quarter, has already made me benefit by the change of nation. He has given me Schroetter's map of Prussia: no money could now buy it. Any other present I should have refused, but a map was too seductive.

Marshal Kutusow is very unwell; Count Wittgenstein has declared himself so, but I believe he is only a little chagrined at Admiral Tchichagow's being nominated commander over him. As this, however, was but a temporary measure, I make no doubt all will soon be well with him; and whether the Marshal lives or dies, I believe the Emperor will make very good arrangements for the executive army.

[1] Soon after the birth of Jesus King Herod ordered the massacre of all children in and near Bethlehem.

Dawson has been unwell. I have therefore sent him to repose and refresh at Königsberg for a few days, taking advantage of his movement in that direction to acquire intelligence, which will be very interesting, on all subjects.

January 28th, Wittenberg.

We arrived here yesterday. That day six years Buonaparte entered this town to commence the operations which ended in the battle of Eylau. What a revolution of events!

The ride to Johannisberg was so cold on the 24th that my nose and cheeks again froze. Charles did not escape with impunity. To this hour I have several knots in my cheeks, which when touched cause most acute pain.

The next ride might have been a more fatal one. I was alarmingly petrified and for some time very sick indeed from agony. An old woman saved me from extreme calamity by rubbing more than half an hour. The Emperor, hearing of my distress and danger, sent Wylie, who ordered additional embrocations. The crone moaned over me with touching, yet almost laughable, sympathy.

This day we received the important intelligence of Austria having made an unlimited armistice with the Russians; of her having, moreover, agreed to evacuate the duchy and retire within her own frontier. At the same time General Kleist arrived, and brought us the agreeable intelligence of the King of Prussia, with his family and guards, having gone to Breslau.

Europe has thus again another brilliant hope, founded upon pretensions more solidly established than any which former coalitions favoured. We have now to pass the Vistula with all expedition between Warsaw and Plock. The Poles can make no effectual resistance. The French have their headquarters at Posen and must be too much alarmed for their communications to assist in the defence of Warsaw. I presume that city will be occupied by convention.

Count Wittgenstein is ordered to take Dantzic, if practicable; I think he will succeed by escalade, if the garrison does not number fifteen thousand under arms.

The King of Prussia will probably act in concert with Austria. He has forty thousand men in Silesia, and his garrisons are well stored; he can raise forty thousand more in Pomerania; there are eighteen thousand with us; and at Colberg as many. This is a formidable military aid in the state of France, which must make another conscription to maintain the ports beyond her frontier, even if Austria is a passive spectatress; but that policy is now improbable. She would not excite vengeance without securing some positions and additional means to resist its violence. I rather suspect that her first acquisition is the part of Gallicia added to Russia, and the promise of the Turkish nibblings being restored to Moldavia. Under every point of view it is a promising moment.

I counted little upon our military powers; the direction, I knew, would be unskilful and our means daily decreased by sickness. We have not now above two hundred men a battalion; but all goes well when fortune is friendly.

I saw an English merchant from Kōnigsberg this day. He tells me that trade was there almost extinct, but that there is great want of coal, of blue, green and grey cloth, and indeed of all manufactured goods. I can add another need of great profit—bottled porter.

February 5th, Plock or Polotzk on the Vistula.

The rides from Willenburg to Mlawa, and from Mlawa to Radzanow, were particularly severe. In the former Charles's nose froze severely once and mine twice; in the latter my ear was frozen, and yet remains greatly frozen and very sore. I do not think that a Marshal's staff would tempt me to make another campaign in this climate. At Mlawa, Morland, the King's messenger from Vienna, came to my quarters; he left the next morning for St. Petersburg. He is a phenomenon of health and activity at sixty-six years of age.

At Radzanow I was quartered in a mendicant's Jew's house or cell. He and his wife wore more rags than all England's rag-fairs ever presented in two garments. Glory was overshadowed and, as I lay shivering during the night on two planks, each eight inches wide and one four inches higher than the other, I lamented that I had not some Downing Street[1] friends as companions.

At Dobrzyn, the next march, I had another such frightful den that I determined to proceed thirty wersts further, and I came yesterday to this town, which is situated on a lofty bank above the Vistula, here about five hundred yards wide, but now ice-bound. There are about five thousand inhabitants, and many of the houses are very good. In the hospital we found about a hundred and twenty half-frozen Bavarians; all have had some amputation. Seven thousand Bavarians, of ten thousand who had only marched towards the Niemen, had returned by Plock. Three thousand had perished on the route and the party left here could be transported no further.

The remaining seven thousand had marched to Glogau, and all declared here that they would never pass the Vistula again.

[1] The Secretaries of State for Foreign Affairs and for the Colonies and War Department had offices there.

North
Sea

Bremen

Hanover

HOLLAND

U

BELGIUM

Westphalia

R

Cassel

RHENISH

HESSE CASSEL

PRUSSIA

Eisenach *Erfur*

Gotha

Wetzlar *Schmalkalden*

Fulda

Meiningen

Hochheim *Hanau* *Gelnhausen*

Mayence *Frankfort*

R.Main

B

Würzburg

FRANCE

Mannheim

A

R.Rhine

Carlsruhe

WÜRTEMBERG

Strasburg

Baden

Breisach

Belfort

Freyburg

Basle

L

A

R

I

A

E. G. Morton

104

Baltic Sea

Colberg

Stettin

Konitz

S · I · A

Kulm

Löwenberg · Thorn

S

Spandau · BERLIN · Custrin · R. Warta

Potsdam · Frankfort

deburg · Gross Beeren · Posen

Ackern

au · R. Oder

pzic · Torgau · Fraustadt · Lowicz

gau · Hoyerswerda · Glogau

penig · Meissen · Bautzen · i · Rawitz · Kalish

nberg · SAXONY · Lask

DRESDEN · Görlitz · Liegnitz · Breslau

Chemnitz · Pirna · Zittau · Jauer · e

Töplitz · Schweidnitz · Reichenbach

Aussig · Leitmeritz · Trautenau · s

ad · Laun · Melnik · Glatz · R. Oder · i · a

R. Elbe · Josephstadt

PRAGUE · Königingratz

Cracow

R. Spree

0 · 100

Scale of Miles

During the course of the day I visited the Polish gaol. I was desirous of seeing whether the public establishments of this country justify the political pretensions of the people. I found all the cells airy, and yet sufficiently warm; the food good, and the superintendence effectual for the nourishment of the unfortunate tenants; but I objected to the want of proper gaol clothing, as several of the malefactors were in rags, and the neglect of cleanliness must produce disease.

I also judged that Polish criminals could not be very desperate men, or the strongest cells in this gaol would not hold them a single night. All the fastenings are so slight, and the facilities of escape so inviting, that I was much surprised to find that any men ever awaited execution; and still more so to hear that sometimes a condemned wretch remained here tranquilly three years; for the laws in Poland are so defective as to allow of appeals to the Court of Cassation, at Warsaw, and afterwards to the King, which protracts the final sentence, if the culprit wishes, to the stated period. Punishment, inflicted after so long a time, is deprived of its chief value, deterring example, and spectators must think that they see the sword of vengeance, rather than of justice, fall upon the neck of the sufferer.

Willanova, Palace of John Sobieski, six wersts from Warsaw.

On the 6th Charles and I proceeded on our route from Plock. We went thirty-five wersts, and came to General Doctorow's headquarters, where we passed the night; the next morning proceeded to the corps blockading Modlin. General Passkewitch[1] went with us to reconnoitre the fortress, in which were three thousand Poles, some French artillerists and two thousand Saxons. Charles went to the right to take a sketch of the works. When he had got very close, the French perceived him and fired repeatedly. He was several times covered with the earth which the shot struck up. I had also their salutes from another battery, but with less precision. The place is a very important one, not only from its actual command of the Vistula and the Boug, but from its neighbourhood to Warsaw. All the works are not complete, but it is most respectable. Charles's drawing was sent to the Marshal with some remarks: they will probably induce a partial attempt that may incommode the enemy.

We proceeded twenty wersts further, and took up our night's quarters with General Kanow. This morning we joined General Milaradowitch, who was quartered in a house where the hostess

[1] Ivan Feodorowitch Paskewitch (1782–1856) took a leading part in the 1812 campaign, and in later years fought for the Turks. In 1831 he suppressed a rising in Poland.

talked faster and shriller than any dame I ever heard in my life. After breakfast we rode ten wersts and arrived at an apartment where the deputation from Warsaw came to present the keys of the city. General Milaradowitch and Baron Arnsted received the magistrates very well, made the most of the opportunity, and dexterously avoided any proposition to quarter troops in the town— which in good truth, from weakness, could not be done.

The town surrendered unconditionally. Near two thousand Austrians are left in the hospitals, and four thousand French and Poles, who are prisoners of war. Prince Schwartzenberg wished to have stipulated for their liberty and for other terms favourable to Warsaw, but Baron Arnsted refused to admit them, after having previously assured himself that the bargain was already struck and could not be broken for such minor considerations.

The possession of Warsaw is entirely due to diplomacy. The military means of obtaining the city did not exist after the fatal march from Minsk to Wilna.

All the great Poles have left Warsaw, but few of the inhabitants of the inferior order have done so. The Senate, and, indeed, the greater part of the fugitives, have gone to Petrikau and from thence to Cracow, where they expect certain shelter. Their protection, however, depends on Prussia; and Prussia gives but a precarious hope, according to the belief at the Imperial headquarters. Certainly the denouement of the enemy's campaign will be most extraordinary; as yet the champions cannot be arrayed. I shall, however, feel great inquietude if we advance without the possession of Thorn, Dantzic, or Modlin. The ground is too hard to be worked for six weeks; the broken ice descending the Vistula will prevent the formation of bridges for a fortnight after the river bonds are loosened, and we must depend on fortune rather than force.

The French exaggerate their numbers and exertions so grossly, that there is no positive confidence to be placed in their statements; but if they can advance to Posen five thousand cavalry and fifteen thousand more infantry—in addition to the thirty thousand already there—before the 20th of this month, we shall be greatly embarrassed to maintain ourselves beyond the Vistula bank; and when we are there, if we have no bridge or *têtes-du-pont*, we shall have additional difficulties. I must repeat again, that according to all military calculations, independently of secret policy, we are unequal for six weeks to the necessary operations for the security of the positions we now occupy. I hear, however, that it is the intention to advance on the 15th.

After the deputation had offered all the generals quarters in their houses and a town dinner, which were refused, we went to Willanova, ten wersts from Warsaw. I was very unwilling to go so far, but sometimes that which is reluctantly undertaken proves in the end very agreeable; so it was with Willanova, which I found to be the Palace of John Sobieski, now in possession of Countess Potoski daughter of the Marshal Czartorysky.[1] The centre is the ancient residence of this celebrated sovereign; the wings, which are brought forward, are modern. The *tout ensemble* is the most magnificent establishment that I know of in the hands of an individual. I could employ several sheets of paper in a description of all its magnificence, and the valuable property treasured in it. I have, however, not leisure: and I shall only note that I was most struck in the old building with the bed of the King; by the preservation of all his apartments in the same state in which he left it, so that every moment the royal owner was recalled by some forcible impression; by a valuable gallery of pictures, many of them most natural; by a richly inlaid cabinet; and by some very fine ancient editions of the classics. In the modern apartments, I had to admire everything but the want of mahogany furniture.

My quarters were most splendid, but I was bitterly cold all night, although I did not undress and brought my sofa to the wood-fire side. I regretted the stoves of the Jews' hovels during darkness.

Baron Arnsted is here by the Emperor's desire. He told me that Lord Cathcart would now be allowed to come up, 'but more for show than use,' was the Baron's addition. Indeed, he frankly said what the Emperor and Baron Budberg did last campaign relative to myself. The fact is, "the times are extraordinary, and require men of pliable form to take advantage of them, not professors of an unbending old school: Lord Cathcart means extremely well, but he shuns responsibility and hates exertion."

Writing to the Under Secretary of State for Foreign Affairs on December 29th, 1812, Francis Werry referred at length to Lord Cathcart, for whom he worked while attaché to the British Embassy in St. Petersburg.

His Lordship acts upon a principle of profound and unexampled secrecy, even in affairs that are the subject of common conversation in other houses, that is to me perfectly incomprehensible. This is, I know, highly pleasing to the Emperor; but notwithstanding the

[1] Adam George Czartoryski, born in Warsaw in 1770 and educated at Edinburgh and London. Having fought against Russia in the Polish insurrection of 1794, he was sent to St. Petersburg as a hostage and gained the friendship of two successive Czars. In 1803 he became Curator of the University of Wilna.

secrecy which is the order of the day at court, scarcely any confidential communication is made from the palace, before it is known at every respectable house in the town. . . .

. . . His coldness and reserve are so extreme, that many persons have told me that they had experienced it too often, and therefore could not, consistently with their own dignity, make any further confidential communications to him. They have therefore addressed themselves to me as a channel for such communications, and . . . I have undertaken, with the greatest reluctance, such tasks of reporting to his Lordship the information they wished him to know, and in every instance he has given me to understand that I was meddling in matters that did not concern me. . . .

. . . We get no credit for our quietness with people who are bred up amongst intrigues, and who are aware that the best course cannot be upheld without them. We are openly reproached with our want of information, and our retirement from society is offensive to all. Neither I nor any one of his Lordship's suite has been introduced *by his Lordship* into any one house in this city; how is it therefore possible to be *au fait* of what is passing? When the Emperor is here himself, his Lordship can only expect to hear one side of the question; and now he is absent, he does not learn even that (147–50).

February 10th, Warsaw.

I arrived here this morning with the intention of staying in the town two days, and then returning to the Imperial headquarters.

This residence is particularly interesting. I acquire most valuable information of all descriptions, as everyone of every country regards me as a common friend.

The Austrians, as I suspect, are marching, by private arrangement, to their Gallicia; but the Austrian headquarters will, for a short time, be at Konitz. The Austrian Government will probably then declare their peace with Russia, which is made without any direct engagement for co-operation; but the force of circumstances will, I think, accomplish the rest.

The Austrian Government could no longer control the will of the army, which is so strong that the officers almost refused to serve, even to save appearances. Indeed, the aide-de-camp of General Meyer told me that if I ever saw him drawing a sword against the Russians again, I might 'spit in his face,' and he declared to me that there was a common sentiment of the same character through the whole of Schwartzenberg's army.

The Saxons, &c., under Regnier, are gone to Glogau. The King of Prussia has promised to throw off the mask early in the spring. I do not know the measures which he proposes to adopt for separation and action, but his assurance is positive.

The occupation of Warsaw is a memorable political and military event: but it is also personally remarkable; for here for the first time since I left St. Petersburg, on the 15th of September last (a hundred and fifty nights), shall I have pulled off my clothes at night, or slept upon a bed.

The thaw is now rapid. This circumstance may check our movement on the 3rd, which is still intended, but probably only for a few days. If we once establish our bridges, I shall have no alarm.

February 16th, Kladova.

During my stay in Warsaw, where I remained until the 14th, I employed every moment usefully or agreeably except one in which I very nearly perished while walking on the middle of the Vistula, by the ice yielding and cracking for many yards around me, and giving totally away whenever I removed my step. I never remember to have passed a more embarrassing five minutes. I was saved at last by the Cossacks putting and fastening several lances together, and thus floating and drawing me to firmer portions of the ice-bed.

Political feelings indisposed the Polish families who remained to the Russians; but I was not only received but sent for by all who were worth knowing, and again had to be proud of British estimation. To be an Englishman is a letter of credit which no rank, no introduction, can procure a foreigner. An Englishman is at once admitted, on the faith of his national character, to the regard and confidence which others must prove themselves worthy of possessing before they can acquire them; and even the most favoured of other countries are never allowed such latitude, nor do they ever obtain such favours as the English. Woe to him who trespasses to the prejudice of his country! Shame be to him who does not augment the fund upon which he drew when a stranger and unknown!

At the house of the Countess Alexander Potoski née Tichawich, whose husband is one of the richest nobles, I learnt many curious anecdotes. Amongst them, that when Buonaparte went to Dresden he sent for the king, obliged him, who never in his life stirred from his palace after dark, to come to him in a chair at midnight, received him in bed, and made him remain three hours; solely to prove that he exacted in adversity more than the homage he required in prosperity.

On another occasion, speaking of the French, he said to the Countess A. Potoski: "I have them, Madame, always in my pocket; I can do with them as I will, only by operating upon their imaginations." This speech was made before his suite, who hung down their heads in humiliation.

I cannot attempt to describe the city, which possesses more palaces and bad houses than any city I know. I shall only observe that the establishments of the nobles are magnificent, and the houses are fitted up with a taste and costliness which are unknown in England. The city in its external appearance, and, I believe, in all its internal concerns, has suffered considerably from war, and the streets are crowded with mendicants of every description, but particularly mutilated men. I went to visit the hospitals. The Polish were in good order; the French frightful. I went to the theatre once, when I saw a good ballet and a handsome building lighted with patent lamps. I indulged twice in the use of the warm baths, which for extent and arrangement would not have dishonoured Rome.

During my stay in Warsaw I gave a fête to sixteen generals who had assembled there, and it merited the *Morning Post* title of a 'grand entertainment.'

At this fête Novosiltzow challenged my toast: "The Princess Potoski," by insisting on giving her again as his own when it came to his turn. I used my privilege and required that the draught should be salt and water, and I drank off a magnum. Novosiltzow shrunk from the contest ignobly, but related the incident the same evening to the Countess, adding: "Did you ever know such a —— as that Wilson?" The Countess replied that she "did not agree with him," and he had his *congé*.

On the 14th I left the city in the morning, and journeyed until four o'clock.

The next morning I proceeded on my route by Lowicz, where I received a command from Princess Radziwil, the mother-in-law of Princess Louisa of Prussia, on no account to pass without paying her a visit.

After a previous visit to the Princess Radziwil at Bommel in July 1807 Wilson wrote in his journal:

This lady is certainly one of the most accomplished women in Europe: and had nature been as kind as to personal attractions she would have been one of the most celebrated in the world. She is the first woman I ever saw who fascinated irresistibly without the charm of beauty; who enchanted the mind without moving the passions.

She exhibits great good sense and large information, without the slightest trespass beyond the bounds of her sex's delicacy; without the revolting hermaphrodisy of the 'blue stocking' (ii, 295).

The Princess's residence was near two German miles from Lowicz and out of my route, but the compliment was imperative and I immediately drove to Arcadia, not in a very high-classed equipage for a British general, it being a common cart with ladder sides, in which I made my journey from Polotzk; but I conceived that I should be welcomed even by the porter when he knew that I was an Englishman, come in what vehicle I might. I did not miscalculate.

Princess Radziwil and the Countess Serivan Potoski received me with the most cordial kindness. After some conversation, they showed me the wonders of their magic creation.

I am at a loss even now to determine whether the genius of conception or the energy of execution is most to be admired in this extraordinary combination of both.

I really look at the Princess Radziwil as a woman calculated to have been a Semiramis. She would have proved another wonder of the world had she been born a sovereign.

From Arcadia the Princess Radziwil insisted on my going to Nieborow, which is the mansion of the property. I could not refuse and I entered her carriage.

Here I saw a noble collection of pictures; some most exquisite drawings, as large as life, by a Saxon artist, who only shades them with bistre, being conscious that he does not equal with the colour-brush his execution with the pencil; and a grove of orange-trees in a gallery a hundred yards long: they were the identical trees given by King Augustus to his mistress. The Countess Radziwil brought them, and transferred them to Nieborow.

We dined early. After dinner I had the affliction of seeing that charming woman and the Countess Potoski shed torrents of tears, at an incident which made them feel that their nearest relatives were exposed to all the miseries of this fatal war. Still, like every other Polish woman with whom I have ever conversed, they spoke with a spirit and a virtuous love of country which does them the highest honour, and entitles them to the sympathy of every generous mind.

At six o'clock in the evening I took leave of these excellent people, for whose personal security I felt no uneasiness as the Emperor had ordered them a considerable guard, but for whose anxieties I felt great regret.

We were carried in their phaeton and four to the post-town, which

now belongs to Marshal Davoust, and which did belong to Bernadotte.[1] From thence we descended to our rustic car, and, having
travelled all night, arrived here this morning, when we learnt that
General Winzingerode had taken Kalish with near two thousand
prisoners, and Woronzow Posen with several hundred.

I was much gratified at finding brother[2] Platow here. He is experiencing the persecutions of jealousy and chiefly because his
portrait was in the English newspapers; but he has the admiration of
every high-minded man in the army, and although he may neither
have the first order of St. George nor a laurelled sword set in
diamonds, he is a happier man, for he will always feel that he has
faithfully served his country.

February 22nd, Kalish.

Having declared my protest against a further advance with the
whole residue of our armies, I determined to come here and see
Kalish, that I might inquire into the late affair of Winzingerode's
and reconnoitre a point which I thought we ought to occupy until
the King of Prussia declared and our reinforcements had reached
the Vistula. I then proposed to join General Milaradowitch, but
on my arrival here I found that general, and the next day, the 21st,
we received advice that headquarters would be transferred here.

Kalish is a small city, but an honourable memorial of the Prussian
administration. The houses are well built; the machinery of the mills
is a *chef-d'œuvre*, and the whole state of the city proves that the
Government was animated by a most liberal spirit of improvement;
for it was the Government who sacrificed temporary revenue to the
permanent advantage of public establishments on a scale calculated
to create public spirit and active industry. I am told that several
hundred thousand pounds were thus laid out in Kalish alone, and
through the Polish provinces several millions.

Many German families reside here, but the patriotic sentiment is
so strong that when General Winzingerode gave a ball not one lady
went to it. What other women could resist the fiddle and the waltz?

I have collected here seventy-five Spaniards, who belonged to a
battalion in Regnier's corps. The poor fellows skip about with me,
and show as much joy and satisfaction as the faithful dog expresses
at the discovery of his master. They will all be sent to Memel to join
Colonel O'Donnell's battalion.

[1]Charles Jean Bernadotte (1763–1844), Marshal of France, had in 1810 accepted the
position of heir to the Swedish throne. After Napoleon's retreat from Russia he openly
supported the Allies in Germany with a Swedish force. In 1812 the French had seized
Swedish Pomerania.
[2]A Freemason.

March 1st.—The King has signed the Treaty! '*Toto certandum est corpore regni.*' This is a most important event. I have no doubt Buonaparte will decree that the House of Brandenburg ceases to reign, and that he will offer Silesia to Austria. But Prussia can put a hundred thousand effective men under arms, and in the need of France such a force acting upon such a base as Silesia ought to determine the superiority of this campaign, if Austria be neutral. It is a most fortunate coup for Russia. We were quite expended: we had not sixty thousand effectives under arms, and many guns had not *one* artilleryman!

Austria's enmity, even if that were probable, would now lose much of its mischievous power, but I think Prussia would not have acceded to the Treaty unless the King had private assurance of Austria's favourable view of such a line of policy.

Some Cossacks entered Berlin the other day. They formed a garrison of seven thousand men. Two guns placed on a bridge, loaded with grape, drove them out of the town with the loss of two hundred men. It was, however, a gallant enterprise, similar to one in a former war.

Since then the French have removed their headquarters from Frankfort to a place between that city and the Oder, probably anticipating the defection of the King.

That apprehension accounts for many of their movements which otherwise, with the actual force they have, would be inexplicable.

The anecdotes collected here of Jerome Buonaparte are very singular. He bathed in a bath of wine every day, provided by the town. Here, as well as at Warsaw, he obliged ladies to be his hand-maids; and levied a contribution of five hundred crowns a-day upon the inhabitants for his expenses. These and similar excesses occasioned his first quarrel with Buonaparte.

The Emperor has given Captain Fanshaw, who acted as my aide-de-camp at Malo-Jaroslavets (when I planted the guns that checked the descent of the enemy), the order of St. Anne, *à coup*. This is a great compliment to myself, and this is the second aide-de-camp of mine whom the Emperor has distinguished with a public mark of his approbation.

The week that has been passed here in quiet has enabled me to refit my tatters and fragments, but the wear and tear of man, horse and property in such a service exceeds all ordinary calculation. I am sorry to say I am in progress to the invalid list. My left shoulder is full of rheumatic pains and my right ankle, where I received my droska wounds, continues enlarged and very painful occasionally.

Frequent opodeldoc [soap liniment] embrocations will, I hope how-ever, save me from becoming a barometer, and consequently an antique before my time.

I have been adding to my stock in hand Admiral Tchichagow's Turkish charger, the handsomest animal of his size I almost ever saw. Harry,[1] if he distinguishes himself, shall have him on my return. I have also increased my establishment by a black poodle, who came of his own accord and sought my protection. His character is very like Pacha's, but in physiognomy and colour he had such properties as obliged me to address him by the name of Pluto.

Dawson has had the severest fall from his horse I ever saw in my life. The animal reared, tumbled back, and Dawson's body formed the bed to receive him. It was on pavement, but, strange to say, he received but little injury, although the saddle was crushed while he was a-straddle.

I much fear that my dragoon left at Polotzk is dead, and also Baron Brinken. The former was to have had the soldier's Cross of St. George, and I believe those who are yet with me will also be so honourably decorated.

5th.—I am going to Winzingerode in a few days, as he will have the most conspicuous and advanced command; but as there seems to be a resolution to put an extinguisher upon my sparks of vitality, unless some instructions come from England to accredit me as a general officer instead of a volunteer—which is my character by im-plication in Lord Cathcart's memorable Wiazma despatch—even His Majesty's Government will never see the records of my existence, to enable them to judge of its utility.

I understand that all my despatches are closed down in a strong box, never to see the light. How, in such a case, can Government know how far I am worthy of the trust actually reposed in me, although it is officially recognised?

There may be good reasons for refraining from giving me public notoriety, but there can be none for total suppression.

I make these remarks without any ill-will to Lord Cathcart, who is in all personal matters very kind and who has certainly reason, from the most marked attentions on my part, to be satisfied that I have no feeling but that of good-will to himself and respect to his station; but he seems rather to have been instructed by—or to have understood—His Majesty's Government that it would be agreeable to them if he kept me as much as possible in the background—out of sight, if not out of action; and I *could say* what I do not think it

---

[1] Sir R. Wilson's eldest son.

prudent to write, as to the very general impression of the existence of such a disposition on his part.

Even in the despatch about poor Tyrconnel, he has so far omitted notice of myself that Lord Tyrconnel's friends and the public must conceive that either no British officers were present, or that we neglected our duty to a countryman, and one so deservedly beloved.

God forbid that I should have paid any attention from other motives than those of affection and duty; but still, an omission of all notice in such a communication as Lord Cathcart made is in fact a reproach.

With regard to all silence about my public services, the officers here, and more than the officers, are far more astonished than myself.

12th.—The last diary advertised a nobility-ball and one to be given by the Marshal. The first was very thinly attended, and if there was much fashion there was very little beauty. The second, by admitting the town ladies, improved the specimens of 'Nature's last, best work,' but presented no remarkable model for admiration.

Kalish is scarcely Poland, and the motley band presents a very unsatisfactory effect. I was also much disappointed in the *élégantes'* robes: the drapery was badly selected and ungracefully worn.

Having a very bad headache the second night, I withdrew after making my bow to his Imperial Majesty, who danced both evenings with the zeal of a certain late British general.

Winter has again covered the earth with her white scarf, and my nose quakes whenever I look upon Nature's shroud.

For the last two days I was indeed not so well as heretofore, but I am again braced to the right tone.

Lord Cathcart will not only transmit any information contrary to the official statement of the Marshal with a long name and unjustifiable fame, but he has positively refused all communications of military proceedings. He permits me to go on a visit to my friends in command, but he "wishes to have no report of what I hear or see, as it would be indelicate to have any papers contradicting the official document." This is indeed zeroing me. *Sed spero meliora.*[1]

I strive to push my bark into a flowing tide, but I can never clear the foul ground. If once I could get my navigation free, I would gladly take the goodwill of my own pilotage. I feel even now like the Russians floating amidst perils, without a port under my lee and without a true compass.

The Russian detachments have been pushing the enemy, and I

[1] "But I hope for better things."

understand have cleared the country to the Elbe. The return of the Emperor from Breslau will probably give us an insight into the proceedings of the campaign as far as they can be regulated by our prescience and power.

There are still supplies both in front and rear; but the operation will be slower to the front, and the distance is so great to the prisoners' depôts that the recruits cannot for this summer be brought into action.

Lord Cathcart went to meet General Walmoden[1] at the frontier the day before yesterday. The journey was to be a great secret, but alas! the whole town knew it before he set off. He reminds me very much of the child who hides its face, and cries "You can't see me."

In private life Lord Cathcart may be, and indeed is, an excellent gentleman and an honourable man, and in the field a good executive cavalry officer, but he has defects in his nature and habits which disqualify him for any public station in which a man is charged with high public interests.

General Walmoden, it is said, will enter the British service and command the German legion. Fame speaks well of him.

The weather since yesterday has again become moderate, and the long-absent sun pierces the misty clouds.

21st. The Emperor has returned. The King is to come here, and the headquarters will remain at Kalish some time longer. The enemy will, I think, be first in the field. His exertions continue most vigorous, and I am still more inclined to think that Austria will not forbid action, except against the Poles at Cracow. Her power augments as the combatants expend their blood and resources. If Buonaparte is a wiser man than he was, he will only endeavour to push to the Vistula this year; the next, if peace be not made, to the Dnieper. His march, however, will cost France much valuable life. The Russians are 'brand high,' and the Prussians seem to have caught the spirit of self-devoting patriotism.

The early hostility of Austria to Russia will alone give Buonaparte an easy approach; so England ought to do all in her power to fascinate the Austrian negotiator.

Pozzo di Borgo[2] is arrived from England. This place becomes now the great diplomatic *foyer*; but the diplomats will, or I am mistaken, have to rest on their arms until the bayonets have clashed. I am going myself tomorrow to see Glogau, then to Custrin, perhaps to

[1] L. G. T. Count von Wallmoden-Gimborn.
[2] Carlo Andrea, Count Pozzo di Borgo, born in Corsica in 1764, entered Russian service in 1803 and carried out many diplomatic missions. He was to represent Russia at the Congress of Vienna.

Berlin, and from thence I shall run along the Elbe, for I suspect the enemy will not be able to move before the end of April.

Admiral Tchichagow, who is just come here, states that the French cohorts are very fine men, well clothed and well exercised; and that the remains of the French cavalry are all remounted, and well mounted. This confirms my opinion '*sous tous les rapports.*'

The Russians have commenced the bombardment of Thorn, and are procuring guns to batter from Graudentz. Thorn is, therefore, I conceive, a sure prize, and its position is of value as a *tête-du-pont.*

One of my dragoons, whom I constituted my factotum as a servant, is, I am sorry to state, in a most dangerous delirious fever, attended with violent vomiting of blood. I must leave him behind and this greatly inconveniences me. It is extraordinary how I escape so much contagious sickness as has been in my family. It is one of the incidents that gives me most hope for the future.

March 29th, Fraustadt.

On the 27th, after having been detained to dine with the Marshal, and again with the Emperor on the succeeding day although my horses were at the door, I left Kalish.

I left Kalish very gladly, because I was tired of diplomatic mystifications which the sword will and must arrange. If the pen could win Austria, then indeed the sword would not be the most important talisman; but as Austria will await the issue of another trial of force, I think the field is the best theatre, and he is the most likely to win who can enter first.

Knowing Austria as I do, I am satisfied that Buonaparte's speech to Baron Bubna[1] is congenial with the feelings of the court, the cabinet, and the nation: "Tell the Emperor to think of the power which Russia has displayed under the most feeble of sovereigns, and to think of her capabilities when ably directed." England could alone check that alarm and counteract its operation, but England is a cipher on the Continent at this time from the character of her representation.

I overtook my horses at Kroeben, and tackled them four-in-hand to my britzska. I fear, however, that for equipage and equipment I should have been voted a dishonourable member of the Whip Club; in all other respects I am vain enough to believe that few of the best coachmen of that society would have rivalled me. I made lame horses go and blind horses find their way over the worst roads for thirty miles. When I came to Lissa I regretted that I had not time to

[1] Ferdinand, General Baron Bubna-Littiz.

overlook the field of battle[1] but I had a passing view that fixed its locality in my mind for instructive purposes.

I reached Fraustadt per post, and there found General Milaradowitch. I had so bad a headache that I could not remain up with him, but a night's repose restored me. I was quite charmed with Fraustadt. It is the prettiest town I had ever seen in Poland, and does great credit to the Prussian Government, under whose auspices it was built.

Here I saw the fine remains of the two regiments with which we stormed Wiazma. The Emperor, in recompense, has made them grenadiers; but alas! there are only five hundred survivors sensible of this distinction. At night we went to a theatre, framed in a small room. In the midst of one of the most interesting scenes there was a cry of "Fire!" which threw the actors and actresses into a real distraction and the company upon one another. Some tranquillity was restored by the advice of its being at a distance. I ran to the spot and found that it was exactly opposite my quarters. The flames burnt furiously. We all worked, and with success. One Russian officer claims the merit of snatching me from a flaming pile which was descending with Virgilian force upon me: '*En lapsa repente, ruinam Cum sonitu trahit.*'[2]

Fraustadt had been burnt down before. Like a phœnix it had risen from its ashes, but a second resurrection by the same process was regarded with terror by all.

At Fraustadt Allen took the fever. This was the last Englishman on my establishment. Thus am I in the hands of persons ignorant of my ways, and national ways; and what I grieve most for is that my stud is without English superintendence. I have taken Spanish soldiers whom I found at Kalish and who had been to Moscow with the enemy. They are extremely well-disposed men and I am sure they will be faithful, but they want instruction.

March 31st, Frankfort-on-the-Oder.

On the 29th I left Fraustadt, passed the Oder at Gollwitz, and made in my carriage for the nearest point to Glogau, that I might reconnoitre that fortress; ascended a hill, within cannon-shot, on which were two windmills; entered one and, with my telescope, immediately saw advancing in my direction a column of several hundred French infantry and some horsemen. Charles having

---

[1] Also called Leuthen, where Frederick the Great beat the Austrians in 1757, during the Seven Years' War.
[2] "Behold, it suddenly collapses, and crumbles in ruins with a crash."

made the same observation, we quickly descended and drove under the direction of a Cossack to the nearest Russian post, expecting every moment a shot from the works, which we passed for the whole distance considerably within reach.

The post was under arms, with two guns to check the sally, but the French did not approach within their range. They kept up the river, and, having taken a walk, returned. This was their general daily practice; and on the preceding day they had done it with a thousand men and some artillery, which they fired against the Russians. Having well reconnoitred the place, which is in excellent order, well palisaded, strongly flanked with a garrison of near five thousand men whose guards and detachments appeared very well clothed and who, two deserters told me, received daily, bread, meat, and wine (and we saw many sheep about the place), we again proceeded and for a distance of two more wersts ran the gauntlet, not by choice but necessity. In the evening we reached Quaritz, where General St. Priest[1], charged with the blockade, was posted; but he was to be relieved the next day by a Prussian General with twenty guns and three thousand Prussian recruits, whom, however, I think the French will remove soon to a greater distance than musket-shot.

We stopped all night with St. Priest, as the weather was very foul and there was no moon—good entertainment for man and beast being offered.

The next morning we drove off early, passed through Grunsburg, crossed the Oder at Crossen, and recrossed it here this morning at daybreak.

Here I found Woronzow and learnt that the King was expected. We went out to meet him. He received me in the kindest manner. I rode by his carriage through the town, and when he got out at the house prepared for him he took Woronzow and me by the hand and made us go up with him and breakfast. After half an hour the King said he would walk through the town to see the troops drawn out to receive him and that he would cross the footbridge, while his carriage crossed the ferry, the enemy having destroyed the town bridge. His Majesty desired me to keep with him, and we entered into a very interesting conversation. He told me that "the French had evacuated Dresden on the 27th, but that they were concentrating their forces in great strength near Magdeburg; that he thought they would make an early effort; that the Russians ought to advance with

[1] Emmanuel, Comte de St. Priest, an émigré French officer in Russian service, had been Bagration's chief of staff.

regularity to anticipate their operations; but that the conduct of Austria in keeping her contingent on the Pilica and covering the Poles at Cracow, caused very great inquietude; that Austria showed an apprehension of Buonaparte's power quite unworthy of her military reputation; that for his own part he had taken his stand; that he was resolved to be an independent Sovereign, or lose all but his honour; that he trusted that England would support him, and then whatever might be the event, he would make a struggle that should cost Buonaparte dear.'' He spoke and felt as a man conscious of, and equal to, his difficulties and I am confident that he will do his duty. Would that I could hope fairer than I do, but I do not think the nation is so steady as its Sovereign, Russia powerful to the degree that the occasion requires, or Austria yet safely bonded to the common interest.

It is Austria!—Austria! which holds the balance, and it is to Austria that we should direct all our thoughts, whilst we afford Prussia sufficient succour to keep her vessel afloat.

Woronzow showed about nine hundred men under arms. He has ten battalions altogether under his command—not making at present fifteen hundred men—and about a thousand horses of every description: all are in good order, and his artillery horses are as fat as if they had never marched above five wersts a-day, and as sleek as if they were out of Newmarket stables.

Frankfort is an old town, remarkable for the fair annually held there, and its neighbourhood to Kunersdorf, where the famous battle[1] was fought by Frederick the *truly* Great; the field of battle is in sight. The fair was this year very thinly attended and the injury is very great to Frankfort. I have not noticed the *carte du pays* through which I have passed, but generally from Fraustadt to this place it has greatly reminded me of British scenery, and agriculture seems in a prosperous state. Sir John Sinclair[2] would not be able to make more of a light soil.

April 2nd, Berlin.

On the 31st I went to Custrin, and approached until I could hear the outposts talk by the dyke on the right. While I had my glass in my hand, I saw an officer running down to order me a salute. I observed him expressing his anger vehemently at suffering so near an approach, and presently the ball of a musket proved that all was on the alert. Having finished my reconnaissance in that quarter,

[1] Frederick II of Prussia was defeated there in 1759.
[2] Sinclair (1754–1835) was a leading agriculturist and President of the Board of Agriculture.

I rode across to the other flank; and as I crossed, a cannon, that had been laid ready, was discharged. Fortunately they had charged with round instead of grape, not expecting that we should move so much within range. The infantry fired again here and showed great jealousy of this point, so that I was convinced that they were vulnerable on that side. I refer, however, to my military report on that subject. Having accomplished what I wished, I rode to the place where I had left my carriage, for I was resolved not to appear before an enemy again in any car but one of victory. The Cossacks' colonel had provided a sumptuous dinner against my return and, after partaking with more pleasure from the compliment than from the dainties of the feast, I proceeded to Berlin, where I arrived at night.

Yesterday I paid visits to all the members of the Royal Family still residing here, dined with Alopeus,[1] went in the evening to see *Romeo and Juliet* operatised with very melancholy music, and supped with Princess Louisa wife of Prince Radziwil. I met a variety of friends here, and a general reception as an Englishman that is most flattering to England, which, with all her throes, still towers aloft in foreign estimation.

April 11th, Dessau.

I passed the Elbe yesterday over a ticklish bridge. I was glad to see works constructing, but the locale is not very favourable for efficient protection.

We have been floating with fortune's tide very long. It will require, however, Leander's powers to swim the Elbe, and I lament the absence of the patent 'anti-submergists.' In this march I saw many Prussian and many new Russian troops. The Prussians have exactly the air and appearance of the original Portuguese. The pride of martial mien is not visible, but the stuff seems healthy and muscular. The Russian *débris* are in good order, and the militia look particularly well and rudely warlike. The Prussian cavalry horses already begin to look thin and broken. I much fear that the Allies will not long retain their cavalry superiority. Extreme need produces abundance and sometimes superfluity. So it will be with France.

Dessau is a very pretty, clean, English-arranged town, with a very fine palace. The Duke of Dessau Anhalt, *père*, is not well, and was a mile off at a château, which has an English garden, the Duke having been in England and brought back an Anglomania. The Prince, his son, is forty years of age, an extremely good-natured

[1] Alopeus had been appointed Governor of the north of Germany by the King of Prussia.

person. His wife is sister to the Princess William of Prussia, and is Princess William embellished with very animated expression. There are two daughters, fine girls, and well brought up, and a son of much promise, with very good manners. It is an excellent *ménage* altogether and kept up in good style throughout. Wallis[1] would, I am sure, be pleased with the residence, the stables, and the stag-hounds; nor would the cellar be disapproved.

I have been dining with the Prince daily, and one evening we went to the theatre, which is larger than the Lisbon theatre, and where a corps of amateurs acted with much effect, particularly the musical parts. This evening we went in a procession of carriages to drink tea at a *maison de campagne*. Prince Henry, the King's brother, an ancient acquaintance, is always of our party: he speaks English perfectly well.

This mode of existence is very different from Russian service in Russia or Poland, and to other *agrémens* we add a glorious sun. It will be painful to break away from such attractions into the scenes we have gone through, but toils, and privations, and mortifications all tend to the bloom of the soldier's laurel.

13th. If I live through this campaign, I shall have seen my share of 'big wars,' and I do not think that without other inducements I will pass a Russian winter to be spectator of the next campaign. I shall prefer English service. I only hope I may have opportunities of being in the present as useful as in the last, and then, if I retire without the approbation of His Majesty's Government, I shall have the satisfaction of bearing away a good conscience and a good fame.

I do not know that I ever felt more flattered than by a trait which Prince Wolkonsky told me. As I was passing by his house at Dresden, he heard a soldier ask some others "Who I was?" The immediate and general answer was, "*Our* English General"—"*Nashe Angliskov General.*" '*Nashe*' is more expressive in the Russian language than 'our' in English: it implies, when said emphatically, 'appertaining to our affections.'

My time at Dessau continues to pass very agreeably. We live with the Prince, and, besides his attention, I experience the most distinguished kindness from Wittgenstein. His countess is with him, and four children. This is a weakness which surprises me, especially in a man of his firm character; but it is of an amiable species, and so long as he does not suffer his affections to prejudice the public service, he deserves charity in commentators: he promises to remove the

---

[1] Wilson's brother-in-law, General Lewis Bayly Wallis.

perilous sorceress as soon as active exertions commence, and I hope she will have good sense enough to seek absence when the very first trumpet sounds.

The situation of the poor German princes is most deplorable. We force them to join and to give men as well as money; Buonaparte will fine them for obedience: and between these two protectors they must perish.

April 15th, Leipsic.

I left Dessau this morning. I had passed a very interesting time there. The Duke whom I went to see at Worlitz was one of those men who would be recognised as noble by all observers. His reign has been one of the most liberal beneficence, and every feature of his polity is characterised by the traits of a wise administration combined with an active personal philanthropy.

I was enabled to give the Duke useful counsels and to render him some good service. He shed tears from feelings of gratitude and regard for the English nation, which he had frequently visited, and with many individuals of which he had formed intimate friendships, especially the Claverings.

The Hereditary Prince and his family were also amiable personages, and contributed to the ornament of this most interesting domain. There were, moreover, several very pleasant families, all English in their manners and establishments.

Walmoden went the day before to take the command of all the light corps on the lower Elbe. He will, or I am much mistaken, be a distinguished officer this campaign.

General Wittgenstein strongly invited me to return, and I felt much flattered by the cordial manners of this accomplished general and honest soldier. He is really a man without guile: confident but not presumptuous; loosely active perhaps in his projects, but still a man of business. He may meet a great misfortune, but he must always acquire honour in the struggle; and he seems one of those enterprising, straightforward characters who by their courage and their patience extricate themselves from difficulties which would greatly baffle, if not ruin, better tacticians.

I had not such good opportunity of judging of General Yorck, but, in a conversation I had with him, he spoke as an officer with a very intelligent and reflecting mind, and I am sure he will feel, that, like Macbeth, he has 'set his fortunes on the die and will stand to it.'

I arrived here about two o'clock, and found General Winzingerode, a brother knight of Maria Theresa and a very kind friend. We learnt

at dinner that Buonaparte had left Paris on the 9th. We shall soon
mself again.'[1]

ough the town of Leipsic amidst a most
as everywhere, the English receive willing

ty, but it has paid dear for its temporary
have levied already one hundred thousand
l the amount of the contributions in kind.
s an agricultural garden. The great fair
tended, and I think every article of every
re.

that the Governor of Torgau has given
in eight days subscribe to the following

and Prussians; provided that the Saxon
friendly, the reigning dynasty guaranteed,
y a Saxon garrison."

at the old Governor is but a feeble traitor
at he has pledged; but in the interim he has
from the negotiation, for he has got from
for his bridge, and a free passage round the
ns to defection must, I think, have an effect
w him that no tyrannic rule can perpetuate
le Archduchess, named Empress of France,[2]
as the audacious, parricidal anti-patriotism
constant career of victory: to vaunt successes
ed her family with distress and disgrace!
of the Duc d'Enghien and of the many
ors slain might scare her to silence! I was
Archduchess Anthony, after the battle of
pplaud that victory, saying in the public
arrived, that defeat was the only way to

ench prisoners were brought in. The officer
y five days. He will have an agreeable and
ask and Siberia! What a derangement of a
s!

me part of the Journal is lost.[3]]

Richard III. 'Conscience avaunt, Richard's himself again.'
leon had divorced Josephine and married Marie Louise
ustrian Emperor Francis II.

April 19th, Dresden.

I left Leipsic on the 17th, and went to Altenberg, where General Blücher[1] and others were. I was much pleased with the town and country. The Duke of Gotha is ruler, and merits the same encomium as at Dessau. His palace is a fine building, and nobly elevated.

The dress of the peasantry was remarkable. The men were all clothed like priests, with cocked hats; and the women had their petticoats as short as the *Milo* ladies. I had the good fortune to see a bride; and her costume was very airy, though not very light. Her garments, which reached only the top of the knee, were hooped out so that between her limbs and the woollen was at least a space of three feet. All the ladies, indeed, in this district seem to be fond of cooling hoops.

I ought not to have omitted that the first strange sight of this morning occurred as we were driving out of Leipsic. Our leaders struck down an old woman, who rolled and rolled, with her clothes over her head, till she settled on her back, when, in a state of stupefaction, she gathered her legs and drew them up as high as she could. In that position she remained at least while a person could have gently told two hundred. There were many spectators, it being market-day. Charles and myself have not yet recovered the terrible vision. I could not help exclaiming: "Take any shape but that, and my firm nerves shall never tremble!" It was truly a sorry sight, and long shall I remember the old woman of Leipsic.

On the morning of the 19th, I left Altenberg, passed through a fine country, the most picturesque and the most mountainous that I have seen since I have been in these parts, but the day was Siberian. The wind blew as cold and the snow fell as thick as if it was the month of December in Russia. Here I found General Milaradowitch, and my horses, &c.; but, alas! Richard had never come up, and Allen was left dying on the other side of the Oder. Thus was I deprived of every English aid.

April 25th, Chemnitz.

I left Dresden yesterday. My residence there had been very pleasant. The Russian generals gave daily handsome fêtes, which produced corresponding attentions from the Saxon nobility. A dance given by General Ouwarrow, with supper, excelled any entertainment of the kind I ever witnessed. The entrée was indeed more interesting; for a superb hall, brilliantly illuminated, was sur-

---

[1] Gebhard Leberecht von Blücher (1742–1819) took chief command in Silesia, and was prominent at Lützen, Bautzen, Katzbach and Leipsic. In 1815 he and Wellington defeated Napoleon at Waterloo.

rounded by Russian dragoons, of extremely martial appearance, harnessed with French cuirasses which their swords had won.

The women were very pretty, very well made, very well dressed, and gracing all with the most accomplished manners. In no country did I ever see a better specimen of female education and presentation. Indeed, in England only have I ever observed anything like the *tout ensemble*; but in England there is a more affected severity, which preserves no more dignity while it prevents an amiability in social intercourse.

The Anglomania is, however, so strong in Dresden, that the society aspires to no greater object of ambition than that of resembling the nation with which they were once more intimately connected.

I proposed to leave my name with the Princess Elizabeth, the King's sister, who of all the royal family alone remained; but so soon as she heard of my being in the Palace, she came out herself and received me most graciously. I do not know that I ever passed a more agreeable colloquial half-hour than with this princess, who, although advanced in years, retains all the vivacity of her youthful spirit, with a most happy manner of expressing herself.

The conversation turned, at last, upon Buonaparte, and I made some observations about his variations of creed, that I think she will repeat to the King, who is more likely to be influenced by such remarks than by any political arguments. My opinion in favour of the Roman Catholic claims enabled me to obtain a complete personal triumph. I quite regretted the moment of departure, and I have quitted Dresden with an intellectual love for an old woman far more, I believe, than seventy years of age.

The Court I understand is melancholy to the highest degree; and for fear of sating the public eye with royalty, all old, antiquated and ridiculous ceremonies to separate royalty from the knowledge of the public, and vice versâ, are preserved.

I am told that the young Prince is, by his seclusion from all intercourse with the young nobility, quite a booby. Princess Elizabeth thus becomes a greater phenomenon in such a family.

The corps of General Milaradowitch filed through Dresden on the 20th and 21st. The cavalry, about two thousand five hundred, was in very good condition, the artillery in unparalleled and *unparallelable* order; the infantry, about four thousand, in the best possible state. But alas! what a wreck in the total! This corps ought at least to be thirty-five thousand strong.

I do not think I am growing a misanthrope, but Childe Harold[1]

---

[1] The publication of the cantos of Byron's *Childe Harold's Pilgrimage* had begun in 1812.

would not find me an unsuitable companion. The flowers of hope no longer bloom in my view. Her roses, her lilies, her evergreen laurels, I can contemplate with indifference and feel no inclination to plant or to nourish them. This is not the momentary sentiment of a testy humour or a vexed spirit, but the product of an extensive observation and long experience. I am not ungrateful for the good which I have enjoyed in my passage, but I see that the order of things is adverse to my action; and even when Fortune is most propitious to others, she can yet establish for me no solid enjoyment.

I have also the peculiar ill-luck not to have been born an ass, that could be satisfied to eat provender without a care for my master's interest. Colonel Campbell[1] from England joined us. He had been with Lord Cathcart and met with a reception which he little expected from what he had heard in England; for Lord Cathcart sent him off with all speed to hide himself, as it were, and now intends to make him 'serve as a volunteer,' although he is colonel on the British staff, and was sent out to obtain and report information. The Emperor approves of his executing the orders which have been given him and yet, to prevent confidence, to degrade the appointment and the officer, the term 'volunteer' is deliberately used and insisted on by Lord Cathcart.

A volunteer is a nobody in estimation, and must be exposed to a thousand chagrins. He has no rights, no protection, and must depend on the favour, not of the general in command, but of the lowest subaltern in the army, perhaps of the very soldiery.

I gave my voluntary aid in battle to the Russians for their immediate interest; but it is a recognised British general who does it, and that increases the power to make the present and enhances its value.

I would rather dig and delve for my bread, than submit to any *avilissement* of my station, to gratify the low feelings of a jealous spirit.

A colourful description of some of the leading personalities in this history is afforded by Colonel Neil Campbell, who on April 6th watched the guard mounted in the square of Kalisch, where he had just arrived. He saw it all from the windows of Lord Cathcart's house.

The Grand Duke Constantine first came upon parade on foot, wearing the uniform of the Chasseurs of the Guard who were on duty, and of which he is colonel. He bowed to the different officers

---

[1] Colonel, later General Sir Neil, Campbell (1776–1827) came out as a liaison officer on Cathcart's staff and was appointed to General Wittgenstein's corps. In 1814 he escorted Napoleon to Elba.

as he walked down the line, the men standing at ease. Soon after the Emperor himself came up on parade, attended by Platoff, the Duke of Würtemberg, brother of the Confederation King, and eight or ten others. Platoff had a Cossack orderly. He was himself dressed something like a Turk, in a blue cloth wrapper with white sash, a sort of turban cap, and half-boots with pantaloons. The Emperor wore a long coat of dark green, with green overalls, gold epaulets, an orange ribbon across his breast, and a huge cocked hat with an immense black feather. All the other officers of the suite were dressed in similar hats and coats, with ribbons of dark or light blue, green pantaloons, and long boots. The Chasseurs passed in slow and quick time, Constantine on the right of the first section, and saluting with his hand to his hat. After this the Guards halted. The different officers, from twelve to fifteen in number, came out to the centre of the square where the Emperor stood, with his hand to his hat. Each then stepped forward in succession, with sword reversed, said, "I am of such a guard", faced to the left with a peculiar flourish of the sword, and then rejoined his guard. After this the Guards marched to their posts, and the Emperor with his suite walked off.

The Emperor is about the height of the Duke of York, or perhaps rather taller, but not so large. The Grand Duke Constantine is stouter and shorter. The Emperor is fair, and has a very good countenance; but the Grand Duke has a most unpleasant physiognomy, like a flat-nosed Tartar. Both of them are very smart, and walk with a quick short step. They never miss the guard-mounting, and perform the duties corresponding to those of field-officer and adjutant of the day. The Emperor has also frequently manœuvred one of his regiments of Guards under Lord Cathcart's windows, and given the word of command himself (pp. 67–8).

26th—Before I left Dresden I had the satisfaction to have an order from the Minister Stein[1] to draw for the full amount of the sums I proposed for the purchase of Stettin and Custrin. If I can effect the negotiation, as he says in the document, 'three months' use of the river will repay the same, exclusive of all the military and political importance of these places as fortresses.' It is a great satisfaction to have such a proof of my judicious application of responsibility.

I may truly say, if my military counsel had been adopted, which was in unison with the counsel of others, Buonaparte would no longer

[1]Karl, Freiherr von Stein (1757–1831), statesman and diplomat, had reorganised Prussia after the defeat of 1806. In 1812 he became political advisor to the Czar.

have been in authority; and if my political counsel had been followed, Germany would now have been clear to the Rhine, and the Allies would have held securities for suitable arrangements.

I certainly feel mortified at the treatment I am experiencing from my own national protectors (from no others, for I have only to express gratitude to all foreigners for general kindness), but I shall in the ensuing campaign endeavour to enjoy a glorious vengeance; and instead of desponding with disgust, I will strive to make courage mount with the occasion, and in such a case I shall ambition the compulsory praise of adversaries.

Although a thousand circumstances combine to make me sick, I feel my powers renovate as the cry "They come!" augments; and if I have not the tranquil mind and content, I am sensible to all the glow of the approaching hour; without, however, setting up the golden calf of glory for worship.

By dint of great personal surveillance and energy I have also got myself in good marching order. I do not think any man can pass me, or remain longer in the field, from the possession of a better stud of chargers. I purchased this day a noble dove-grey, or rather milk-white, on which General Ilovaisky was killed at Wilna and which was wounded with General Winzingerode on his back at Kalish. They think in Russia 'Luck's all in man or beast' and so they sold the unfortunate a bargain, considering his real value. My creed is 'Every bullet has its billet,' so I coin with my faith. The 'little Turk' is the admiration of soldiers and citizens. He is the greatest beauty that can be seen of his kind and I hope he will survive to make his appearance in England. I have various others; but my stud, although as good as the countries afford, is not British, and a British general and horseman should have British horses for his credit as well as for his pleasure.

This is a very pretty town, and extremely prosperous: indeed I never saw throughout a richer and finer country; all is pleasing to the eye and the mind. But, as an Englishman, I am chagrined to see a very extensive spinning manufactory set up by an *Englishman*: it has succeeded so well that he is going to build another at Rochlitz. He has not called on me; if he does I shall frankly say I can make no acquaintance with a man who injures his country from any selfish motives. The Prince Royal of Prussia passed through this place this morning on his way to Dresden. I went to see him, and he really is so friendly that I am sure, by his manner of showing his attachments, he has a good heart. His departure at such a moment makes me suspect that the King intends to keep him at the Imperial

headquarters during these critical times; and that the army—
GRAND from the grandeur of its chiefs and merits, but not its numbers, alas!—will not advance.

April 30th, Altenberg.

I left Chemnitz on the 29th, and went to Penig. Here I discovered that an English horse belonging to me and another belonging to Charles had the glanders, so I was obliged to shoot them both.
I had given in Russia fifty pounds for mine and Charles gave sixty
pounds for his. I shall be satisfied if the first misfortune is the last;
but I greatly fear for the rest of my stud, especially as many of the
Prussian horses are glandered.

I came here this day: my military report will state why and
wherefore, and the et cetera. It is a most critical moment. God
protect the good cause, and make us victorious! If we triumph, it
will indeed be a success beyond human powers and Russian courage,
as we are situated, and all Europe should sing *Te Deums*.

I see as visibly as my own a higher hand in all our late operations; but whether its working be for good or for evil to us, the
event must show. While I was here, a Mr. Gordon came in search
of Lord Cathcart. This Mr. Gordon, who is a very fine young man
apparently, has entered into the Russian hussar guards, although he
is on navy half-pay as a lieutenant. Lord Cathcart, on quitting
Dresden, would not name to him the place where he might rejoin
headquarters, but told him to steer west and he would find it: which
was very diplomatic, as well as nautical, but not very indicatively
precise.

May 3rd, Langdorff.

Charles joined me on the 1st, and brought me a carte blanche
for my movements to the centre and left of the Russian army.

In the evening I rode towards Borna, where I heard the Imperial
headquarters were; but as a cannonade commenced, I turned off
as I was entering the village and rode towards Zwenkau; but the
firing having abruptly ceased, I returned, after a ride of fifty
wersts.

The next morning I packed up bag and baggage, and moved from
Altenberg in the direction of Lützen, where I proposed to find
General Winzingerode. When I had ridden about fourteen wersts,
the cannonade commenced again and I pushed on with all speed
to the field of battle, distant about two more German miles. I
reached it about ten o'clock in the morning. From the moment I
entered, until eight o'clock at night, I do not think I was thirty
minutes out of a continued storm of shot and bullets.

It was a furious combat of artillery, more especially, and such as modern wars only present.

It was my good fortune—aided by Colonel Campbell, my aides-de-camp Charles and Brinken, and at the moment Dawson whom I met in the field—to rally the Prussians, as they were flying from Glogau and extending panic through the Russians; to enter with them, sword in hand, and carry the village, which was maintained until night when three French columns again threatened to retake it. I then rode to acquaint Count Wittgenstein. The Emperor met me, asked me the tidings, and, with his and the Count's orders, I took a Prussian reserve, put myself at their head and, uniting with the Russians still disputing the skirts, again drove the enemy back upon Lutzen. I do not mention these traits from a vanity that would derogate from the acts, but I have two motives: first, as a family memorial for the imitation of my children, who, I hope, will always be ready like myself to sacrifice their all for the public good; and secondly, to show, that although I pronounced a strong opinion previously against the possibility of successful resistance on this side of the Elbe, still I did not let my judgment and prediction influence my action, but endeavoured to do all in my power to prove their fallacy. I hope, also, it will not be suspected that I exaggerate the advantages of my efforts. To British evidence I can add General Charnhotzh's, and, for the last exertions, the whole of the spectators assembled round the Emperor.

It was a severe day, but I never felt more equal to the need. Such is the effect of a moral excitement; for as to food, I had none, nor even one drop of water, for thirty hours! I was quite unhappy to see the poor Prussians slaughtered from mismanagement. They are fine material, but they require exactly what has been done with the Portuguese—the loan of British leaders to train their own.[1] The cavalry, however, are perfect. I never saw such steadiness: it is quite incredible. I was obliged to ride up to several squadrons, to express my admiration. The King was on the field and behaved very well. I had two or three opportunities of seeing him and I lamented to him the unnecessary exposure of his brave horsemen, which he also regretted. The young Princes also were present and showed much firmness. The eldest, Prince Ferdinand, had a horse killed under him.

Poor Charles was wounded immediately after quitting me. He told me he would take the horse round the village, while I pierced

---

[1] In 1809 Marshal Beresford had been appointed to reorganise the Portuguese Army, which he and a number of British officers achieved with great success.

with the infantry. His wound is a great injury to the public service. I do not dwell upon my predictions respecting the passage of the Elbe, but never was a military calculation better verified.

I passed a cold night and, as Charles was missing, a very uneasy one; but he turned up in the morning. I lost him in the attacks of the enemy at Gera. The next morning I quitted the field with the rear-pickets, as I wished to see the enemy's deployment of forces. He showed a considerable body of infantry and cavalry in his position, but no great number advanced. Hitherto he has suffered us quietly to retire, although he might have distressed us greatly. I hope he will continue to be as forbearing on this side the Elbe.

During last night's march I lost my servant, my horse, with all my baggage on him, box with papers, money, &c., and a fine mare; but I am still in hopes that they have not taken the road to Leipsic, although there is great probability. This second loss would be great, and the capture of the papers mischievous.

We are now, I presume, on march for the Vistula, although I think I could keep the war between the Oder and the Elbe afloat through the summer. When we get behind the Vistula, I conceive Buonaparte will not this year press us much further; and, if he returns, I will hie to England on leave.

The Marshal's death[1] is kept a secret. He died most opportunely for his fame.

[FRAGMENT]

At four o'clock we received an order to retire from Wilsdruf and pass the Elbe. The execution of this service was very creditable to the Russians, but much otherwise to the enemy. The commander must have very little confidence in his troops, or he would certainly not have been so cautious at the last moment. His previous forbearance was to be accounted for by the hope of the Bavarian corps getting in our rear.

The temporary bridges were burnt and removed without difficulty; but the principal bridge of the town, which Davoust had destroyed, and which had been repaired by a wooden arch, did not consume so rapidly as could be wished.

*   *   *

Fortunately the horses were stopped and the traces cut at the foot of the bridge.

I was desiring the sentry at the furthest ridge of the broken arch not to fire when the French entered, and several of their dragoons

---

[1] Kutusow died at Bunzlau in Silesia on April 28, 1813.

galloped forward into the great *place* opposite the palace and sent their balls at our heads. I was determined on revenge for such an unhandsome proceeding, and soon had it, for I mounted a 12-pounder on a ruined bastion of the New Town and, having a skilful artillery-officer, the first shot fell among a mass of persons riding in confiding complacency along the water-side; the second and third with shells fell into the midst of a body of cavalry, who flew in all directions.

*   *   *

The appointment of Wittgenstein, who is a younger officer, occasions great jealousy, and the whole army, from this and other causes, is disorganizing. It is a pity: Wittgenstein is a valuable executive officer, and perhaps the best. Russia has no chief. Unfortunately in Russia there is great selfishness in men engaged in the public service and the defects of government institutions are sensibly felt to the prejudice of the public interests—by this cause the motives of action are contracted not expanded, individualised not nationalised.

I have suggested in the proper quarter what ought to be done to secure the restoration of a necessary spirit of perseverance in this struggle.

Last night was a very uneasy one: there were sharp cannonades occasionally, but the enemy made no attack. They had in the morning prepared to put ladders for workmen into the broken arch, but I planted a gun, which by the first discharge with grape made all the survivors ascend with expedition.

This morning we mounted at daybreak, and being wearied to a degree which I scarcely ever experienced before, and suffering some pain from a blow which a piece of bursting shell gave me on my shin bone at the close of the battle of Lützen, I determined to come on here after I was certain that the army could not advance against General Milaradowitch to harass him this day. Tomorrow he comes here and I wish to receive him. My leg has been dressed. From neglect and great exercise it has suppurated a little, but like my ankle it will proceed, while I am at work, on its cure. I did not mention the accident before, as I was afraid of giving uneasiness and I really attached no importance to the laceration which it occasioned. Now I can note it, because there is self-evident proof from the elapsed time that there is no serious injury. It was just as I was leading the Prussian and Russian battalions to resist the French attack that I was hit. It was a momentary severe sensation;

but this passed, leaving only an aching pain that continued. On first looking at the leg, there appeared a swelling, and the flesh was cut. If I could have laid still a week I should have been well without any inconvenience: now it will take me a fortnight, and a little more punishment from inflammation; but vinegar and water will soon conquer its anger.

The army marches tomorrow to Bautzen. There are many offensive projects in agitation, but I fear we have not the means to fight and cut down the difficulties of our position.

We may reduce the enemy by active operations with our cavalry, but we must evade with the main force desperate extremities until we are very much reinforced. It is of importance to show to Europe that the Allies have the power and the will to continue the war. This mode of proceeding will, I think, eventually engage Austria and if there be but wisdom enough to make terms with the Poles, Buonaparte's power in Germany will not endure; but this policy requires many sacrifices which Russia, I fear, will not make with a good grace, although she may lose that which would preserve the rest.

The King of Prussia is much to be pitied. He is really a stout fellow, which is a rude but expressive compliment, and his troops fought with a courage which redeems all their ancient character, and engages the deepest interest for their success.

May 14th, Bautzen.

On the 12th the enemy attacked Milaradowitch at Weissenkirsch. They showed great intrepidity and advanced against grape fire very frequently: but latterly they were driven from the open ground, and obliged to gain the woods on their right, where they manœuvred so successfully as to dislodge the Russians from the position which covered Bischoffswerda, and obliged them finally to evacuate the town. There was also a subsequent very severe contest to gain the wood in front of Bautzen, in which the enemy succeeded by a superior fire of artillery.

During this affair Stewart[1] joined us in the field. When it was terminated I went into Bautzen to nurse my leg, and lodged with Stewart in the bishop's palace.

---

[1] Lieut.-General Sir Charles William Stewart, afterwards Baron Stewart and Marquess of Londonderry (1778–1854), was half-brother to Lord Castlereagh, the Foreign Secretary. He commanded a cavalry brigade in Portugal in 1808 and was for three years Wellington's Adjutant-General in the Peninsula. In 1813 he was appointed British Minister to Prussia.

Mr. George Jackson, a diplomat who accompanied Stewart, described him as "a very active and dashing officer, and, socially, a most pleasant and excellent fellow" who was always preaching the doctrine of "the necessity of suppressing every appearance of *aigreur,* and allowing only the *suaviter* to appear, in order to encourage our Allies and keep them firm and staunch in their warlike resolves."

The 13th was quiet. The army had on the 12th moved into the celebrated position of Hochkirch, and the Emperor was lodged in the same house in which Daun slept after his victory,[1] and which still retains shot-hole memoranda of the action. This day the enemy have made no movement, but two hundred prisoners, taken by the Cossacks on the Königsbruck road, were sent in. They were Bavarians, Spaniards, Croats, and Tyrolese of Macdonald's corps— mostly soldiers of three and four months. The Emperor sent his surgeon to dress my leg; but Count Wittgenstein's surgeon has regularly attended and, if I had been an obedient patient, inflammation and suppuration would have ceased. But the exercise I take only protracts cure and gives me pain; it causes no danger: I suffer the evil therefore to obtain the good, and shall not regret the inconveniences I endure to maintain my post.

15th—This morning the enemy advanced, and General Milaradowitch fell back behind Bautzen, keeping the town and his advance behind the Spree River. The enemy lost a good many men in their progress by several successful cavalry charges, but still they gain ground and do not appear intimidated.

The French force is now posted within cannot-shot of the Spree, but their strength is not known, and indeed, nothing is known of the movements of the enemy, except that a large column is advancing from Camenz, as I think, to Hoyerswerda, to turn our right while the corps now opposite to us will march through the mountains on our left, as Daun did when he turned Frederick the Great.

Either movement will oblige us to quit the position of Hochkirch and, if Austria does not join immediately, the sooner we pass the Oder, in my opinion, the better.

Count Stadion[2] has arrived at headquarters, but I do not think, from what I hear and observe, that Austria is about to declare war on the part of the Allies, although she is desirous of doing them service.

The Swedes seem to have totally withdrawn from co-operation and Denmark has been playing the game that I surmised her to be meditating when I first mentioned her propositions.

May 20, Graditz.

On the 18th the enemy made a show of movement which disturbed us early, but they returned to their position without action.

---

[1] Leopold Joseph, Graf von Daun (1705–66) drove Frederick the Great back from Prague and out of Bohemia during the Seven Years' War, and on October 14, 1758 he gained a crushing victory at Hochkirch.

[2] Johann Philipp Stadion (1763–1824), Austrian Minister, who had been Ambassador in St. Petersburg.

In the evening I rode to see Sir C. Stewart at this place, but he had gone to Gorlitz. I however remained in his quarters, and he returned in the night. Yesterday Barclay de Tolly, Yorck and Kleist, with a force of about thirty thousand men moved to Königswerda and attacked Lauriston with success; but the enemy, having information of his design, detached from Ney's corps a force which fell upon Yorck and resisted his progress with a loss of two thousand men.

Hearing the cannonade, Sir Charles Stewart and I rode out to Bautzen with Mr. Vernon, who had just come from England on his way to Vienna; but the enemy in front of Bautzen only made a feint to disturb our attention and prevent any reinforcement being sent to Yorck, &c.

General Milaradowitch, at Bautzen, told me that he had received the Emperor's commands to put in writing the services which I and my staff had rendered at the passage of the Elbe, and in the affairs of the rearguard.

This communication gave me pleasure on account of others more than on my own. I am not ungrateful for intended royal favours, but I have more satisfaction in the consciousness than in the recompence of utility.

Last night I read Stadion's note. It will, I think, excite much displeasure in England, as she wishes, contrary in my opinion to her interests, to make a conjoint peace.

The answer of the Allies is extravagant, but they are perhaps right to make huge demands in the first instance; I suspect, however, that in doing so they are favouring the protracting policy of Austria, who actually by Stadion dictated the pretensions. He was I know present when the answer was being penned.

Provided that Buonaparte permits continental traffic with England, the continent, that is the people, will quietly submit to his rule and not care about our private interests. The policy of England is always charged with self-love, and though our loans and gifts prove the contrary in the contracted sense of that term, we continue to displease by the mode of eking out our liberality; and the person whom we choose to represent our interests in the great crisis has invariably injured them by his manner of conducting the negotiations. This is no prejudiced opinion, but a positive fact broadly asserted everywhere by the friends and foes of our connection.

May 23rd, Gorlitz.

The last preceding three days have been replete with great incidents. I had scarcely finished my diary, and sent off some letters by Mr. Broughton, when a heavy cannonade on the right mounted Sir Charles, James,[1] and myself. We rode forward and found that Barclay was vigorously attacked on the right, and that the action was commencing near Bautzen. When we arrived there, which we did, as the French would say, '*ventre à terre*,' we found the left of our line in a warm fire, and that the enemy was passing the Spree on the right of Bautzen to take the town in reverse, and act in the rear of Milaradowitch.

A battery on the hill, which ought to have covered the ground below, on which was a Russian battalion, was withdrawing from the enemy's fire upon it, and the battalion was also retiring.

In a few moments the enemy appeared on this side the river and drove back rapidly all the tirailleurs, &c., who opposed. Not an instant was to be lost. The point was the key of the position of the advanced-guard, and the most prejudicial results must have been the consequence of its premature occupation.

Sir Charles agreed with my opinion. I brought back the guns and the retiring battalion. We then advanced at the head, caps in hand and accompanied with loud cheers. The enemy fell back, but again we were obliged to retire by fresh succours sustaining the fugitives. Again and again we rallied and charged; and finding about forty Prussian lancers we dashed in among the enemy's infantry, while our own pressed forward to help our inferiority. The enemy threw their fire upon us before they gave way and in flying singed us, but we were revenged. It was my lot to strike the arms out of three men's hands; one at the level, whom a Russian Yager instantly stabbed with the bayonet. A few were spared—a good many taken; and if we could have procured but one squadron, I would have engaged for at least five hundred prisoners. The importance of the success was not, however, to be measured by the numbers slain or taken. It was the preservation of the ground that was of chief moment and that was saved until Kleist was enabled to reinforce the point with guns, infantry and cavalry: here he gloriously maintained himself for some hours against all the enemy's multiplied and powerful attempts to batter and storm him from the post.

It was hot work: little more than pistol-shot distance for near two hours and considering that we were conspicuous *à cheval*, and in glittering kits, it is wonderful that no marksman fired with unerring aim; but this is another proof that 'every bullet has its billet.'

[1] John James, a relative of Stewart's, serving as a volunteer and attaché to his mission. He was later decorated by the Czar. See Sept. 27th.

The rest of the day I was here, there and everywhere, but as this is more a personal than a general diary—for I have made a separate memorandum of the military occurrences—I must note two occasions of some interest. The first was that when in the evening I was on the battery of the conical hill at the right of our position—which the enemy took the next day—we were collected *en masse* as spectators, and the enemy, seeing the group, directed the fire of a battery against the height: every shot struck, and many persons were killed and wounded around the Sovereigns. As they were retiring I remained to look at the enemy's motions after such a fire, and three Prussian officers were seated in the battery: a ball came and struck the earth under my horse's girth, and passed thus completely under him. The animal I thought would have shaken to pieces with terror. The Prussian officers came to me and said:"*Je vous félicite sur un tel coup de bonheur!*"—and in verity it was one. Colonel Campbell had his horse killed in the next battery by a cannon ball on the neck.

Second.—In the evening, when the French were endeavouring to force the mountains, the Emperor sent me to desire Milaradowitch to sustain himself until the arrival of the guards and grenadiers who were ordered to repel the attack which, if successful, would have carried our main position. The troops were informed of the Emperor's wish and in a short time I had the satisfaction of saying to the Emperor, that, with the use of his name, the enemy had been repulsed and driven down the mountain. He took me by the hand, grasped it in the most affectionate manner, and said the kindest and most gracious things, assuring me of his eternal friendship, although attempts had been made to estrange it. I knew by the hints he gave that it was not a foreign foe that had endeavoured to poison his mind. At night, I was told afterwards, notwithstanding all his anxieties and business for the morrow he descanted largely before many persons on the good service I had rendered, the exertions he had seen me make, and those which he knew I had made on every occasion without concern for my own person, but only for his interests.

The next morning at day-dawn we were again in the field; and Sir C. Stewart[1] and myself keeping company we rode to see everything, and I was the bearer of many important communications from various points, particularly from Barclay in his extremity.

[1] On June 5th Wilson wrote to the Duke of Gloucester: "Sir C. Stewart's arrival has greatly improved my position. He is truly a most excellent, gallant gentleman, and is very much liked by the Prussian and Russian courts and camps."

This message first made the chiefs think of the question—whether they would retire or endeavour to retrieve the fortunes of the day? The Emperor seemed to wish for an offensive movement; but I could not help suggesting the question whether, if successful, the recovered point could be maintained, or others equally important might not be lost by the removal of the troops? I had seen the enemy's superior force acting against us, and their redundant force in movement to our line of communication. I thought it better to save the brave remains of an army than lose all, and with all our honour.

While this matter was under discussion, Blücher sent word that he was overpowered, and had ordered a retreat. There was then no option; but it was necessary to prevent confusion and preserve order. I begged of the Emperor to reinforce Kleist in the first instance, who still—but scarcely—held the post in the rear of our right, which commanded our line of retreat. The Emperor ordered me to march with the grenadier division and lead them to the ground. I obeyed the order; but as soon as we began to descend the line, the enemy from the ground left by Blücher opened upon us at least eighty pieces of cannon, which played upon us for a mile and a half. *C'était un feu d'enfer*; but firmness was necessary: a bad example would have ruined our affairs.

When we had got to that distance, another order came for the grenadiers to take the road of Reichenbach by Hochkirch, and for Blücher's retiring force to sustain Kleist, which was done. Having escaped this pounding I went to Kleist who had occupied an old battery in front of Wurschen, and there I remained until all the troops had passed. It is surprising that the enemy did not attempt to molest the march, but they were satisfied with cheers of victory and a furious discharge of artillery. This was not permitted to pass altogether with impunity, for we opened a heavy fire, particularly from one battery of forty guns, and checked their cannon for half an hour. We did not lose a single gun or tumbril. Above six hundred pieces and eighteen hundred ammunition-waggons, exclusive of regimental ammunition-waggons, were thus withdrawn in presence of the enemy. Is not this a strong proof of the respect which our conduct had imposed, and of Buonaparte's little confidence in his own people when employed in masses, except on ground much covered by wood where he can throw forward tirailleur swarms and support them by columns working their progress from point to point as in a game of chess? If he had advanced, he must have submitted the fortune of the day, thus partially his, *à l'arme blanche* [to cold steel]; and I am sure not one of the Allies would have declined the challenge. The action lasted fourteen hours, during twelve of which we remained intact on our line. On the left we were completely successful throughout, and here the enemy suffered most considerable loss. Poor Osterman was shot through the neck, and the ball lodged in his back, yet this hero—for he really is one—kept his station for two hours, animating his men to efforts which obtained and preserved victory.

The scene with the Emperor, King and Royal Family was most truly affecting. Their gallant conduct, their firmness and self-possession, the dignity of their resignation, excited deep interest the impression of which can never be erased.

In the morning when I first saw Buonaparte, I prepared some guns for him; but the first law of nature operated too strongly upon him, and he was so skilful an artillerist as just to keep out of range both of shot and shell. He was, however, most distinctly visible to the naked eye.

When the sun set Sir Charles and I rode to Reichenbach, where we had a very poor lodging for the night. The next morning Sir Charles went on to write his despatches, and I remained to make my Memorandum. I had just closed it when I heard a cannonade and rode out to see the action, which was not yet begun in earnest, as the French infantry had not arrived. I was much pleased to see the good order of the troops forming the rearguard. One would have supposed they were in review order and had not yet entered upon the campaign, instead of having fought in such a conflict within a few hours. The heights in front and in rear of Reichenbach afforded our position.

The object was to gain time, but of course not to maintain ourselves with ten thousand men against the whole French army. Buonaparte came in person with the troops and directed the attack.

The cannonade was very heavy. After some time he threw some cavalry into the town, which were instantly charged and all put to the sword. The Russian infantry, however, fired and killed some of our own people in their eagerness to weaken the enemy. After an obstinate conflict, the enemy, by throwing troops on the different flanking heights, obliged us to leave the town, but the action did not diminish in violence.

Our guns, and particularly the Cossack artillery, kept up a heavy fire, and caused disorder in his columns.

As a *coup de fou* [act of a madman] rather than of a general, Buonaparte at last ordered his cavalry to charge round the hill on

which our batteries on the left were placed. Eight hundred of the
Imperial Guard, sustained by a regiment of lancers and about three
thousand horse in reserve, made the desperate attempt. Some
Cossacks and hussars in advance fled before them; but a regiment of
hussars charged down in flank, the others rallied, ran, bore on them
and in a few moments the enemy were rushing back with the loss
of several hundred killed, wounded and taken. Buonaparte then
made another attempt of a different character, and with more success. He opened a battery of forty guns against our eight on the
left, and in the same proportion against the others. This fire obliged
us to fall back and we occupied Reichenbach, but we had been
detained till near night and could make no further progress. He
had hoped to intercept Milaradowitch returning by Luckau on
Reichenbach, to find his troops dispirited and in disorder, the train
encumbered with fugitives, wounded, artillery, baggage, &c.; but
in all this he failed, and did not find one single carriage of any
description from the field of battle to his present ground. The next
morning we leisurely returned but very slightly pressed. Yesterday we evacuated Gorlitz, and the enemy entered; but as he does
not seem disposed to make any great efforts, I am come over to
Count Wittgenstein, who has his quarters in the town, for the night.

I have done my duty to the Emperor and King in staying to the
last, in encouraging by my language and example, and in aiding all
in my power, but now I want myself two or three days' repose for
several reasons.

May 27th, Jauer.

I rode in from Jauer this morning to suggest to the Emperor the
utility of looking at his troops who were in position between Göld-
berg and this town. He immediately seized the idea and mounted
his horse. He was received with rapturous cheers and every one
present will witness that they were toned on the heart-strings. The
Emperor spoke much to the officers and men and on one occasion
he said—which was very true—that he wished to attempt the recovery of the lost heights of Kreckwitz, but that he was overruled.

When he came on the left of the first line of the Imperial guards
and on the right of his cavalry of the guards, he turned to General
Augerausky and said—"Now is the proper time for me to show my
gratitude to Sir Robert Wilson for all the services he has rendered
me. General, I request you to accept the order of St. George of the
third class as a memorial of my esteem for your courage, zeal, talent,
and fidelity to my service." Then turning to Sir Charles Stewart,
while General Augerausky gave him the cross and ribbon, he added:

"General, I give this to Sir Robert Wilson for a long series of distinguished services through the campaign—through the war" (which last words were very emphatically expressed to Sir Charles, while with a gracious smile he made me understand the full meaning of the words). The Emperor continued some time to speak in the same strain, and then in the most gracious manner presented me with the cross and affectionately grasped my hand in his: His Majesty almost during the whole previous time having his hand upon my shoulder, and only raising it to place it again with a motion of approbation. Sir Charles behaved most generously and kindly on the occasion, saying all that could be said, and perhaps exaggerating my merits. The guards, &c., crowded round to salute me, and I received the additional compliment of an assurance that I wore a cross to which every man in the army would acknowledge my title. I do not mention my answer to the Emperor, &c. My expressions and my feelings must be imagined. It was not merely the Cross of St. George of the most distinguished class that could be given to one who did not command an army; it was not only the additional honour of having this cross presented by the Emperor himself, before his army in the field and in the immediate front of his guards, but the manner of the Emperor, the tone of voice, the look and the gesture, which animated me with pleasure and gratitude. It was a gratifying and proud moment, rendered more satisfactory by the further good-will which prevailed for my honour.

We returned home, and Sir Charles immediately wrote a despatch to Lord Cathcart, with the intention of sending a copy of it to the Secretary of State for Foreign Affairs,[1] lest the original might not reach him.

This document, penned by a friendly hand, still is a true record of what passed; and as such it must convince His Majesty's Government that I have not deserved ill, although no statements may have been made of my having merited favour.

Perhaps if inquiry were deigned it would be found that while I was thought an agitator and an encroacher on authority—while my acts were censured, my credit unsustained, and my power of doing good restricted as much as possible—I was promoting the best interests of my country and maintaining its professional honour.

The best intentions may err in action; but the most impartial examination, the most rigid scrutiny, the most mature reflection on

[1] In a letter dated May 27th from Imperial Headquarters Stewart described the scene to Lord Castlereagh, referring to "the gracious manner, the well-chosen moment, and the pride I felt that one of our companions in arms should be thus decorated in front of the Allied army."

my whole conduct acquit me of any indiscretion under the circumstances in which I was placed, and secure to me the consciousness of having been a most disinterested, zealous, and useful public servant during the whole of my mission. I can charge myself with having done nothing wrong; and I have left nothing right undone that was within my intelligence and power.

May 29th, Schweidnitz.

Yesterday I determined to ride with Stewart to Schweidnitz that I might pay my *devoirs* to the Emperor, write letters, and make other arrangements. Since my arrival I have been overwhelmed with affectionate greetings; but none pleased me more than that of my old Cossacks, who kissed the cross[1] twenty times, and quite cried with joy.

Schweidnitz was once a strong fortress, memorable for a very daring and successful surprise. The French have partly destroyed the works, but the Prussians are working to restore them. Why and wherefore I know not, as there are no guns to place on the fortifications and there cannot be time for the ramparts to be restored sufficiently for any defence.

June 4th—Since the dispatch of my last notes we have been in treaty for an armistice, and made frequent short suspensions of arms, which the enemy have converted to their own advantage, since they have occupied Liegnitz, Neumark, and Breslau, which they offered in the first instance to leave in the hands of the Allies. I believe if we do not immediately accept the armistice as now offered, we shall lose Berlin also and then finally make a very disreputable arrangement, when we might by early decision have masked inferiority.

I think an armistice necessary, although the Russian army is much strengthened and greatly improved by Barclay's regulations, and notwithstanding that the king has augmented his army from twenty-one to near thirty thousand men, by throwing in some Landwehr and the blockading corps of Glogau, so that the Allies have a total force between Schweidnitz and the Oder of near eighty-five thousand men.

We cannot live where we are: our communication with the Vistula is almost in the power of the enemy, and perhaps, and probably, Polish insurgents will endeavour to close the only narrow route yet left us. I also believe the enemy to be in far greater force than ourselves.

[1] Colonel Neil Campbell describes "a small white cross, with an image of the Saint, suspended at the left breast by a ribbon of orange and black stripes."

The arrival of the Emperor Francis and Count Metternich[1] at Jung Bunzlau in Bohemia prove that the Austrian Cabinet are very anxious to make some pacific arrangement. But I do not believe that Austria will assume the previous character of a belligerent, which is necessary to extort from Buonaparte the cessions which are useful to her, not all those which are required by the Allies.

I have a notion, however, that Hymen is about to play a principal character in the last act. The King of Prussia[2] has long been politically courting an Austrian archduchess, and the Grand Duchess Catherine would again put on the wedding garment if the interests of Russia required her to plight again her troth. I am sure she would not suffer one of the Corsican relatives to ascend her bed; but she would not think that an alliance through the wife would dishonour her.

I confess that I expect a family compact. Buonaparte, though in a better position than recently, has still many difficulties that are of a nature to make peace more desirable than war for the next two or three years. A thousand circumstances prove this feeling on his part and in the late negotiation for an armistice he was most particularly anxious that the agreement should have for its title: 'Armistice for the purpose of forming a general Congress to restore Peace.'

Perhaps the state of France requires such an opiate.

The Cossacks *vont leur train*. Every day several hundred prisoners are brought into Schweidnitz; but the majority, I am sorry to say, are very fine men, and very many of them 'resurrection men' from Moscow.

I have been passing my time between Schweidnitz, the Emperor's headquarters, and Stewart's, with whom indeed I am chiefly living; for the food of the mind rather than the body's entertainment, although he banquets more sumptuously than any person in the army.

His appointment has been very agreeable to the Prussians. There is a great store of good sense, honourable feeling and engaging candour in his character, which inspires respect and confidence. I do not know any man whose policy is more loyal, in the liberal sense of that term.

---

[1] Clemens Lothar Wenzel, Count Metternich (1773–1859), became Austrian Foreign Minister in 1809 and negotiated the marriage between Napoleon and Marie Louise. Wilson wrote of him: "He adds to the talents of a minister all the accomplishments of a liberal host, a gallant gentleman, and *bel esprit*; so that his table and his soirées are very delightful points of rendezvous."

[2] He had been a widower since June 1810.

5th—Yesterday being the King's birthday[1] Lord Cathcart gave a commemorating dinner. The hall of festivity was a barn. Showers of rain prevented the *fête champêtre*, as was proposed, in the miller's garden. We mustered fourteen English, and all not assembled.

June 5th, Plauendorf.

The armistice is concluded: the period, six weeks. The Katzbach river forms the line of demarcation; but Breslau, and the posts now occupied by the enemy on this side the Katzbach, is neutral territory.

Hamburg and Lübeck are to remain with the power which shall be in possession on the 9th of June at midnight. The whole line of the Elbe and the Baltic is to be included in the armistice, and the enemy's fortresses are to be provisioned from five days to five days, I believe at the expense of the Allies. The terms are more favourable than I expected, and they prove the disposition of the enemy to make peace or be better prepared for war. The Emperor Francis is expected at Reichenbach, where the Imperial headquarters will be established to-morrow. The next ten days will be interesting.

June 11th, Reichenbach.

"Now are our bruised arms hung up for monuments, and grim visaged War has smoothed his wrinkled front." Famine, however, still hovers around the field and endeavours to scare us from Silesia.

The British Ambassador still insists that Austria only robes herself externally in the pacificator's pontificals, while she is locked in mail and, resolute in action, strides to the field of battle with the guileful step of the '*marche politique*.'

Bubna's first note on the 18th of May, the *Moniteur*[2] advertisement on the 24th, the Emperor of Austria's known family consideration, Metternich's character and avowed predilections, Austria's steady and palpably illustrated policy, the diminished chances of success by force, could not influence any variation in the British Ambassador's speculations: speculations which also confided in the enemy's total ignorance of what was passing in the Austrian cabinet, in the daughter's want of information, in Buonaparte's illusion and his ministers' enchantment by the superior genius of a power whose standard was at the same time planted in the camp of his adversary.

The rejection of the terms proposed by the Allies as the basis of the best mediation, which terms were represented by Lord Cathcart

[1] King George III was born on June 4th, 1738.
[2] *Le Moniteur universel*, founded in 1789, was the official newspaper of the French Government.

as the sanctioned and indeed dictated terms of Austria—and the proposition now made by Austria, of which Nesselrode was the avant courier the day before yesterday, that the Allies should join in Congress to settle the base of a general peace—can not shake the faith of the British Ambassador. He still sees the Austrian army with the *feldzeug*, or laurel-sprig in their caps (which is always worn by the Austrians when in war), descending from the Bohemian mountains and forcing with their bayonets the boundaries of the French empire. So did he dream of battle on the very day on which the armistice was signed.

I shall now, however, leave the British Ambassador to his dreams with more satisfaction, because I know his colleague, Stewart, is not asleep.

Three days since, the Emperor reviewed or inspected four thousand two hundred new troops for the foot-guards and grenadiers, and twenty squadrons of cavalry. These infantry had since November last been marched as recruits from Yarisloff, &c., via St. Petersburg, where they were trained, and they themselves and their appointments appeared as if they had not moved further than from barracks to the parade during that time. The horses and men of the cavalry bore the same freshness of appearance. Man and beast certainly in Russia afford the most surprising material for powder service.

If English battalions had marched a tenth part of the way they would have been crippled for weeks and would scarcely have had a relic of their original equipments. Our horses would all have been foundered, and their backs too sore even for the carriage of the saddle.

The day before yesterday I dined with the Emperor in a family party; yesterday with the King at a great dinner; and this day I dine with the Emperor, who gives a banquet. The Emperor the other day was gracious enough to present to me two crosses of the Junior or Soldiers' Class of St. George for my two dragoons, observing, when I thanked him, that he had 'always pleasure in doing what was agreeable to me.'

These attentions evidently mortify a certain person. His even more than female jealousy of the Emperor induced him to tell Stewart, the other day, that 'he must not approach so near the Emperor.' I could mention a thousand of the same ridiculous traits.

I did propose to go to Prague; but I fear Lord Cathcart will oppose that wish, although the military information I could obtain from the use of my eyes and the knowledge I have of

Schwartzenberg[1] and others, with the favour of the Emperor of Austria, would enable me to make a useful expedition. Great numbers of the Russian officers are already gone there and to Vienna.

I shall, however, persevere in the project.

I am sorry to be obliged to remark that the enemy, in withdrawing from Breslau, have left a good name here behind them. Everything was paid for in ready money. It indeed appears that Buonaparte has introduced a very strict discipline into his army and, according to the report of the Russian officers, his camps are completely camps of instruction. The report of peace is prevalent in them, the wish universal and loudly expressed; and, aware of Austria's resolute interference to obtain it, the troops do not hesitate to applaud her reported menaces against the dissentient party.

June 12th, 8 o'clock p.m.

Yesterday the King did not come, as was expected, to dine with the Emperor; he found himself unwell.

We want a *Morning Post* to advertise all the grand fêtes. Cooks now are in more estimation than any other class. The diplomatic campaign is to me, however, more terrible than any other; gout, &c., awe me with a thousand alarms.

This day is Count Stadion's.

It is said that the French have occupied the Tyrol, and that the Bavarian fortresses are provisioning.

July 1st, Berlin.

The daily occurrences of a Berlin residence at this time cannot be very interesting to strangers. The Royal Family's hospitality and attention made our sojourn agreeable; but there is no other society.

5th.—On the 2nd Prince Radziwil gave us a super-fine specimen of French cookery. It was pronounced by judges to be unparalleled. It certainly had the merit of satisfying my appetite for two days.

After dinner we inspected the Berlin Landsturm. The cause was more agreeable than the effect to a soldier's eye; but, nevertheless, military progress had been made.

At midnight I entered my carriage and found myself in solitude with a cheerless imagination. The pleasant society of Sir Charles, &c., was now a source of melancholy. Thus vagabondagers pay for their temporary pleasures. Pouring rain completed the discomfiture. Fortunately, I had exchanged *Queen Mab* for *Apollo* at Berlin, or I

---

[1] Karl Philipp, Prince Schwarzenberg (1771–1820), was Austrian Commander-in-Chief.

should have been drenched; but notwithstanding that *Apollo* rolled on elastic springs, with all the *légèreté* without the rudeness of *Queen Mab*, troublesome busy thoughts, and perhaps Radziwil's conjurer, banished sleep from my eyelids.

The next night I arrived at General Tauenzien's [1] headquarters near Stettin, still cheerless, for I had not seen the sun the whole day. I had imagined a spiritless expedition altogether, but the intelligence that no armistice was in force at Stettin restored me to the *qui vive*.

At daybreak I mounted my horse, reached within six hundred yards of the body of the place and saw enough to assure me that Stettin ought long since to have been taken by the bayonet, if powder failed for the siege.

I then passed the Oder and its branches, which, with their sinuosities, occupied me in a boat an hour and a half. On the other side a Colonel Roedler, who had been aide-de-camp to Mack,[2] was waiting to receive me, and I was shown by him the *tête-du-pont* at Damm, which remains still in the possession of the enemy, to the great reproach of the Allies. Indeed, there is so much military, political, and commercial importance attached to the re-occupation of Stettin and Damm that very few objects can be put in competition.

I was much pleased with the order, &c., which I observed in Colonel Roedler's command. The officer was in everything perceptible; but, although this man has been thirty-two years a soldier, esteemed by the most estimable, as his letters prove, and acknowledged to possess the most eminent military qualities, he has with great difficulty succeeded in obtaining the rank of Colonel.

From Damm I travelled all night, rain still pouring down, and arrived this morning at Colberg.

July 6th, Colberg—This morning I mounted the Commandant's horse in a pouring rain, to reconnoitre the intrenched position and the fortifications of the town. As I wished to return by ten o'clock to breakfast with the French Princes,[3] I went *ventre à terre* and astonished man and beast, but I could not save myself from a wetting or secure a cut of the first round.

However, I found amiable hosts, who did not impatient themselves even at the weather, and that is an infallible sign of good temper in such a month of July. Last night the vessels in the road drove considerably. As they were laden on Russian account, I have directed them to proceed to Pillau.

[1] Commanding Prussian 4th Corps.
[2] Field-Marshal Karl von Mack (1752–1822) had surrendered after the defeat of his army at Ulm in 1805.
[3] The Comte d'Artois and Duc d'Angoulême.

July 15th, Warsaw.

I quitted Colberg on the 7th of July, after breakfasting with the French Princes, whom I could not serve, but to whom I was anxious to pay every attention.

The weather instead of improving became more tempestuous and on the day of my departure it blew so heavy a gale dead on shore that I feared for the safety of the transports.

The country from Colberg to Oliva, the headquarters of the Duke of Würtemberg,[1] was *goose* domain and very fully occupied by the family.

There was only one good town in the whole line, Coslin, where was a statue of Frederick Augustus,[2] handsomely decorated. On the 9th I arrived at the Duke's headquarters, with Colonel Willeminew sent to take the ammunition, whom I found a pleasant companion for the few miles he travelled with me.

I would not disturb the Duke's family so early and therefore deposited myself under a balcony, where I slept four hours, lulled to repose by the falling water of nine fountains.

I was sorry to find afterwards that the Duke was very ill. Until he could see me I rode out to view the left of his posts. As I passed, some Frenchmen approached, and it was singular enough that the first man was of the ci-devant regiment of Artois. I took that occasion to mention the neighbourhood of the Count himself, with other matters which I thought might tend to a good effect hereafter in the garrison.

The Duke having had a relapse and still being invisible, I dined next door with General [Mikhail] Borasdin, where I met two French officers, both very well bred and well-informed men, one the aide-de-camp of Rapp.[3] After dinner the Duke sent for me. On their mentioning my arrival he had fainted, but, recovering, insisted on my going to him. I was much shocked to see the great alteration in his countenance. I sat by his bed about an hour and then, in obedience to the Doctor's commands, withdrew. The next day the Duke was not better. I passed the morning in visiting with General Borasdin all the corps, posts, etc., and was very much gratified with the arrangements. The camps were, indeed, more beautifully arranged than I ever saw, although I have seen many ornamented camps. Perhaps that architecture is better understood among the soldiery of barbarous than civilized nations: but it required instructed taste to obtain the perfection which existed here.

[1] The Duke commanded the blockading corps before Dantzic.
[2] King of Saxony and Duke of Warsaw.
[3] General Jean-Baptiste Rapp (1772–1821), for many years Napoleon's A.D.C., had received four wounds at Borodino and another at the Beresina.

In the evening I drank tea with some merchants who had lived in Dantzic several weeks since the blockade. There were one or two ladies, who assigned to me as their reason for withdrawing that they could not bring themselves to eat horseflesh, which the carnivorous townspeople are obliged to feed on and the garrison partially. The Hindoos would have a great advantage in a town so situated.

At night, after passing some hours with the Duke, whom I again left better, I proceeded on my course to Warsaw without any accident occurring which is worthy of note, unless I thought others would feel a sympathetic interest in my disgusts at the sight of the Jews. I was satisfied that it was only in twenty and thirty degrees of frost that I could enter their habitations and submit to their presence.

I arrived at Warsaw, where I found Beningsen, Novosiltzow, Lanskoi, Doctorow, and a number of my best friends. Next to the pleasure of a British welcome was the gratification of that which I met with here. There is not much society in the town, but I am free to the best, and last night was at a very animated political conversazione, where, of course, the ladies were the greatest orators, for I believe they take most interest in the fate of their country.

My hatred of Buonaparte and French connection, yet friendship for Poland; their struggle for independence, yet aid for the oppression of Spain, make a fine medley and afford much opportunity for self-contradiction if great precision of expression is not preserved, so as to keep the fine-drawn lines always distinct.

July 24th, Reichenbach.

On the 21st, after passing several very agreeable days and obtaining much information, I procured passports, but not without the most positive pledges to return if the armistice was prolonged and, if war broke out, to join Beningsen provided that I could make the arrangement with Lord Cathcart.

I am sorry to find that civil war among the Russian chiefs is still probable. Barclay and Beningsen are contesting for command: Beningsen also wishes to have his army in a direct communication with the Vistula, so as to assure his retreat on Plock. Barclay desires to throw him up to the right of the Kalish route and post him about Lissa, Winzingerode having marched to be under the orders of Bernadotte. These discords all tend to peace. They distract the Emperor, terrify the Allies, and destroy the confidence of the armies.

25th—Lord Cathcart came to me this morning and requested me to visit all the outposts of the army, beginning my tour tomorrow. I saw that his object was to remove me from the Emperor, but as His Majesty asked me at dinner to accompany him on Wednesday to the review of the cuirassier-squadrons, nine German miles distant, where the Grand Duke is, I shall not go till Thursday.

The Emperor was much pleased with the report which I was able to make of the state of the fortresses and troops: but I could not help again observing the total indifference of Count Stadion to all military intelligence and this observation has been made at different times by many others. He actually thinks the sword a secondary, if not an unimportant consideration. If Austria were about to become a belligerent, could he regard the military powers of the Allies as a minor feature?

27th—This day I had an interview with the King, who assured me that he had a hundred and eighty thousand regulars and Landwehrs under arms. I afterwards dined with him and met the Emperor; General Barclay de Tolly took me in his carriage, the King living three English miles off, and in that drive to and fro I received much interesting information. Barclay confirmed the King's statement, and assured me that he had in Silesia a hundred and eighteen thousand Russians, and seventy-five thousand Prussians; that his army was now put in good order, and that he had provided ten thousand waggons with two horses each for the transport of provisions.

He estimated the enemy's force at above four hundred thousand men, including a hundred and fifty thousand between Mayence and Wurzburg, and the garrisons on the Elbe. The troops which have been ordered to Spain have been countermanded.

He thought complete success certain if Austria joined; but a good peace with her aid better than a precarious war without her.

From the King I went to Stadion's, with whom I was to have dined, and thus passed an hour. In the morning I had previously read the late correspondence between Metternich, the French and the Allied plenipotentiaries. That correspondence convinces me more and more that Austria will not be a belligerent.

The late irritation of Buonaparte inspires hope in some that she will be brought to action by a misunderstanding, and the temper of the army and people encourages others to speculate on the Cabinet being compelled to adopt warlike measures. These, however, are vague speculations. The feeling of the Cabinet points to the only reasonable deduction.

July 20th, Reichenbach.

The Emperor's departure, which occasioned the removal of Count Stadion and other diplomatic chiefs, produced a painful change in our society; and extreme bad weather has greatly increased our *ennui*.

I, who am certainly a creature of climate, yielded to the oppression of a sky holding suspended unusual proportions of moisture for some days. The 'foul fiend' completely possessed me. Such was the load of the atmosphere that no vivacity of spirit could contend against it; and if the sun this morning had not burst through the condensed darkness, Reichenbach might have been memorable for a 'bowl, rope, and dagger' catastrophe. I am still so cold and cheerless that I could quarrel with any man who now presented himself in good humour.

It is fortunate for Brinken that he is gone to Vienna and for Charles that he has started for England, out of reach of the effects of my present villainous disposition.

I did intend, as politics and war no longer engrossed my attention, or rather employed my time, to make various excursions, that I might see and describe the generally-praised beauties of Silesia; but where there is not a *beau ciel* I cannot be just to the earth, and my personal dissatisfaction would make me a prejudiced observer.

22nd—Rousseau[1] did not appreciate ill the English military character when he described it by the remark: "*Les Anglais se donnent avec gaieté à la fatigue et même à la mort, mais ils ne peuvent pas supporter l'ennui.*" To fly from the terrors of this most terrible *ennui* I have resolved to make a journey, which will night and day occupy my attention.

During the time that the armistice is still to continue, I propose to visit Berlin, Colberg, Dantzic, Bialystok, Warsaw and Cracow. The objects of my inspection are various, but I hope that the results of my observation will promote the public utility. At all events I shall ascertain where and in what numbers and in what state the so-long-talked-of reserve forces are. They shall not fly from me as Wills-o'-the-wisp. I will grapple whatever substance they have.

Mr John Spencer Stanhope, having spent over two years in detention, first in Spain and then in France, was travelling in Germany at this time and became involved in the campaign. He wrote in his journal during the armistice:

We took up our abode at a village near Reichenbach, which had been fixed upon for Lord Cathcart's quarters; and, as soon as he himself arrived, we proceeded to report ourselves to him. He made some remarks about our long absence; and, upon my stating that we had been hunting after the headquarters, he somewhat dryly

---

[1]Jean-Jacques Rousseau (1712-78), French writer and philosopher.

observed, "I should have supposed that the Emperor of Russia was a mark large enough to be hit."

. . . Our life was monotonous enough. We rode about, lounged about and dined every day with Lord Cathcart, who now kept a *maison montée*; unfortunately, he was not on the best terms with Sir Charles Stewart, nor with Sir Robert Wilson; therefore, instead of our diplomatic authorities endeavouring to relieve the tedium of an inactive life by mutual festivities, they kept aloof from one another. We, however, had the advantage of not being excluded from the society of other missions, though they did not join in ours. They were each established in different villages. . . .

Sir Robert Wilson had amused himself in tacking four horses, by means of harness and rope, to his old campaigning britzska, and there he was, with all his orders, driving his four-in-hand, to the great astonishment of the natives, who were amazed at such an exhibition of an English General. To add to the absurdity of the proceeding, George Cathcart proposed to me, that we should turn out an old carriage of Lord Cathcart's and with the help of ropes, drive our three horses. Thus established in our unicorn, we made a point of following Sir Robert in all his drives, to the great amusement of the spectators (pp. 542, 544).

July 28th, Berlin.

Lord Cathcart made me dine with him again on the 23rd and before my departure gave me carte blanche instructions for my movements, but I consider them as most peremptory on my zeal. "Do what you think right," is a mandate to do what is possible.

In the evening I set out with Sir Charles Stewart, Captain James and Bidwell[1] in Sir Charles's English coach. My britzska followed with servants. Dawson did not come with me: there were difficulties in the way of his departure which it was not prudent to force for either person's interest. The road, always bad, was rendered worse by heavy rains. On the whole, however, the journey was very agreeable.

It is my intention to leave this city tomorrow evening: Stewart will remain several days longer. Newspapers to the 21st have put me in possession of English story nearly down to the epoch that interested me most; but still I am anxious for intelligence from them to a later date on various accounts. My private letters only reach to the middle of May.

July 20th, Reichenbach.

On the 27th I tackled my five horses to the *Apollo*, neck or nothing, and drove to Strehlen, five German miles. The King overtook me,

[1] John Bidwell of the Foreign Office.

but I kept up with him afterwards, although he had eight horses. The Emperor at Strehlen appeared by another route and found me on the box: this served for more than the minute's amusement, as I accused Lord Cathcart at the Grand Duke's table yesterday of this Anglomania and stated that his non-appearance in the coachman's character was because I had disarmed him by reclaiming my whip. The truth is that Lord Cathcart also drives, but he has done so at an early hour. From Strehlen I went to Grotkau, where I found quarters prepared. The next morning we assembled at the Emperor's, in the house of the Grand Duke, and thence proceeded to the ground of review, where seventy-one squadrons of cavalry were drawn up and exercised. It was a fine sight. Five-sixths were cuirassiers. One regiment was armed with the enemy's spoil. After the review, which lasted several hours, we returned to dine with the Grand Duke. Not more than twenty persons were at table. The Emperor and King presided. After dinner I went per post to Strehlen, thence to Count Langeron's[1] headquarters at Heinensdorff, where I passed a very pleasant evening; and this morning I returned to Reichenbach, after an expedition of above a hundred English miles: rain pouring as usual.

From Strehlen I had on the preceding evening driven my own horses; and I thought that I performed wonders in saving my neck: but this day's journey was terrible. I am sure no member of the Whip Club would face the danger; but I arrived without any accident.

Aug. 8th—On the 1st of August, Barclay gave a grand banquet. On the 2nd, Princes Czartorysky, Radziwil and myself were to have followed the Emperor to Landeck, but Prince Radziwil preceded us and we remained until the 3rd, proposing to reach Landeck in time for the dinner of the King on that day, which was his birthday. Prince Czartorysky was ill in the morning and we did not arrive in time by several hours. We, however, went to the ball, where we paid our respects to the Sovereigns. I danced afterwards with the three young Princesses, with the Princess of Würtemberg and the Countess of Brandenburg, the King's illegitimate sister, a most accomplished and very handsome young woman, twenty years of age. The ball lasted until midnight. About a hundred ladies were present, and a hundred and fifty men, forming a very brilliant assembly. The architecture and decorations of the *salle* added greatly to the effect.

[1] Alexandre Andrault, Comte de Langeron, an émigré French general in Russian service.

The next morning Czartorysky, Radziwil and myself went off to the bath. The Emperor and about twenty gentlemen and ladies were already chin-deep in water, and their nodding heads reminded me of the dancing angelic group who wanted the '*de quoi*' to repose themselves. The spectators, however, in the upper gallery pierced with their eyes to the planks below, and could frame no incorporeal illusions.

Our arrival caused more than ordinary gaiety. After an hour's assembly in this Neptunian court the ladies retired to their barrack-room, and the gentlemen to another—where tubs full of hot water were ranged in rows—in which we removed our court dresses, and then renewed our toilettes.

Countess Golz, the wife of the minister, gave a breakfast in a shady bower and the morning was passed in admiration of the Landeck establishments, which are after the plan of Cheltenham, and of the surrounding country which is far more beautiful.

Not having an Udolpho[1] pen I must leave each imagination to conceive mountains covered with thick pine-woods, slopes and valleys waving a golden harvest, and the rapid Neisse with various tributary streamlets pouring down abrupt rocks, or "kissing every sedge, and making sweet music with the enamelled stones."

The whole must be tossed together on the mind's entablature with this impression: that it is possible to diminish, but not exaggerate, the charms of this locality.

We dined with Prince Biron, whose princess is a most amiable woman—in all but language, English. After dinner we went to the ball given by the Prince. The Emperor, the King, etc., were present. The dancing was in the same order as on the preceding evening.

The next morning at seven we reappeared at the bath. Platow was the sun of this day, but an April sun which poured torrents on our heads without distinction of persons.

The Emperor afterwards challenged me to a combat, on the condition that I should not respect him more than I had done Czartorysky, etc., for every man's hand had become a scoop against me. I soon drove His Majesty from the field, which enabled me to say with truth: "Your enemies, sire, are more formidable when they throw water than when they throw fire against you."

After breakfast the Emperor and King left Landeck. *We* were prevailed on to remain another day, which we passed in reconnoitring the country, &c. The next morning we retired without bathing, which very much disappointed the *old* ladies at least.

[1] This refers to Mrs. Ann Radcliffe's *The Mysteries of Udolpho*, published in 1794.

On summing up the *agrémens* of Landeck we were of the unanimous opinion that it was a most delightful asylum from the solicitudes of the cabinet and the camp.

About a mile from Landeck we passed the residence of Princess Faustenburg, which, being English in the arrangement of the grounds, attracted us irresistibly, and we continued to walk through them for a considerable time notwithstanding heavy rain.

At Glatz we waited on the commandant, who conducted us to the citadel, where we viewed the fortifications, entrenched camp, etc. The citadel is formed out of a solid rock which rises loftily above the town and presents a noble feature of strength and majesty, in contrast with the surrounding scenery of milder character.

In one of the casemates we visited the celebrated Madame Orsinew, who admits that she endeavoured to poison her servant twice that she might know the effect before she took a dose to terminate her grief for her husband's death.

She, however, was suspected, not only of poisoning him and her uncle, but various others, and one night she was suddenly arrested and taken to her husband's grave and there told that, if she did not confess, the body would be taken up and examined. She persevered in denial: the grave was opened, and in her presence, before her eyes, the winding-sheet was unclasped from the mouldering remains; and, although two years had elapsed since the decease, the surgeon believed that he perceived the proofs of poison in the bones.

Her own apparatus for death could not have presented to her so terrible a spectacle. But as the surgeon would not swear and her servant did not die, she was condemned to perpetual imprisonment, and here she had been ten long years. She is yet only fifty years of age and seems in perfect health.

I looked about to see if there was any score of years, months, weeks, days, hours, minutes—any note of weary time. I found only some books and was told that she had composed a system of education.

This woman had once possessed fortune and all the advantages that society, accomplishments and a cultivated mind could bestow. What a dreadful change! Her countenance was masculine, but her manner was that of one who had learned to bow to misfortune, and who had known little indulgence in the course of it. We endeavoured to prevail on the governor to allow her a little plot of ground for a garden, as she had implored permission to walk once again where her feet might press verdure; but I do not think we obtained our entreaty. Her criminality has been very great, but ten years is a very long period of correction.

10th.—Yesterday evening General Stewart arrived. I was most happy to see him and to find that he had not been seduced by Bernadotte, whom he describes as a great *fanfaron* [braggart] unworthy of trust, and one who desires general peace with France that he may renew the ancient relation with Sweden. Colonel Cooke,[1] who had seen a great deal of him, tells me that he has said that "if anything happens to Buonaparte the French people would select him or Moreau as their chief.' With this view he fears to make himself unpopular by vigorous action against the French interests.

Stewart, writing later as Marquess of Londonderry, described Bernadotte in these terms: Whenever the Prince Royal conversed, it was always with the greatest affability and cordiality. It is impossible to resist the fascination of his eloquent expressions, or be indifferent to his insinuating tone and manner; and when armed, as he always is, with a bottle of Eau-de-Cologne in one hand, and a white handkerchief in the other, inundating lavishly every thing around him with the perfume. It requires some hardihood to be quite collected, and insensible to beautiful phraseology, so as to discover the drift or solidity of the extraordinary man into whose presence you are at all times admitted, and accosted as '*Mon ami*' (*Narrative* p. 88).

All is in motion around us, and war to almost all seems inevitable; but I cling to the expectation of peace, or a further extension of the armistice.

Stewart proposes to Lord Cathcart that I shall be sent to the Austrian army, which is my wish, that there may be no more ground for jealousy. At the same time I am entitled to this field, which gives me a more conspicuous position: I have been kept long enough in the background.

11th—All this day troops have been moving, and Count Wittgenstein's corps enters Bohemia at Trautenau. His headquarters are to be on the 19th at Melnik. Still I believe that Buonaparte will accept the ultimatum which the Emperor wrote with his own hand, and which is a repetition of the six original articles.

There is not one person—Russian, Prussian, or English—who is not satisfied (Lord Cathcart only excepted) that Austria never seriously intended war; that her objects are at total variance with the views of the Allies. That she merely seeks to satisfy the hostile feeling of the nation and army; to obtain security, and not press the dynasty.

[1] Henry Cooke, Stewart's adjutant.

That she is as much afraid of Russia as of France, and that she is by no means a believer in an easy victory; but circumstances within this fortnight have *entaméd* her further than she originally intended.

The Spanish victory[1] increased her confidence, and Buonaparte's impracticable temper excited her resentment. Nevertheless I am still an infidel as to actual war. I am sure that it is the interest of Buonaparte to concede, *pro tempore*, and that by so doing he will be able to divide the Allies, who will quarrel about the arrangements of Poland.

If he suffers a shot to be fired he can no longer control the cabinets, and all his fortunes must rest upon his bayonets.

The arrival of Moreau[2] at Berlin must still more dispose him to gain time and recover influence with his father-in-law. Moreau's arrival facilitates this object as his views are hostile to the Emperor's daughter and to Austria's hereditary connection with France.

Moreau refuses to command foreigners. He will only fight in company with Frenchmen. It is feared that Bernadotte will be more slippery in consequence of Moreau's sentiments.

Tomorrow is the important day of final decision. At all events I hope to reach Prague, for which place I start in the evening, and join the Emperor there.

I had promised Princess Lieven[3] when at Berlin to pass by Nieborow and call on her mother-in-law, Princess Radziwil, as I could thus see the ground to be taken up by the army of reserve at Lowicz by taking that direction. I did not much regret my engagement, and still less did I do so when, for the second time, I entered Arcadia, to which I found that the Prince and Princess had gone after their dinner. I confirmed all my former opinions of the extraordinary charms and interest of this place. The Princess took me back to Nieborow, gave me tea and supper, which was my dinner also; and then, notwithstanding all friendly entreaties, I entered my calash again and braved desperate road, pitchy darkness and rain torrents. I never was more weary with any journey. I remembered that it was July, and I found the season of November. After three nights and three days I reached Reichenbach, to my great joy and

[1] Wellington's victory at the battle of Vitoria on June 21st ended Joseph Bonaparte's reign in Spain.
[2] Jean Victor Moreau (1761–1813), victor of Hohenlinden against the Austrians in 1800, was accused by a jealous Napoleon of plotting and in 1804 was banished from France. He went to New Jersey in America, returning to Europe in 1813 so as to accompany the Czar on the march to Dresden. He was wounded mortally on August 27th and died at Laun in Bohemia six days later, being buried in St. Petersburg.
[3] Dorothea, *née* von Benkendorff (1784–1857), married a Russian diplomat who was sent to London as Ambassador.

my servant's; he fares but ill in my journeys, as I seldom take more than tea twice a day en route, and allow no time for kitchen operations.

I found here the original *corps diplomatique* with one or two exceptions. Lord Cathcart received me *au mieux*, approved of all that I had done, and has been ever since very communicative and attentive. Yesterday I went to the Emperor, who was most gracious; but as he was about to review a regiment of guards I was obliged to attend, which annoyed me for two hours. I am sure I shall never be able to do the duty that will be expected of me when on a peace staff, for I hate the exercise of troops.

Aug. 15th, Landeck.

At length on the 12th we received advice that, Buonaparte having sent no answer, Austria had declared war against him.

I certainly did not expect that Buonaparte would have withheld amicable propositions so long, although I knew that at Erfürth he said to the Emperor of Russia: "When I negotiate myself I am always endeavouring to be the last person to show fear." He has probably miscalculated the character of another Emperor.

Events will prove how far he wished hostilities; but certainly Austria was most anxious to obtain peace, and the renewal of hostilities has been a surprise to all her allies.

If Buonaparte did not wish war, he has only to thank his own errors and impracticable temper.

Sir C. Stewart wished me to go with him to Landeck where he had to exchange the ratifications of the treaty. We had so much to arrange at Reichenbach during the day that it was nine at night before we could leave it.

I went away with low spirits, for I had to separate from Czartorysky, who, from the misfortunes of his country, has become quite melancholy and who inspires these feelings in his friends from love of him as well as of his cause. He is certainly one of the most highly gifted of the human race, and the more I see of him the more I attach myself. He possesses a playfulness of temper in his moments of indulgence that is congenial to his natural character, and fits most aptly to his natural mildness of disposition.

We arrived at Landeck on the 13th. The Emperor and King are both here, and at the ball in the evening received us all most kindly. Indeed the Emperor's good will and favour seem hourly to increase.

The Emperor danced until ten at night, when the company separated. Yesterday morning he went away to be at Prague on the

16th. The King remained, and remains until the 16th, when he joins the Emperor. Yesterday the King invited Stewart, Colonel Cooke and myself, to one of his family dinners, and we had a very agreeable entertainment. In the evening the royal family went to the assembly-room and a small dance was made up. Stewart and I danced with the two elder Princesses, who have been my almost constant partners and who are truly most amiable girls. They will credit any Court at which they are destined to preside.

This morning I am going to Prague. Stewart remains the day here to finish his despatches. I would have cheerfully remained also, but I think it my duty to be present when the Emperor arrives.

We have just come out of the tub bathing-room—not the bath where the gentlemen and ladies hold their social meeting, into which I have not entered on this visit, but—where the tubs are ranged all in a row, and where so many Adams are floating. Stewart was much shocked at first, but he did as the Romans at Rome, and left his blushes for reflection.

Aug. 20th, Prague.

I quitted Landeck with Stewart on the 15th. The Duke of Cumberland[1] had arrived the preceding evening. I presented my respects, as in duty bound, was coolly received, made my bow and retired. Afterwards we met at his saloon and I was obliged to surrender the Princess Charlotte to him as a partner, according to etiquette: she was the eldest and entitled to this honour. We spoke no further.

After a toil of two days and two nights over wretched roads, rendered worse by heavy rains, we reached Prague early in the morning. On our route we had passed the fortress of Josephstadt with thirteen thousand men and five hundred pieces of cannon, and Königingratz with three thousand men and two hundred and fifty cannon. The former place is one of the most formidable in Europe; the latter not so strong, but strong and in high order. Here I found Charles. I passed the day in reading my letters and looking about me. The busy note of preparation animated the scene, and everywhere vigour, with system, presented itself.

---

[1] Ernest Augustus, Duke of Cumberland (1771–1851), the eighth of King George III's children, was to become King of Hanover in 1837. Thanks to the unsavoury exposure in Parliament of the Duke's interference in an election at Weymouth, the Prince Regent and his ministers were obliged to recommend that the Duke should leave the country and travel in Europe. He left London in April 1813, and went primarily to see the Hanoverian troops. Roger Fulford, in *Royal Dukes*, says Cumberland wore a "green morocco travelling cap made in the Russian style, lined with fur and ornamented with gold lace and buttons. With his moustaches, whiskers and scars, the whole effect, as an observer complained, was 'very outlandish.'"

In the evening I went to young Prince Esterhazy's.[1] The Emperor of Russia and the King of Prussia, who had arrived during the day after breaking down three times, came in to visit the Princess of Thurn and Taxis, and her daughter the Princess Esterhazy. After some time I withdrew, although the Emperor said: "*Où allez vous? Ça a l'air comme si nous vous chassions.*"

The next morning, although I had but lain down two hours, I rose at three o'clock, A.M., went to Stewart, and we mounted in a little calash provided for us by Prince Esterhazy to go and see the review, distant, as we heard, forty-two wersts, but in fact fifty wersts. We found on the road relays of the Prince's own horses, and on reaching the ground I found to my great surprise sixty-nine battalions of Austrian infantry, of which seventeen were Hungarians and three of them grenadiers, and twelve regiments of cavalry. The total above sixty thousand infantry and six thousand cavalry, under the command of Prince Schwarzenberg.

Prince S. received me as an old acquaintance; and, as I could not find the horses provided by the Emperor, he mounted us.

After some time the Emperors and the King came to the ground, when the whole army passed them.

It was a fine spectacle. Not quite so fine as the grand review in 1794 on the plains of Landrecy, but equally so as far as regards the Austrian portion. The infantry were active men in the best military order; the cavalry, both cuirassiers and hussars, superb—especially the hussars of Hesse-Homburg.

I thought the artillery not so good as heretofore, but perhaps the excellence of the Russian artillery has prejudiced me as well as General Moreau, who said the other day: "I have seen as fine infantry, but never as fine artillery, as the Russian."

The column did not clear until near five o'clock, P.M. The Sovereigns got into their carriages and I undertook to conduct Stewart by a shorter route to the village where I supposed our stud to be after it left the field where we mounted. All happened as I had anticipated and, although I had never passed through the country, except in a carriage ten years before, I succeeded as a guide and found our calash. We arrived a full hour before the Emperor at the city of Prague. This town was very important for men who had gone a hundred wersts, and toiled many hours besides on horseback, without tasting a morsel of food since the foregoing day at dinner.

[1] Prince Paul Esterhazy (1786–1866), member of a powerful Hungarian family, was for many years Austrian Ambassador in London.

After a repast, I came to my quarters very tired, and with a cold which still distresses me.

I had been disappointed at not meeting Moreau on that day; but I saw Jomini,[1] who left the enemy five days since. He estimates the French force at five hundred thousand men, and calls Buonaparte "the ablest of men." I admire his sincerity, in his circumstances; but I cannot, from what I have seen, acquiesce in his opinion. He further told Stewart that the re-establishment of the French artillery was the most prodigious effort, accompanied by the most scientific distribution of the work, that had yet been made by France.

In the course of the morning, an incidental opinion gave me the confidence of General Radetsky[2], the Austrian Quartermaster-general. I had long wished to know this officer—the auricular intimate of Metternich. I found him, as I anticipated, very able and intelligent.

General Radetsky told me that the Russian and French[3] advice for offensive operations had prevailed, contrary to his judgment. He felt assured that the enemy wished us to attack him immediately and put the defiles behind us; whereas it was our intent to put *him* in that situation. The doubt he entertained of sufficient ability in the Chiefs to direct separate columns of attack, further induced him to prefer a system of defence combined with offensive operations on a smaller scale, to a general offensive movement which might win much, but might lose all. He feared the issue of the measures now proposed.

I perfectly agreed with him: for "if we forced Buonaparte to attack, we obliged him to do so under many disadvantages; and experience proved that, although he might gain the field of battle, he could not obtain a decisive victory where eighty thousand Russians were present." And I said further that "if we waited until he commenced operations, we might be able to bear with all our means upon some weak but decisive point."

The question of command has been one which threatened and still threatens much mischief.

The Emperor of Russia earnestly wishes it, and I never saw a man more anxious than he was yesterday to obtain it; nor did I

---

[1] Henri, Baron Jomini (1779–1869), served in the Swiss Guards at Versailles and rose to be chief of staff to Marshal Ney. He attracted Napoleon's attention in 1804 by his book *Traité des grandes opérations militaires*. In Russia he served at Napoleon's H.Q. as historian, but was offended at the treatment he received, and entered Russian service. Jomini later wrote a *Précis de l'art de guerre*.

[2] Josef Wenzel Radetzky (1766–1858), afterwards a distinguished Marshal. Strauss's *Radetzky March* was named after him.

[3] Presumably this refers to Moreau.

ever see disappointment more strongly expressed than when it was not offered to him. The Austrians wish to retain Schwarzenberg. If the Emperor does not get it, I, as well as others, much apprehend that his zeal will greatly diminish under the notion that success will be more precarious.

As a corps of the enemy, stated to be about forty thousand, had entered Bohemia by Friedland, this was certainly not the time to be selecting the commander; nor does the definitive nomination admit of delay.

The Austrian force in Bohemia may be estimated at a hundred and fifteen thousand men. Three divisions of Kleinau, at Brix, were absent yesterday, and three of light troops along the cordon. There are thirty thousand watching Bavaria, and nearly sixty thousand are in Italy. All the troops we saw yesterday were of the line—of course many recruits, but none of the Landwehr battalions. The Russians have about seventy-five thousand men in Bohemia, and the Prussians above thirty-five thousand.

General Radetsky thinks that Buonaparte can invade Bohemia with about two hundred thousand disposable men.

Buonaparte, when he proposed to surrender Illyria exclusive of Istria, and Poland for an indemnification of five hundred thousand souls to Saxony, and to raze the fortifications of Dantzic, said: "If these terms are not agreed to, *peut-être le plus beau moment de ma vie est en réserve*"; and certainly, if he can maintain present superiority of force and of position, he will have reason to consider all his other achievements as minor glory.

This morning I was presented to the Grand Duchesses of Weimar and of Oldenburg. Had I been of their own family my reception could not have been more gracious. Without, however, any feelings of acknowledgment for their good-will, I must, as an impartial person, note that these two princesses appear to me the most intelligent in Europe.

The Emperor was so busy that I could not be presented to him in form; but he desired that I would come to him at his headquarters on the first opportunity, as an old acquaintance.

This day I have sent off my horses and propose to join the Emperor of Russia to-morrow at Laun, on the road to Töplitz. I could not go before, as I have to settle all my accounts, &c., which appear so confused in England from loss of letters and inattention to the representations I have made as to the inadequacy of income, considering the rate of exchange and extraordinary expenses even of the most moderate establishment. It is too much to give private income to the public service, in addition to toil of mind and body.

Good news from Spain is circulating, and if verified must have a great influence here; for Soult[1] demands fifty thousand soldiers who have never been in the Peninsula.

This moment Prince Paul Esterhazy has been here to say that the Emperor regretted that, from a mistake, we did not dine with him yesterday; and that he waited for us. We are however innocent, as his invitation was positively not received by us.

Aug. 26th, Freyburg.

On the evening of the 21st I quitted Prague, though unwell with a most violent cold and highly-inflamed sore throat, which caused me the severest pain. It commenced as I was going to the review of the Austrian army on the 17th. On my return, I hoped it would pass with a night's rest; but, although the soreness of the throat has diminished, the cold to this hour has rather increased.

On the 23rd I found the Emperor at Commotau. That night we marched through heavy rain and chaotic darkness, confusion, &c., to Marienberg. The Emperor's cook taking a wrong direction next day led us to Chemnitz instead of Sayda. When my guide found his mistake he fled back, but I remained, forming guard and garrison for the town, although the enemy was only three miles distant. At night the Swedish minister pursuing my steps joined his forces, and I had much pleasure in alarming him with tales of peril which might possibly exist, but which I did not believe to be probable. However, I did not myself think it prudent to brave them at three o'clock in the morning, so we marched again in pelting storm, and I joined General Kleinau at this place, where thirty-six thousand men whom I had not seen before are now defiling, although drenched to the bones; most of them without shoes, many without great coats, but still marching with animated step.

If such is the commencement of this march—if such is to be the weather, what will be its end? I shudder to think of it.

General Kleinau received me with the cordial welcome of a brother soldier, and put me *au fait* of all his orders, opinions, &c. I found him worthy of his reputation, and am sure that he will always do his duty with energy. The general of his advanced guard, General Metsko, having already invited me to dine, I was obliged to decline

---

[1] On hearing of the *débâcle* at Vitoria, Napoleon sent Marshal Soult, Duc de Dalmatie, to the Pyrenees from Saxony to act as his Lieutenant and restore the situation. Soult advanced to the relief of besieged Pamplona, but was beaten back by Wellington on July 28th.

General Kleinau's hospitality; but after dinner I went again to him and was presented to many of the generals, who all in virtue of my badge admitted me at once into the rights of an old friendship and of national connection.

August 30th, Töplitz.

I did not expect to be so soon again in Bohemia; but I have not erred in my calculation of events. We have made an experiment of the power of courage against the science of war. We have failed, and afforded a memorable lesson for the regret of the present age and a subject for tacticians in future ages to treat upon.

On the morning of the 27th I rode towards Dresden a little before daybreak. When within five English miles I heard a cannonade and pushing on found the whole Allied army drawn up round Dresden, and partially attacking the advanced troops. After waiting some time on the left with the advanced guard of Kleinau, which had been marching all night, I rode to the centre where the Austrians were, thence to General Kleist, and afterwards to Count Wittgenstein on the extreme right and at the distance of five English miles from the extreme left.

A cannonade was maintained at all points, and some tirailleur firing extended along the line. The enemy during the whole of the morning kept up the heaviest fire and threw their shot wherever they could find an object, but happily for myself not with a precision equal to their ardour.

Orders were given about two o'clock that the Allied batteries should commence their operations against the town at four o'clock; that an outwork of the enemy near the garden on the left of the centre of the town should be stormed, and the town assaulted from that point, if practicable.

It was an interesting interval.

Various opinions were entertained. The Emperor and General Moreau were against the assault. I thought success almost out of possibility, as the town was surrounded by a thick wall, many feeble parts strongly palisaded, and as we knew that above sixty thousand men were already in the place. I was glad, however, of the intention to take the redoubt outside the wall; perhaps from a spirit of revenge for some very malicious salutes.

About three o'clock I slipped from the Emperor's circle and went to Prince Maurice Lichtenstein's, who was to command the Austrians, and under whom Count [Hieronymus or Jerome] Colloredo was to lead on to the assault.

About four o'clock the cannonade commenced against the enemy, and particularly the redoubt, with fury. In about a quarter of an hour some guns outside the redoubt, and between it and the town, were withdrawn. In another quarter of an hour the fire of the redoubt was much diminished. Count Colloredo perceiving the effect ordered his troops to advance. The distance was above an English mile over open ground. They moved forward; they increased their step; they pressed into a run, gave three cheers and reached the ditch of the redoubt, which was stockaded in the most formidable manner. While these brave men were endeavouring to tear down the palisades or climb over them to ascend the side of the redoubt—eighteen feet high, smooth and almost as hard as stone—others drove the enemy by their musketry from the eight guns and out of the redoubt. At the instant of the huzza, Prince Lichtenstein and I could no longer restrain ourselves: we galloped down to the redoubt and animated the men to mount. Some by their bayonets had already loosened the cement in one or two places and reached the crest, but did not like to pass over the parapet, as the fire from the town wall, distant only fifty paces, was too heavy. I remembered what I owed to Austria, England, and myself. I dismounted, climbed over the palisades, with extreme difficulty reached the crest of the parapet, sprang on it, took off my cap and gave three cheers—Charles at my side—(who would not leave me, though I repeatedly ordered him not to follow me, as I thought it not necessary to expose him) and then leapt into the battery. My cheers had been answered by all around me of all ranks, and instantly hundreds mounted and manned the redoubt. This being accomplished, I descended. Count Colloredo came up to me, gave me his hand, said various handsome things and so did all the other generals. It was a satisfactory moment. I then asked Prince Lichtenstein's permission to bring up some guns to batter the wall in breach, and force one of the doors of the town which opened immediately behind the redoubt.

Having got up the guns and placed them at the distance of sixty paces, we were in hopes of obtaining an entrance; but the enemy, through the loop-holes of the walls, killed all the artillerymen of the first six guns. We brought up then another battery of twelve, and while this, under a murderous fire, was battering in breach, Prince Lichtenstein received advice that the enemy was making a sally upon our left with the view of taking us in rear. Stewart, who had come up to the redoubt almost at the time I did, and who as usual made every effort to aid and assist, with his adjutant Colonel Cooke, and Captain Dering who also shewed most conspicuous zeal and courage, now accompanied me and Prince Maurice Lichtenstein who galloped off to make dispositions for the retreat. After ordering forward some cavalry to support the infantry across the plain, we proceeded to another body of troops and to our great surprise found their batteries and themselves facing our own position and receiving a heavy fire from the ground on which our army had been standing. Around us were at least thirty thousand men—some formed in squares, others in march to form—and a long column in movement. We rode up to the guns confused and amazed. It was then that I began to suspect our situation and, pressing up to Prince Lichtenstein, who at that moment had made the discovery, I said: "We are not right here." Prince Lichtenstein replied: "Follow me"; and I gave this answer to Stewart, who had just come up to me to express his surprise at our position; but he was not quite aware of its actual character. We darted along the column advancing from the town, occasionally calling to the soldiers on the way to clear to the right or left, many of whom were crouching from the shot which momentarily struck around and almost infallibly with effect, and then finding an opening turned to our right, and happily rejoined our own, after having been in the midst of Buonaparte's guards for a quarter of an hour.

I can only attribute our non-discovery to the presence of the Austrian force which seemed to engage every man's attention, and to the darkness of the evening which obscured the colours of our uniforms.

As soon as we were clear I proposed to Prince Lichtenstein to go back with a body of cavalry and charge the enemy in rear. The Prince, however, was too anxious for the safety of his troops left at the redoubt to think of offensive operations; but I had the satisfaction of hearing General Moreau greatly approve of my idea and lament that it had not been carried into execution. I verily believe that I could have thrown into flight with eight hundred horse the whole of the force which sallied, taken their guns, and perhaps Buonaparte, if present; for of course we should have made, with that object, at all the mounted officers.

The troops were withdrawn and night closing in terminated the combat. The loss of the Austrians on this day may be calculated at four thousand. Of the troops which stormed and so long held the redoubt two thousand were killed or wounded, and many of them of the best regiments of chasseurs.

The intrepidity of the Austrians could not be excelled, nor the perfection of their dispositions, but they were required to do that which was physically impossible.

The next morning a little before daylight we marched again in heavy rain and fierce wind. The worst English December day was never more bleak or soaking. The Emperor, soon after the firing commenced, desired me to go and see what Wittgenstein was doing, as the enemy seemed to be pressing most on that side. In going there, and while I was in front of the Prussians, a musket-ball struck my oil-skin cloak, which I had bought new at Freyburg weary of perpetual humidity and foreseeing the continuation of this year of 'Pluviose.'[1] As the oil-skin was not lined, the ball tore the cloak greatly; the wind seized the rent, and as the tatters began to fly with a cracking noise my horse became almost mad. With one hand I attempted to tear the cloak off, and with the other to hold the raging animal. For five minutes I was in extreme danger of being dismounted, of having my bones broken and being taken; but at last I succeeded in getting rid of my black streamers and I pursued my course to Count Wittgenstein, whom I found with only one division and two regiments of cavalry, pressed by a superior force. He requested more aid. As I went back by the Prussians I entreated Prince Frederick not to abandon the village of Strehlen—as he was ordered to do by General Kleist—since the occupation of that village by the enemy would render Count Wittgenstein's position extremely hazardous. I then rode and made my report to the Emperor, entreating him to direct that the Prussians should keep Strehlen. General Moreau approved and orders were sent. Prince Schwarzenberg coming up I renewed the subject to him, and he requested me to go and order eight battalions to remain and defend Strehlen. On my arrival there I found the village already abandoned, except by one battalion, and that in retreat. By prayers as well as authority I prevailed on the officers to remain half an hour and check the enemy already approaching. At the expiration of that time we received orders to retire and I had the mortification of seeing all the troops withdrawn from a village which could have been kept by fifteen hundred men against ten thousand, and a village which was of great consequence to the general dispositions. I could only send notice to Count Wittgenstein of the Austrian intention. On my return to the Emperor and Prince Schwarzenberg they both expressed great regret at the evacuation, and Generals Kleist and Barclay with two divisions of grenadiers on the flank were ordered to retake it; but the enemy were too strongly posted before the arrangements could be made, and the attempt was abandoned. The

---

[1] Strictly, the fifth month of the French republican calendar (January-February), but Wilson must mean *pluvieuse*, 'rainy.'

conduct of the Prussians on this occasion greatly displeased me. Such skilful officers as they have are generally pedants and the majority of their officers are good for nothing. The soldiers are willing, but rather brave raw clowns than soldiers.

The enemy showed a force of about a hundred thousand men and, having the city to sustain their centre, threw with security their principal forces upon the flanks, while Vandamme with fifteen hundred men advanced from Pirna in view of our right, and against the corps of Count Osterman who was left to mask him and Königstein; but whenever the enemy attempted to beat back our artillery and dislodge us, he was driven, and all his efforts were vain to make the smallest impression.

Baffled in the flanks he thought we had weakened our centre, and about midday made a great effort with artillery; while great masses (probably of fresh troops from the other side of the river) advanced under that protection; but, after half an hour's thunder, he was obliged to withdraw his guns.

A little after this, as the Emperor, General Moreau, Lord Cathcart, myself and suite were passing on the right of the centre in the wake of a French battery which still played, a ball came and struck something about us. For a few seconds no effect was seen or heard, but then General Moreau cried "Oh!" and I perceived him, for I was next upon his left, struggling and endeavouring to dismount. I immediately said: "Sire, General Moreau is wounded." And almost at the instant I saw him throw himself from his horse, with one leg shattered and the inside of the left knee all mangled. His horse which had stood firm till the General fell, now staggered and threw himself down close to his master. The violent struggles of the horse alarmed General Moreau, who said: "Keep the horse down." But the horse died before any one could get near him. Moreau then lifted himself up a little, looked at his legs, and said: "*C'est passé avec moi! mon affaire est faite.*" The Emperor, on riding away, ordered him to be carried off the field. Some Cossacks lifted him on their pikes and removed him to the nearest village. The operation of amputating both legs was performed by the Emperor's surgeon, Wiley. Moreau bore it as a soldier, and during the whole day kept a cheerful serenity that proved the possession of extraordinary powers of mind.

I never saw a more amiable man—more modest—more intelligent. It was my good fortune to be with him a good deal during the day, and to hear him express his opinion on various subjects in a manner that convinced me that he was fully entitled to all his fame.

About half an hour before his melancholy accident he had seen me drenched to the bones, for I had not even a great coat after the loss of my oilskin, and in the kindest manner he had given me a Spanish cigar which he told me he had brought from America, saying that he was happy to have preserved one for my use on that occasion. He had come from America by the Emperor's invitation and in his first combat in presence of his rival he loses both his legs, and probably his life. I asked the Emperor about him yesterday. He told me that there was no certainty of his death, but less of his doing well. Thirty soldiers carry him: the roads are too bad for his transport by ordinary carriage.

Towards five o'clock Prince Schwarzenberg, &c., assembled to deliberate on what was to be done; and they resolved upon returning into Bohemia. The place of council was a field, round a wet wood fire; the canopy of state the blackest clouds of the heavens, which for thirteen hours rained their streams upon us. The Emperor and King, with the Crown Prince of Prussia, had chairs which they did not use, and their footstool was a board to keep them out of the mud, but which was not thought so good as the embers till the leather of their boots began to burn. I was present and heard all. The King of Prussia's observations were particularly just and apt. Few officers in Europe have juster notions. The Emperor of Russia with great reluctance consented to withdraw; but the fact was, that we should all have rotted before Dresden: it could never have been taken with a garrison of above two hundred thousand men that Buonaparte could throw in or manœuvre with against us from Königstein and Torgau. What the sword and the ague did not kill, famine would shortly consume, as the line of communication was not practicable for the transport of provisions, &c., from Bohemia. The order given, execution was immediate. At about seven o'clock the chiefs quitted the field. The first part of the road to Dippoldiswalda I accompanied the Emperor through a sea of mud; the second, I rode with General Jomini; and the third, with Prince Schwarzenberg. Miserable as I was, replete and loaded with tons of water, I still thirsted for the cold but sober comfort of mathematical arguments from Jomini and I refused the cuisine and quarters of Schwarzenberg to find my people and get a change of clothes.

I only remember once in my life to have made such a night's march, and that was in Flanders—a memorable night in the Flanders annals.

After a fruitless search for Charles, I pitched upon Stewart, who, like a friendly brother, a truly good Samaritan, gave me raiment, food and lodging. I should have been comfortable if my cold had not been so excessive, but the nasal suffering kept me wretched all night.

The next morning word was brought me that I had lost my Turkish horse; and after having arrayed myself in comparatively dry clothing I had the misfortune to be thrown into a river by a cart, against the wheel of which my stirrup caught. The stirrup gave way as the horse plunged to extricate himself, and he and his rider were pitched from the road. The mud in which I was obliged afterwards to walk was worse than the river; but I reached Altenburg, and from Altenburg came here to write. I must leave off, as the cannonade rapidly approaches. The army has been defiling through the most difficult roads, through the most desperate country, through the most impracticable woods that Europe presents. When the traveller hereafter passes through these mountains he will not believe that an army of two hundred thousand men, with all its train of equipages, &c., could have got through, especially when pursued by an enemy.

The cannonade on our right lasted till twelve o'clock last night. Buonaparte says: "Now or never!" but I think he will only maim not ruin us. If we reach the Eger without the loss of more than thirty thousand men since we marched from Laun on the Eger, we shall be fortunate; but I think our loss will amount to so much killed and wounded, sick included. It will, however, require three weeks' time to reorganize us, and time is of more value than men and guns.

It has been, on the whole, an ill-advised enterprise executed with great vigour: honourable to the troops, but I fear very beneficial to Buonaparte, who will acquire great consideration by our faults. He may strike a decisive blow against Bernadotte (if *Bernadotte is his enemy*, which the Grand Duke, with whom I dined yesterday, does not believe), or again attack Blücher, whose loss on the 21st Stewart tells me amounted to five thousand men, instead of two thousand as stated.

As far as I am personally concerned, the expedition has been favourable. I have been enabled to make some very valuable friends and to obtain the good opinion of the whole Austrian army.

If the enemy enters Bohemia we shall not fight, I believe, a decisive battle before we reach Prague, but there is a good entrenched camp on the Eger, where we shall make a partial stand.

August 30th, Töplitz.

I mounted my horse as the cannonade increased and approached. Outside the town I met the King very uneasy about the Prussian column which, together with Barclay's and Wittgenstein's, had been obliged to leave the main road and take to the mountains, the enemy having moved from Königstein and strongly lodged themselves on the Töplitz road from Dresden. Osterman, who was now engaged and who had been left to mask Königstein, had been himself intercepted and twice compelled to force his way with the bayonet.

The enemy now pressed Osterman and, having occupied the village of Kraupen, menaced seizure of the *embouchure* of Eichswalde, at the distance of a werst, where it was supposed the Prussian corps, &c., would attempt to break out. Indeed the danger seemed imminent, for the whole army still remained fixed in the mountains, unable to move from the breaking down of carriages and other impediments. The distance from Kraupen to their *embouchure* was but five wersts, and, if that pass was gained, ruin was inevitable for above a hundred and fifty thousand men.

I rode forward to the scene of action and found Osterman with eight thousand men, mostly of the guard, engaged with near forty thousand. His left was thrown into the mountains covered with thick wood; his centre was commanded, his left well protected by cavalry in open ground. The enemy made various heavy efforts to force the left, but were always repulsed. About midday two strong columns advanced from Kraupen, but the lancers and dragoons of the guard charged through garden-ground and ravines upon the right column, which threw down its arms and fled with the most rapid haste, but many hundred were killed and several hundred made prisoners. The other column retired with more order but not less speed.

It was soon after this that a shell burst and carried away the arm of Osterman, who still lives but in great danger. Never had the Emperor a braver or more zealous officer; never did any man deserve more gratitude than he for this day's conduct.

The Russian 'eight thousand,' notwithstanding a loss of one half, for fourteen hours continued the action and finally remained masters of the field. The enemy could not gain an inch of ground, but as night closed in withdrew beyond reach of fire, with a loss of certainly not less than six thousand men.

Never was an action more gloriously fought by the Russians—never was success more important. The safety of the whole army was insured, and with it all the high interests with which it is charged. It is impossible to describe the general anxiety of this day; how troops were sent for in every direction, and how disappointment constantly accompanied the returning messenger. I myself rode no less than twenty-one wersts backwards and forwards in a gallop, bent on fruitless search for infantry and twelve-pounders. At last, however, I did find two battalions and brought them up. It was not until six at night that the first division of infantry arrived, so great were the impediments; and certainly it will require two days more to clear the defiles of the baggage, &c., which still remains in them. To-morrow we shall have troops enough, but those survivors may think themselves happy who can boast that they fought on the 30th of August at Kraupen. The enemy may be reinforced and make another effort, but we have nothing to apprehend: indeed we ought rather to wish for the attempt.

I fear, however, that the loss of his guard, added to other griefs, will greatly exasperate the Emperor of Russia and weaken the conditions of co-operation. Indeed I have long seen, speaking in reference to that subject, more than I choose to note to others; and I have heard more than I choose to repeat.

I must not omit to record that in the course of the day I saw Schwarzenberg. In a conversation with him I find that either he will resign, or make over the command, if his Sovereign wishes it, to the 'military college' that accompanies the army. I think he is right, for without unity of direction it is impossible to command an army.

Sept. 1st—I had been told by Prince Schwarzenberg on the evening of the 30th that he would attack Vandamme next morning: a plan which I greatly approved, upon a principle which made me adverse to our movement into Saxony—viz., placing the defiles immediately on our rear.

Stewart and I rode out early, and as the action was commencing we were passing to the right of our position to advance with the Austrians when a shell fell close to us and burst. The splinters flew around, but not finding myself hit, who was nearest to the spot where the shell burst, I hoped that Stewart had escaped; but almost at the moment he said to me that "he was hit." I found that a piece of the shell had struck his thigh. Cooke and Kinnaird coming up we led him off: as he complained much of sickness we took him off his horse and placed him on the ground; but the shells came so thick around us that we were obliged to set him again on horseback and conduct him to a greater distance, when he was again taken from his horse and dressed by a soldier, aid to the regimental surgeon.

The blow was severe; and it appears from Wiley who attended him in the evening, that the sharp point of the splinter had entered deep but done no serious mischief. After the dressing, and when the sick feeling had passed, Kinnaird accompanied him to Töplitz with two soldiers whom I obtained to attend him; and Cooke and I returned to the field.

I refer to my military report for the transactions of the day. As far as concerned myself, I was not idle; and I was enabled to lead a charge, with several Austrian squadrons of cavalry, into the flank of the enemy on retreat, while General Radetsky led the Austrian infantry. Our success was complete, and several battalions were broken and taken.

Here I very nearly lost my life from an act of humanity. I saw some of my dragoons pursuing an officer who most gallantly defended himself, but who kept shouting like a madman. On approaching, I recognised him as a Cossack officer. I cried out to the dragoons to desist; but the unfortunate man flew forward (in the hope of joining some Russians), followed by the dragoons, one of whom fired into his horse. The animal rushed on impetuously, breaking over the pole of an ammunition-waggon, and almost immediately afterwards fell and expired. The Cossack was instantly again on his legs. Seeing his peril I rode to him and parried several cuts which the dragoons aimed at him; but at last one fell on his hand, and another cut off the flesh from the right temple and made a terrible gash on the head. It was only then that I could persuade the dragoons that he was our friend. They galloped off and I remained a moment to give him up to some Cossacks whom I saw approaching. The man, however, mad with vengeance and pain, seized at my horse's bridle and told the Cossacks that I had wounded him. In a moment their lances were couched at my body, but another Cossack darted forward and cried out: "He is our English General!" The others withdrew their pikes and I preserved my sword, which a Russian dragoon was attempting to wrest from me; but I was not altogether extricated till Prince Galitzin came up with other officers.

After this I rode up the Peterswalde Mountain in pursuit of the enemy passing by that route, who either threw down their arms or were making a faint resistance. To my astonishment, however, I also found the road covered with the Prussian artillery. I could not believe my own sight, and therefore I do not wonder at the King's being astonished when I sent to him to say that we had recovered the Prussian artillery but wanted several hundred horses to remove it. The King, in the evening when I went to him, told me that he was never more astonished, and could not for some time make out what had occurred; but that in consequence of my message the Emperor had lent him the Russian artillery-horses for the occasion.

It is almost incredible that a body of cavalry should charge up such a mountain, at least two miles of ascent, force through a hostile column on march, and effect its escape, while thousands of flying infantry should profit by the panic and also pass.

It was a great fault in General Kleist to descend the mountain with his guns. He should have remained on the height with them, and only sent down some carriages to barricade the road, as thick wood prevented passage to the right or left. The general should moreover have sent some troops to line the wood, and take post at points which in a few places commanded the road through openings in the wood. But with all these faults of the general, the troops also behaved extremely ill, according to the report of their own officers who all denounced them to me as I came up; and indeed they were as much in disorder as the enemy. Many of them also were killed by the Austrians and Russians under the supposition of their being flying French. I released, moreover, numbers who were marching as prisoners by the Austrians.

If the Prussian corps had been well posted, not a man of the two French corps could have escaped. The plan was admirable, but unfortunately that part which required the best troops failed by the employment of the worst.

I must be just, however, and add that the greater part of Kleist's corps is composed of Landwehr and raw recruits.

The whole scene was most extraordinary and the day most memorable; presenting another subject for tacticians to treat upon hereafter.

The Emperor was obliged to keep aloof. Count Osterman, who had lost his arm, had been presented in the morning with the Order of St. George; but he returned for answer, that if the Emperor wished to reward him it must be in another manner. The Emperor wrote to Osterman to know his wishes; when Osterman, and a number of generals, implored the Emperor not to expose himself, as he had done, to the hazards of the combat, and finally obtained his word of honour that he would not.

On my return I went to Stewart, whom I found in pain, but soon afterwards Wiley arrived. I then went to the King, who was in high spirits having just received Blücher's report of a victory in which he took fifty guns. But I must pause to know all the particulars before I can believe that the Prussians obtained this success by force of arms against anything like equal numbers; so low do I esteem the Prussians, from want of officers and experience.

The cry now of the Russians and Prussians again is—"Advance!"

but they forget how much is due to circumstances and the errors of the enemy.

It will require three weeks to reorganize the army completely, and provide it with shoes, &c. The best thing we could do would be to detach more aid to Blücher, or threaten a descent by the pass of Zittau, on the other side of the Elbe, while we struck a blow in Bavaria with the corps now on that frontier reinforced by such troops as could speedily be added.

Buonaparte would be greatly alarmed if we made much progress on that side without weakening too much the army destined to protect Austria.

All the details of what has passed in the mountains cannot yet be collected, but it appears that Wittgenstein by tackling his cavalry to the guns has saved them all.

I fear that the Austrians have not been so successful. The baggage, however, of the whole army has been nearly all taken or destroyed; and the enemy must have made an immense booty, but not easily transportable. One of their columns is already on this side of Altenburg, but I presume must soon retrograde from yesterday's occurrences.

I understand that the scene in the mountains was most horrible from the shot of the enemy which occasionally fell among the baggage, and the confusion which the terror of the drivers, &c., created when no enemy was near.

Evening—This morning many more prisoners were brought in. The total number exceeds five thousand, and above sixty guns have been drawn through the town. It appears also that seven generals were either killed or wounded.

Vandamme[1] has been sent to Moscow. He made some complaints against some supposed indignity of treatment; gave offence to the Russian officers by complaining of the Russian Emperor to the Austrian Emperor; and after being exposed in a cart to the view of all the passing Hungarian grenadiers, as he pretended on purpose to make a spectacle of him, he had his sword taken from him by a Cossack at the Grand Duke's order.

After dinner I saw the Duke of Cumberland, who to my great surprise was very courteous: so much so that, on a Russian officer asking whether I had been in the action yesterday, the Duke replied: "Oh! I will answer for him never being out of one if within possible reach!" In various other instances he was equally civil and begged of me to go over the ground of battle with him in the morning, which

[1] General Dominique-René Vandamme (1770–1830) had capitulated at Kulm.

I must do if no attack is made on Marmont's troops, who have been pursuing the Austrians and Wittgenstein, and who are now themselves embarrassed with their spoil in the defiles.

I shall, however, keep well on my guard, and take care of every word I utter. I could not refuse his civility altogether; it would not only have been personally injurious, but nationally improper. The Duke will, I presume, remain with the Prussians.

Stewart is to-day feverish, but I still hope his wound will not be serious. He will go to Prague as soon as he can be removed.

Moreau is, I hear, worse this morning. All the French officers taken express great interest in his welfare.

2nd—I have received advice of my servants and carriage, which retreated by the route of Freyburg. The carriage behind them was taken and the French were coming to mine when they espied four pieces of cannon which they preferred. My aide-de-camp, Brinken, is taken, and Charles's baggage is lost. Dawson's baggage is also taken, and his servant in flight passed fifty Austrian cannon abandoned. I have no doubt that the Allies in this retreat have lost above a hundred guns and several hundred ammunition-waggons; amongst them some Russian. The carriages lost must exceed three thousand.

6th—After the action with Vandamme no military event of any importance occurred on our side. The news from other quarters began to pour in with many favourable details till yesterday, when going to Peterswalde I brought back tidings of Buonaparte having marched the preceding day to Bautzen with his guards, leaving about twelve thousand men in Dresden, and St. Cyr's corps on the Peterswalde road. It had been the intention to dislodge this corps from its position in front of Peterswalde: I went to see an operation which I disapproved, being satisfied that the enemy would find the least inconvenience from a movement into this part of Saxony, and we the greatest. The columns, however, destined to pass out of the mountains upon Dippoldiswalde and menace the enemy's rear at Bautenau and Velser did not move—perhaps could not move—with sufficient speed, and the enterprize was abandoned. The spies which came out of Dresden further informed us that about thirty thousand prisoners, including wounded men, were in the town, and a vast quantity of spoil; many cannon, &c., had also been brought in with much parade. I had reason to believe this statement not exaggerated, and my former statement of the Allied loss underrated; for the Austrians estimate theirs alone at above twenty thousand, and I know that of the Russians seven thousand wounded have reached the environs of Töplitz. Add their prisoners taken with their baggage, three battalions on the Peterswalde road; their killed; and the Prussian loss, with the subsequent casualties by sickness; and I fear the total will fall little short of fifty thousand men. It is true some will be restored from the hospitals, but at least a force of forty thousand men must be extinguished.

On my return to Prince Schwarzenberg with Barclay's message, I found the Prince very anxious to make a movement on the other side of the Elbe to check Buonaparte's progress into Lusatia. As we could not pursue our own plans and were obliged now to confine ourselves to the counteraction of the enemy's, certainly this was the most feasible measure, the least hazardous and the most immediate in its operation. I went to gain the Prussian assent and Schwarzenberg undertook the Emperor's.

After a long conversation with certain personages and Hardenberg[1] I perfectly succeeded in convincing them of the propriety of the project, and as the Grand Duke called me up to drink tea with him as I was passing his balcony I gained another friend; but I was happy to find that he was still more anxious for a movement to the left, where we could in our turn resume the offensive. Schwarzenberg's contest was more difficult, but after hard battle he obtained sanction to move with sixty thousand Austrians, in two columns, by Leitmeritz and Aussig towards Zittau. The Emperor of Russia would not let his Russians march. Certain political views in Saxony, I believe, retain them on that frontier. The Austrians had wished to throw the Russians on the right, hoping to get them out of Bohemia; for it is now a fixed principle with the ministers as well as the generals that the armies must act separately, as otherwise the discord arising from disputed command will not only occasion the greatest detriment to the general interests but prevent the possibility of political union for six weeks longer. I found the Austrians at daybreak this morning in transports of joy at the idea of separation, and the morning in consequence has been quite a jubilee.

Schwarzenberg and Radetsky both cheered upon it as if a victory had been gained. As this movement promised to have the greatest interest, and as the Austrian service was more immediately connected with my personal views, I obtained from Lord Cathcart permission to accompany this corps, and Schwarzenberg to my application answered: "You come not by favour but by right, and I only hope you will consider yourself inseparable from us."

[1] Karl August, Prince von Hardenberg (1750–1822), was Prussian Chancellor.

Among the Austrians are some new battalions of Landwehr. They really are apparently as effective as their Line, and composed not merely of boys as the Prussian Landwehr are, but of grown men rather under prescribed military height.

I have just seen the troops pass and certainly they are in better order than could have been expected after what has occurred; but still many shoes, &c., are wanted.

The Prussians, all of whom I have seen, are in the very best condition; and the day before yesterday, the Duke of Cumberland, after he had viewed their infantry, cavalry and artillery, said to me: "It was really worth coming from England to see such troops."

No man can form a conception of the vigorous state of the remnant of the Russian army now here. No man ever beheld such guards and such artillery. Infantry, after two successive seasons, is rarely in similar order; and the cavalry is in as high condition as if it had never marched more than five wersts a day, and never encountered a cold or wet night.

The Prussians here, being chiefly Landwehr, and Silesian Landwehr or recruits, are not fit subjects for notice, especially after their late misfortune.

They are, however, diligent, and if not too hastily brought again into the field may become useful; but youth is the great fault of Austrians and Prussians, so that a winter campaign is almost impracticable. Five-sixths of both armies after six weeks would be in hospital or the grave.

The Emperors are still here, but I believe the Austrian will go to Aussig and the Russian to Duchs. The King has not fixed his quarters. Yesterday Hardenberg sent for me and asked whether I would receive a Prussian decoration. I answered—"As an honour conferred by itself, and further as a mark of favour from a Sovereign so highly entitled to esteem." He told me that he was desired by the King to put the question.

I do not recollect that I mentioned the Emperor of Austria's having told me the other day not to get another cross for the one I lost in the redoubt, as "he would charge himself to replace it."[1] I only mention these incidents to show that the former gift has not been forgotten though delayed, and that I rather make progress in Royal favour than otherwise, which is not a low ambition under my circumstances.

[1] In the attack at Dresden on August 26th Wilson had lost his Cross of Maria Theresa. On learning this, the Emperor instructed Metternich, as Chancellor of the Order, to send Wilson another. See Sept. 15th, evening.

The Duke of Cumberland, strange to relate, has also added his meed of approbation and assured me that he shall represent to the Prince Regent that I am acting here no insignificant or useless part.

I can truly say this change in the Duke's own sentiments has taken place without any *strategy* of mine. I sought it not—I expected it not: it was perfectly a feeling created by the evidence of the senses. I think the eulogy will astonish friends and foes in England.

It is impossible for me to trace all I see, hear and do. My life is most incessantly passed in action; and in these times a thousand incidents occur daily which might engage the attention of others more remote; but to record them I should need a warehouse of paper, and friends would be years deciphering the narrative of the events of a few hours. Much may be imagined when it is recollected that in a small village three Courts, Cabinets and Councils of War are assembled, and that within the eyes' range three armies of three different nations are in position.

Moreau's death cast a great gloom, and is too memorable a catastrophe not to excite lasting regret. Stadion and Metternich passed the last four hours with him, and he died dictating a letter to Alexander.

Stewart, who is getting better, will remove tomorrow to Prague. He has given me a beautiful English blood-mare, and I hope that I have not been wanting in liberal regard towards him, as the *Gazette* in a short time will show. He is an excellent fellow, and merits all good-will.

September 9th, Leitmeritz.

On the 7th I left Töplitz to join the Austrian army in these environs. Stewart went to Prague with the intention of proceeding to the Prince Royal when a little more recovered. I separated thus from a friend and *camarade de guerre* with whom I had associated in some pleasures and more perils, of which we mutually entertain a durable impression. I found, however, in Lord Aberdeen[1] not altogether a new acquaintance, but a man with a spirit of good-will towards myself which engaged reciprocity of interest, and established, as I hope, the solid foundation of a permanent friendship.

I have seen too much of the errors into which a hasty judgment of men leads—I have known too much of the difference that frequently exists between the first presentation and the real character

[1] George Hamilton Gordon, Earl of Aberdeen (1784–1860) had arrived as British Ambassador to Austria. Wilson described him as "a liberal politician and a man of high independent spirit, with a very reasoning mind, in which there is no inextirpatable prejudice." He was to become Foreign Secretary in 1828.

of men, not to hesitate in forming new attachments until time has afforded sufficient opportunity for full investigation; but in the few days in which I saw Lord Aberdeen I had such conversation with him as assured me that his general views of foreign policy were enlightened; and his application for my transfer to Austria, "as a special favour to himself," after these conversations was an incontrovertible proof not only of concurrence in sentiment, but of personal partiality created by the candour and tenor of our opinions. In communicating with him I cannot but gain, as his mind is highly endowed—in service under his superintendence I cannot lose, as he is a man of honourable feeling and just principle.

Before my departure I dined with Lord Cathcart and took leave of the Emperor, who expressed to me his wishes confidentially as to the execution of the projected movement. I also made my best bow to the Duke of Cumberland, who bade me farewell as if I had all my years possessed his affections.

The day was the 28oth '*Pluviose*.' The roads were knee-deep in mud; the sky yet black with the accumulated vapours which drenched us thoroughly as they discharged their condensed waters.

Waggons with dying horses—waggons without horses—waggons without wheels—waggons with waggoners imploring the thunder of Jove to smite all men including themselves, and all beasts also themselves included; guns which had been spiked by the fugitive French, and which were being withdrawn to be made capable of redeeming their honour; Hungarians without boots—Austrians without shoes—men without energy—women without spirits (in their barrels which they carry on their backs)—and Cossacks without mercy—covered the road. It was a scene of utter devastation.

I had ordered Allen and my Spaniard, with my two best horses, to proceed to Theresienstadt, which I wished to see, especially as the Marquis de Chasteler[1] commanded. I could not reach the outer gate till half-past nine, as I had waited for the servants who accompanied me above an hour. They had stopped behind to pick up and re-pack the things which had fallen off one of my led horses.

All the shoes had also come off my own horse and for the last mile he had gone consequently lame on all fours. In this condition to be at the outer gate of a fortress with rain still pouring furiously and my servants as I supposed within with the parts of my dress most necessary for a change was certainly a military misery; it was aggravated by the apprehension that I might not be able to enter at all.

[1] J.G.J.A., Marquis du Chasteler, an Austrian general.

My fears were realised, or rather my patience was exhausted, and I turned my horse back to Leitmeritz, where I should find Schwarzenberg if he had left Töplitz.

The Burgomaster sent me to the Bishop's palace where the Bishop received me; and, as Prince Schwarzenberg had countermanded his staff, &c., I occupied his apartments.

Some tea consoled me for the past, but as I could learn nothing of Allen I apprehended the morrow, foreseeing that the garments which I drew off could not be drawn on again in the morning. Necessity sent me to bed and a thick feather-bed as a covering kept me in sweltering wretchedness all night.

The next morning at daybreak Allen was sent for to the fortress; but no Allen had been there.

I would rather have dressed as a bishop than lain in my bed any longer, so I rose and with Herculean toil got on my boots, for, as ill-luck had ordered, I had sent Allen forward with my short untwisting boots and trousers to get others made by them and I had ridden in pantaloons and tight half-boots.

It was a day of thanksgiving for the preservation of Leitmeritz from the enemy by the defeat of Vandamme, and the Bishop had very wisely judged that the physical man should be cheered while the spiritual man rejoiced. His Sanctity therefore ordered a sumptuous banquet, which was served in a very magnificent hall with the most splendid accessories.

I am told that the Bishop, who has seven hundred and twenty thousand souls in his diocese, is a most excellent prelate, and I can testify to his being a most worthy president.

Sept. 13th, Töplitz.

I was called upon to mount in the middle of the night of the 11th, as the enemy had driven back the Russians with some loss from before Pirna and the Austrian army was directed to return by a flank march to Töplitz. I found the enemy on my arrival at Töplitz, near Peterswalde, and learnt that on the preceding evening he had broken out unexpectedly from the mountains near Töplitz, almost seized the high ground and surprised the Sovereigns, &c., in the town. The panic had scarcely subsided when I came here.

In the evening I rode out and found the enemy pressing back the Russians and already masters of the height of Nollendorf. Before dark he had descended the hill and reached our abbatis that had been made nearly at the foot. His force was stated to be thirty thousand in front, and Buonaparte was declared to be following with his Guards and a force which made the total a hundred and thirty thousand. The half of the Austrians only had arrived, and the Russians had been diminished in the combats before Pirna three thousand men. The night presented a magnificent scene of illumination in the positions of the hostile armies. The hills were lighted to their crests, and the valleys blazed with a sheet of fire. This morning, as I—and I believe I almost alone—suspected, no attack was made, and the remaining Austrians have now time to file through the passes and gain the position between Töplitz and Moden. But I much fear that, exclusive of Kleinau's corps guarding our left at Commotau and Marienburg, the Allies cannot bring into the field more than ninety thousand effectives; and a great portion of the cavalry included in this number are almost exhausted.

I have been of the constant opinion that Buonaparte was endeavouring to draw the Prince Royal [Bernadotte] and Blücher near to the Elbe that he might strike his blow and not be removed far from the base of his operations. And I suspect that he has only thrown a force here to mask his march against them. The *têtes-du-pont* at Königstein facilitate his rapid progress. There are others who believe that he is retiring altogether, and found this belief on the removal of his hospitals, &c., from Leipsic. I see in that arrangement only proper precaution and expedient relief of the capital which must need supplies.

This morning we had advice of the Prince Royal's victory near Wittenberg. It is strange with so much success as is announced on the other side of the Elbe that Buonaparte should still be able to present the powerful force he does. I hope we shall not at last take more prisoners than ever there were enemies.

The ministers all remained here during the last anxious few days, but from all that I see and learn peace is still the desire, and Hardenberg told Stewart that it would be made before the winter.

I have heard from Brinken, who is a prisoner at Dresden. He had some grand conceptions if ever taken; I hope he will execute his designs. I shall remind him.

I had the satisfaction of finding Allen and my horses. We have been moving at cross purposes, but the pleasure of recovery makes me forget my vexation.

15th—Yesterday Prince Schwarzenberg ordered a grand reconnaissance and went himself to superintend. The enemy's posts were found at Nollendorf. Their force in the environs amounted to ten or twelve thousand men. These retired by the high Dresden road.

Buonaparte has no doubt sustained heavy losses; but he is not yet disposed to prostrate his arms and sue for mercy, although Berthier[1] has certainly counselled peace in the strongest terms and although it is proved by an infinity of intercepted official and private letters that his troops are shattered by fatigue, disorganized by various discomfitures and morally enfeebled. The cry is also universal for peace; but Schwarzenberg told me yesterday that Buonaparte had replied to one of his observations: "*Bah! vous ne connaissez pas la France. Ce n'est pas la guerre que je crains, mais la paix: une paix déshonorable peut seulement me casser le cou.*" And the Empress, in a flood of tears at the apprehension of the Austrian war, said to Prince Schwarzenberg on another occasion: "The Emperor is in a position extremely delicate. He cannot do as other Sovereigns: if he makes a discreditable peace, opinion sooner or later will ensure his ruin."

15th, evening—I now understand that the Austrians are to march upon Commotau and Saxony by the Freyburg route. There is a defile at Zschopau which I much dread, and I think the whole movement very critical. As Wittgenstein and Kleist remain here we shall be very weak. Good intelligence and mobility may, however, preserve us from a *coup-de-maître*, although I speculate upon an early retrograde movement. I shall go to Kleinau, who commands the advanced guard. The Emperor of Russia is to move with the Austrians; this causes great dissatisfaction as they hoped to be disembarrassed of the weight of the Courts—for no doubt all the Sovereigns will follow.

I have just received my Maria Theresa Cross, with a very handsome letter. The Red Eagle, as Hardenberg tells me, awaits but arrival from Berlin.

19th—On the morning of the 17th, I rode with the Prince-Marshal [Schwarzenberg] to reconnoitre the enemy, who had reached Nollendorf with fifteen thousand men, and whose camp in the rear contained about fifty-five thousand infantry and six thousand cavalry.

As the enemy appeared quiet, I returned with the Prince in his droska and profited by this opportunity to receive many more curious anecdotes of incidents that occurred in Paris, &c. Among them I learnt that Buonaparte had intended to avoid battle with the Allies when they marched upon Lützen, until he had crossed a strong corps and gained the right bank near the new town of Dresden. Buonaparte had even said to Schwarzenberg: "If the Allies have not two hundred thousand men, *I will turn their right* and make

---

[1] Marshal Alexandre Berthier, Prince de Neufchâtel, was for many years Chief of Staff to Napoleon.

Alexander repent of his playing the general." On Schwarzenberg observing that he thus exposed himself to be thrown upon the sea and to lose his communications, he replied: *"Bah! Est-ce que je ne suis pas à cheval sur l'Elbe, à Magdeburg et à Wittenburg?"* "And as to communications, what ill can result if I am obliged to draw my line from Wesel? *C'est à l'ennemi de penser à sa ligne de communication."* I note this because it proves my opinion to have been Buonaparte's, as my reports will certify.

We had scarcely sat down to dinner when the cannon commenced briskly. We were obliged to return to the field, and found the enemy pressing the Prussians—who had given way at the *abbatis*, and thus encouraged the enemy's advance to Culm—with about thirty guns altogether, and eight thousand men. The Russian reserve checked the enemy's progress, and the Marshal having ordered Count Colloredo with his corps to attack in flank, which movement was executed with great steadiness and intrepidity, the enemy fell back and regained the hill. The Prussians lost some men, though not many, but a General Kreutzer was taken, whose people abandoned him when he thought they were following to charge. Kreutzer signifies a piece of money worth about a farthing, and this *équivoque* gives occasion to many severe *calembourgs* [puns]. The fact is, that the Prussians did not make a proper defence, and even the King censured them; but they were so very raw and youthful, that pity is rather to be excited than resentment. Thick rain and almost substantial vapour prevented much observation. The flame from the guns was, indeed, the only means of direction to the troops.

We returned about ten at night, wet to the bones, and leaving the poor troops in all the miseries of a hard bed under their bodies, and water from the heavens occasionally pouring upon them 'in pailfuls.'

Many expected a general battle on the ensuing morning—I did did not, and proved right. It happened that Buonaparte only came on to see what we were about, and probably with a hope of crushing some rashly-advanced corps. He had been in the affair, and had his horse wounded in the shoulder. I have spoken with a soldier who saw the accident and his exchange of horses with a lancer of the Guard.

The next morning, when Merfeldt[1] advanced from Klein Kreitnau and took the village of Kitzin, he was also present and ordered the troops forward, which rendered it expedient for the Austrians to withdraw.

[1] An Austrian general.

During the day I rode to see what was going on, and met the Grand Duke, who obliged me to return to dine with him at twelve o'clock, which assured me a meal without an appetite; but I fortunately overtook the Emperor, with whom I had a long conversation of great utility and I had the satisfaction of hearing the Emperor say that he now saw the danger of a new Saxon invasion, at least until the arrival of Beningsen, and that he approved of Schwarzenberg's reluctance to make it.

This gave me an opportunity of doing justice to Schwarzenberg and of engaging the Emperor's influence with the King of Prussia to effect a reconciliation between him and the Marshal, which is now done from this and other measures which I took. The King was certainly *trop vif* and severe in his expressions: he wounded the feelings of the man and the dignity of the chief, but Schwarzenberg happily has good sense enough to set due limits to the excitement of his *amour propre et fierté soldatesque*; and the King, with an ardent temper, has an excellent heart and sound understanding.

The Duke of Cumberland has left us, very angry with the Emperor and in great hatred of the Russians; hatred augmented by the fear of their power.

I had the pleasure to find that I had exactly attained the position which I wished and ought to have in relations with him as the King's son in a foreign country.

20th—Last night we were making a calculation of the loss of the Allied army which formed in Bohemia and it appears that there is a deficiency of thirty-six thousand Austrians, forty thousand Russians, and very near thirty thousand Prussians up to yesterday, including killed, wounded and prisoners of all descriptions.

The Austrians in Bohemia, including their garrisons and Landwehr which have joined their armies, have still a hundred and thirty-three thousand; the Russians muster forty-thousand in their lists; and the Prussians little more than fifteen thousand.

With the weather which daily becomes worse, we shall soon have only skeleton battalions: the more especially as the Austrians are ill shod and clothed, and the Prussians are almost children.

Blücher's loss since the 17th of August is estimated at twenty-five thousand. The loss of the Allies under Bernadotte at fifteen thousand and the little finger of a Swedish chasseur. The whole comprises a tolerable expenditure of men.

Beasts, however, have not suffered less in proportion; and we have now no longer that mass of cavalry which swarmed not only on this plain but in every plain between the Saal and the Vistula.

The reserve cavalry is in good order, and has not suffered greatly, but the light cavalry is now not sufficient for the service of the army; and these, from the difficulty of procuring forage and the constant soak of their bodies, daily diminish.

I doubt whether the enemy's cavalry suffer equally. He is in a better country, has better lodgment and does not employ it so much as we do ours. I always fear that he is nursing the main body to re-appear; as he did after the battle of Eylau[1] with a force which by numbers and condition gave him at once the superiority.

His infantry is certainly hard pressed, but still he affords them relief by constant exchanges of garrison, and sustains them by the neighbourhood of his magazines which contain sufficient means, although we say here that the enemy are starving.

25th—My pacific negotiations have completely succeeded. Schwarzenberg and the King, and Radetsky the Austrian Quarter-master-general and the King, are now quite reconciled; and all is proceeding in that quarter with important good-will. The service is felt and acknowledged by them and many others, among whom are Stewart and Aberdeen.

I am anxiously expecting a Government answer to my application for a transfer to Austria.

I adhere to my original resolution on that subject. It is not worth my while, nor consistent with my credit, to play an under-character as I have been so long doing.

8 o'clock.

The news of Buonaparte's march[2] is confirmed, but as yet his object is not manifest.

It is strange that he should feel himself sufficiently safe in his rear while Bavaria is refusing his control.

The more I consider the importance of Bavaria the more I am sure that we are but imperfectly informed.

I saw the Emperor of Austria this morning, who was remarkably gracious and pleased with what he had heard from Schwarzenberg and others.

To conclude: in the middle of last night I dreamt that I saw preparations for the assault upon this town. I beheld the cavalry mount—I *heard* the trumpet sound the charge, and the crash upon the pavement. I jumped up—seized my sword—rushed to the stair-head—awoke—and found that at the precise moment a courier blasting his horn was rumbling by my window in a waggon at full trot!

[1] February 8th, 1807, when the Russians were driven back in a snowstorm.
[2] Over the Elbe and towards Bischoffswerda.

27th—In the interval of war we have been occupying the time with chivalric banquets. Yesterday the Russian Guards gave a dinner to the Sovereigns on the festival of the Emperor's coronation. Previous to the fête there was mass. A tent perched upon a sloping hill was the temple of worship and about nine thousand men, picturesquely grouped in columns, formed the congregation. After the service these troops filed by and merited much admiration from the *belle tenue* in which they presented themselves. The Prussian Guards were particularly clean and well appointed.

After this inspection we went to the hall of entertainment, and really it was one of the best constructed fir, mat and woodbine *salles* that ever was made. The taste of the artificers deserved the highest encomiums.

About forty or fifty persons sat down at the principal table, and about two hundred more at other tables. I was fortunate enough to obtain a place not merely at the first, but between the two Princes Lichtenstein, who are two of the most interesting persons I ever met in any land. They would have honoured King Arthur's Round Table.

We had scarcely sat down when the kitchen fired, and the flames approached so closely as to cause inquietude to the guests, but happily the wind changed and the store-room as well as the banqueting-room was preserved.

The accident greatly distressed Schwarzenberg, who remembered the fate of his sister-in-law at Paris.

We made excellent cheer, and broke up about five o'clock.

I must note here some particulars with reference to the order of the Red Eagle. Hardenberg gave me, at a banquet at Sir C. Stewart's afterwards, his own insignia, as a compliment additional to his master's *bienveillance*. It has been obtained without any other interest than that which my own services have created. I have won it from a Sovereign who has been gracious enough to consider those services as worthy of the reward of a decoration which the bravest of his warriors heretofore on the scene of Prussian glory have been proud to win and which he now gives with a very sparing hand. This war not more than six have been given; and he proposes to render it as scarce as possible consistently with legitimate claims. The 'Black Eagle' is more general, though higher, as it extends to diplomatic services, and shadows those on whom other Sovereigns smile from whatever cause. I was not within its reach, because my rank in the army was not that of a Lieutenant-General. The Red Eagle is rather considered as the badge of the House of

Nassau, and this in my eyes augments its value. In the last war I had obtained the Fourth Class.[1] In this war how many toils, how many perils, how much privation, what extremity of climate have I not encountered before I received this reward! I have indeed had it measured out to me with an extraordinarily distinguishing favour, but not without an approving army and empire.

I have had the good fortune to force my progress through formidable impediments. When I think on all my difficulties, I scarcely can believe the success that I have realized.

Children ought to be very grateful to parents who give them hereditary consideration. It levels many obstructions and ensures many a helping hand; it makes those payments gold which abstract merit would receive in baser metal.

This day the Emperor gave a grand dinner to all the English. About thirty assembled and the banquet was sumptuous. The Emperor wore the star of the English order of the Garter, recently conferred, and the 'garter' *above* the knee as the boot came up to the top of the knee-cap. It was probably the first time that it was ever so worn. I could not help thinking that the place of the Garter where I had seen the Legion of Honour marked a strange revolution. I am now going to the King *en cordon* to perform my part of chivalric ceremony, and I truly have great pleasure in appearing before the King as one of his knights.

I hope, however, to prove my sentiments by deeds rather than words,[2] and add honour to the Red Eagle, so that I may feel acquitted of every military obligation before the campaign closes.

Mr. George Jackson was also present and wrote:
Between five and six, all the English assembled by appointment at Lord Cathcart's, to be present at the ceremony of investing the Emperor Alexander with the Order of the Garter. His Imperial Majesty kept the three English missions waiting till nine o'clock. We were then introduced, and witnessed a scene that disgusted every Englishman present. There is a degree of impressiveness in the customary ceremony of an Investiture; but on this occasion everything of that sort was discarded, even to the omission of Garter's admonitions to the knight. The whole thing was treated, in fact, as a sort of farcical entertainment. The Emperor was in a little nutshell of a room, with his brother, the Grand Duke Constantine, both of whom were in a broad grin the whole time. With

[1] In April 1807 for his services at the battle of Eylau two months earlier.
[2] *Res non Verba* was Wilson's family motto.

difficulty the Emperor had been persuaded to wear shoes and
stockings, and the whole ceremony consisted in Count Golowkin
reading the commission in Latin, very badly, and in the Commis-
sioners then buckling on the Garter. The company present consisted only of Russians, with the exception of Count Metternich
and the English colony, all crowded together about the door—for it
was impossible to enter the room—with as much noise and want of
decorum as the rush to get to supper in England is usually attended
with.

. . . The next day a party of twenty English dined with the Emperor. He made his appearance with the blue riband and star, and
the garter *round his thigh*, above his great boot!!—some of the party
could scarcely refrain from a burst of laughter, others from looking
their indignation at this undignified treatment and novel mode of
wearing our most distinguished Order (ii, 287–9).

I had the great satisfaction to see Beningsen at dinner. Time is a
powerful corrector of ills. What a variety of considerations is
connected with his return to the Emperor's head-quarters.

His troops have, I understand, suffered much en route. He describes
the roads as almost impracticable. We have had, however, two days'
fine weather and I hope it may continue for a week, when the road
will become a little consolidated.

The Austrian army made a short movement yesterday but brought
up at anchor very near this town as it appeared that Buonaparte had
concentrated at Pirna.

I do not believe he will invade Bohemia except under some new
circumstances, but his lingering so obstinately on the Elbe creates
great uneasiness.

12 o'clock, Sept. 27th

I have just come from the King, who told me that it was necessary
some time or other to treat; and that when Buonaparte showed most
pliability was in his opinion the fittest occasion. I observed that, at
all events, the Allies ought to avoid a line of conduct which would
rally every Frenchman and every ally of France round the Government and its chief; for although the desire of peace was prevalent,
the enemy was not prepared to lay down his arms and surrender
at discretion as a preliminary. After some conversation on this subject, the King told Stewart he was very glad that he was going to the
Crown Prince's [Bernadotte] army, as distrust as well as difference
of opinion was rapidly gaining ground in that quarter, and threatened
great inconveniences to the general service.

I have been with the Austrian Quartermaster-general [Radetsky] this day, advising that Zamosc should be a neutral fort during the war, that is, garrisoned by Prussians in the first instance and until the fate of the Duchy is determined. It is a very important fortress, greatly affecting Austrian interests. Its transfer to Russia should not be lightly admitted at the present moment if the balance of power in Europe be the real object of the other contending parties.

Aberdeen has the same view and works in his own *foyer* of action. I don't believe that we have yet differed on any one subject; and if we should do so, it would be only until the truth was ascertained, for that is the object of his researches as well as mine. Neither he nor I admit any bias from partial feelings. He is, however, the only countryman of my own on the Continent yet encountered with whom I can with safety and advantage candidly talk on war and politics. All others, without exception, have either limited understandings or narrow principles on these subjects. I have resolved, therefore, never to trace a line or open my lips to any one of them on these matters beyond mere narration of facts.

The King of Prussia has just sent Charles and Brinken (unfortunately now a prisoner) his Order of Merit. James (Sir Charles's aide-de-camp) also gets it for service under my orders.[1]

I rejoice that these are honours which distinguish brave friends whose merit I have witnessed.

Dawson also will get a decoration for his service with me, and he truly deserves it.

I transmit a piece of my new order ribbon. It is not in itself beautiful, but it becomes so when cannon-smoked.

Stewart leaves us tomorrow for the Crown Prince. In addition to his ministerial duties he has the superintendence, &c., of all the troops in the north, surveillance of the Crown Prince, &c. Government, I suppose, thinks him gifted with the powers of omnipresence.

Oct. 1st—The news of the day is Platow's success, which will be sent *en bulletin*, so I do not enter into details. Platow does, however, deserve my notice. I was guarantee that he would win the Cross of Maria Theresa: tomorrow he will wear it, with the Emperor of Russia's picture—a most distinguished honour among the Russians. General Thielmann,[2] who was in the neighbourhood, writes that he has taken two guns, and made some prisoners of the fugitives from

---

[1] Wilson had recommended these officers for the Cross of the Military Order of Merit.
[2] Johann Adolf, Freiherr von Thielmann, born in 1765, had fought on the French side in Russia in 1812, leading a Saxon cavalry brigade. In 1815 he commanded a Prussian corps at Ligny and Wavre.

Altenberg. The Saal covered them from further pursuit. Buonaparte, it is said, has gone to Leipsic. The distribution of his army on this side the Elbe is said to be as follows: thirty thousand men on the Töplitz route; fifteen thousand men in Dresden; fifteen thousand near Freyburg, Chemnitz, &c.; thirty thousand Meissen and Torgau; one hundred thousand Leipsic, where he has taken up his own abode, since the 28th, and where he proclaims: '*Gare à celui qui m'approche trop près et à l'aventure!*'

At Erfürth he has not many men, but it is now certain that fifty thousand men from the Rhine are to march there between the 14th and 20th of this month. They are half of the *arrière-ban* and have been organizing by Kellerman.

I always suspected and insisted that some force was forming to supply the vacancy between the Maine and the Saal: it was only this day that I could ascertain the fact. Buonaparte has committed faults, and occasionally adventured desperately, but in general he has made scientific war and attended to the consolidation of his military distributions. He particularly values support, and prefers successive aids to a superior advanced line. Bavaria, however, greatly astounds me. The news from the negotiators received this day assumes that the treaty only awaits the King's signature and that this signature will be given immediately. How Buonaparte can suffer that negotiation to proceed and appear indifferent, quite baffles my calculation. The defection of Bavaria appears, in my judgment, to secure Germany to the Allies. It is an event of such magnitude, that until the deed is irrevocably done I must be an infidel.

This day twenty-four thousand five hundred of Beningsen's infantry passed the Sovereigns. They are well-armed, efficient men, in martial but not in parade order. Their toilette arrangements seemed to mortify the Russian Emperor, but every one else was highly gratified at the sight of such a reinforcement. In five days the bearded twenty thousand under Tolstoy will arrive.

Prince Schwarzenberg, as a proof of his favour and confidence, has ordered that I shall daily have a copy of the report he makes to the Sovereigns (and the Sovereigns only) on the changes made in the location of his own troops and the intelligence he has received. This trait of amity and consideration is of great value. I, of course, shall give the reports to Aberdeen and they will be regularly transmitted to Government, who will thus be able to check the published accounts and keep a correct *tableau militaire*.

It is an additional pleasure to serve with men who feel an interest in promoting every wish I frame and who put so much liberality in every transaction. If ever I were to quit the British army, I certainly would take an Austrian uniform.

I have this evening received another proof of Russian favour. A most flattering rescript has been sent me by the Emperor, stating the motives which induced him to give me the Order of St. George, and that in the manner he did. It is almost too flattering to send home; but I shall do so by the next courier, that it may be inserted in the Herald's Archives with the grant of the Order by the Prince Regent. There it may rest for posthumous consideration; but I desire the boys may have a first perusal, that they may ambition to merit higher encomiums under more favourable British auspices.[1]

Oct. 9th, Chemnitz.

I give a soirée this evening: tea and punch to the Marshal and all his Generals here. The Emperor has even moved the furniture of my quarters. We need such recreations after the toils and soakings of our days.

Oct. 13th, Altenberg. 130th Pluviose.

On the 11th we quitted Penig. Rain as usual. We came to Altenberg, and I was glad to find myself again among the Vandals. On the 12th I rode with Prince Schwarzenberg to Borna and Espenheim, that we might reconnoitre the enemy. My military reports note the posts, occurrences, &c.; but not an observation which I made of the advanced guard being most rashly hazarded and liable to total extinction. Marshal Murat might not see the occasion presented for his glory, but if Buonaparte had been present I am sure the Russian army yesterday evening would have had seven thousand men minus. When we came back to Borna, drenched and covered with mud, the Prince thought it better to relieve our horses and go in post-waggon, so I accompanied him; but we soon regretted the change, as we were obliged, from the shortness of the carriage, to sit with our knees almost up to our breasts. Good-will, however, produces conformity, and in a short time we thought no more of our posture. In the course of our journey the Prince repeated to me various anecdotes which greatly interested me. Among them was a conversation of Talleyrand with Buonaparte, after his Moscow campaign. Talleyrand told it to the Prince at Paris.

"It is now, sire," said Talleyrand, "the general hope that you will make yourself King of France. You are Emperor of the French, but your conquests and that title belong to the army, not to your people.

[1] Alexander praised Wilson's indefatigable zeal and outstanding courage, his devotion witnessed by the Czar at Bautzen, and many other proofs of daring.

Your people have not known you as a sovereign, only as a general. If you will show some concern for them they will support you and your dynasty—if you will only be a military chief, your own reign is doubtful and the loss of the sceptre to your family certain." Buonaparte was displeased and T. remains in disgrace.

On another occasion Berthier told the Prince that he had said to Buonaparte: "Sire! it is time to make a peace that will allow others to live as well as ourselves. It is natural that when sovereigns feel humiliated and nations distressed they should seize every occasion to improve their condition. Hence these perpetual defections and wars. Besides, sire! if you fall during some contest it is almost certain that your child will not reign. The spirit of the people of France is awed, but not conciliated as yet." Buonaparte answered— "Berthier, you know nothing about the matter," and turned the conversation. "But," said Berthier, "I return frequently to the charge, for if these wars go on Jacobinism will sooner or later again prevail."

Schwarzenberg assures me that the Empress also feels great apprehension that her child[1] will not succeed to the throne, or rather that a greater misfortune than that may occur in the troubles of the times which would follow Buonaparte's death. And Buonaparte is himself convinced that the Jacobins are still a most powerful party in France; not the *sans-culotte* Jacobinism, but consular Jacobinism, which the want of a pre-eminent chief to assure the suffrages of the army would extend through the troops.

On our return we heard the joyous news of Bavaria's accession. This is indeed a substantial acquisition: well managed, it is decisive of the independence of Europe. If we will only ask Switzerland to form defensive connection I am sure she will grapple to the link, and then the equilibrium of Europe is almost re-established. I presume that Buonaparte calculates upon the advance of new troops from France to secure Franconia and his line of communication by Mainz and Wesel, but we ought to be masters of the field before they can take solid post, although Kellerman is already in march with some troops. If I commanded the Allies I would not attempt to dislodge Buonaparte from the Elbe; on the contrary, I would do all in my power to keep him there, and uncover Prussia to bring the troops from thence and place them on the other side of the Saal. I would have échelon on échelon to the Rhine.

Metternich has just arrived: he brings the treaty between Russia,

[1] Napoleon's Empress, Marie Louise, and their son, the King of Rome, born in March 1811. The latter never reigned, and died in 1832.

Austria and Prussia for signature. Each party is to have always on foot thirty-six thousand men for co-operation.

14th—I rode yesterday eight German miles to see men greatly fatigued, drenched to their bones, and doing nothing but what ought not to be done. The fact is, that Wittgenstein did not choose to make the reconnaissance and therefore marred it expressly.

This morning the Prince-Marshal, having seen an officer from Blücher, wished me, as I was acquainted with all the parties, to ride and stop the action if circumstances permitted. I went like the wind more than four German miles and arrived in time to stop the infantry before it advanced from the village of Gossa, and to be in several brilliant charges: in one of these I thought I saw Murat, and was making to him, when a body of French horse charging in flank threw us into complete disorder. The two Austrian dragoon regiments then darted in and saved us, or we should have been all spiketted I verily believe. I never was in greater mêlées; and when in them and out of them we were all covered with mutual shot, shells and grape, so that it was in good truth '*multum in parvo*.' When the action ceased I clapped spurs into my best horse and rode a race against time to Borna. There I put four horses into a little calash, almost too light for two, that I made fly like the famous Queensberry car:[1] but 'man proposes and God disposes'; before I had gone a werst one of my wheels locked in a cart. I was thrown out and the axle-tree broken. I had no alternative but to mount one of the postilion's horses and ride him to Altenberg, tackled as he was and unfortunately, as I still feel, with a piece of wood as a stirrup leather to the right stirrup, that the pole of the carriage might not break the leg; but it appears to me that if I had ridden twenty miles in this way instead of ten I should have had a wooden leg all my life.

The troops, &c., passing in the wood stared not a little. The inhabitants of Altenberg were astounded, but I clattered on quite indifferent to their regards and thoughts until I met the Emperor in a droska, to whom I first told the tidings of which I was the herald, and then joined with him in a laugh at myself: for certainly I was a strange figure, and the more from being covered with mud from head to heel. He was, however, much pleased, and, as good or ill luck would have it, when I went to the Prince-Marshal's he and Metternich were looking out of the window, so I passed another review.

The Marshal was much delighted with the manner in which I had executed his wishes and, although he had dined, would not let

[1] William Douglas, Duke of Queensberry (1724–1810), 'old Q', millionaire, patron of the turf and opera.

me stir out of the room before his cook had produced samples of his active skill.

I have been obliged to write my despatch to Lord Cathcart and I am not a little tired, but if I were not to snatch the few moments when I am not on horseback or employed on indispensable business, I never should be able to keep my diary.

I must not omit to note that the Crown Prince has had a battle royal with the foreign generals and ministers about his person. He told them that he wanted no counsel, and would have no counsellors; but Blücher will not obey his order to retreat.

I must be just, although I do not like the man. I think the sacrifice of his communication with Sweden is too much to require of him. He has natural cause to fear such a position, as it may affect his royal interests and personal security. I am more inclined to think so, as I do not believe his thirty thousand men would win a battle. After what I have seen today I am sure we shall have more on our hands than is generally expected, and that we shall find the enemy more powerful, as well as more numerous, than is encouraging. If we fight in a semicircle from Ackern to Naunhof, a distance of at least seventy-five wersts, I am sure we shall be beaten. Concentration and échelons can alone give us a chance; and with these a new formation of cavalry is necessary, or the enemy will ride masters in the field.

For the benefit of *country gentlemen* I must state that the enemy has not less than two hundred thousand disposable men, of which above forty thousand are cavalry, and that Leipsic is a walled city with a castle and a wet ditch.

Oct. 15th, Pegau.

We are now to give battle tomorrow to Buonaparte. The events of war are most uncertain and events frequently contradict—and in the public estimation shame—good counsel. But certainly if I were Commander-in-chief I would not have fought Buonaparte in his position, where I believe him to have one hundred and eighty thousand men. I would have opposed, as I have before said, successive *barrières d'ailes* to his communications with France. I would have forced all the states of the Rhine Confederation[1] to have acquiesced in the wishes of their people and armed against his passage; and then when I had proved that he could not with reasonable hope of success attempt to force my ramparts, or in any case

[1] Formed under Napoleon's protection in 1806 to further his imperial plans, it gradually embraced every German state except Prussia, Austria, Brunswick and Kurhessen. It broke up in 1813.

derive succours through them, I would have proposed to him terms of peace. If he accepted them—and they should have been such as he could not refuse,—or refuse without revolting all the chiefs about him—I would have left to the indignant spirit of France and six months' time the completion of what would have remained to do that the world might have better chance of tranquillity.

He now has great advantages, especially since the troops from Magdeburg—probably Davoust's advanced guard—have taken Bernburg. His communication with Magdeburg and Wesel is now assured, and I still presume that he will form a screen against us, keep turning the left of the Swedes and, when he has sufficiently advanced, throw a corps out between the right of Blücher and the Austrian left to prevent Blücher's junction with us. If he makes this attempt, and succeeds, Blücher and the Crown Prince must soon disperse for want of ammunition, &c. The Austrians will, no doubt, in the interim be driving back the screen; but the screen keeping its right upon Leipsic can roll upon that pivot and recede as the main army advances. The Allies extend from left to right above a hundred wersts! and Bubna with ten thousand Austrians, and Beningsen with twenty thousand Russians, from the corps blockading Dresden, cannot be up for three days to co-operate. They, however, secure our right and communications at this moment, and so far they are very useful.

To add to our difficulties, there is great variance in opinion between the Russian *fainéants* [idlers] and the Austrians. Disputes run high frequently, and Schwarzenberg cannot obtain obedience to his orders, much less preserve subordination.

This morning he was obliged to send Wittgenstein a very severe but merited reproof, as he pretended that the order which I carried yesterday prevented his '*extermination* of the enemy'; whereas I particularly told him that he was not to desist from the combat if he was likely to lose any advantage or experience any detriment. The fact, moreover, was that man and horse had had as much as they could digest for the day, and failed in appetite. Three Prussian weak regiments of cavalry alone lost twenty officers killed and wounded.

Perhaps what I have written here with regard to my apprehensions may be realized; perhaps my fears may have been premature. Fortune has so much influence in war that calculation is more frequently in error than in unison with events; but I submit my judgment to the awful test which is to determine its value; and certainly if occasion offers I shall make the same efforts as I did at

Lützen, at Bautzen and at Dresden, to help a conclusion different from my predictions.

If the worst come to the worst on this occasion, it will be some consolation to think that nature is not idle in our cause. Buonaparte we are assured is grown so fat and unwieldy that he cannot get on horseback without help; and he is so averse to exercise that he now always accompanies the troops in a carriage. He is thus *Kutusoffizing* very fast.

I shall conclude this medley by noting that Ney advised Buonaparte to fall back on the Rhine, recruit during the winter and give the law to Europe in the spring. Ney received an answer brought by a French colonel, chief of the staff of Berthier, who was taken yesterday, and to whom Ney having told what he had written said: "And the Emperor has sent by you that it is *des sottises*. I am sorry to have offended the Emperor, but I am too much attached to him and France not to retain and repeat the same opinion."

Berthier continues too ill to transact business, but perhaps the cannon will rouse him from his couch.

The country through which we are passing is in great distress. The Cossacks have devoured or destroyed the little that the stagnation of commerce had enabled the inhabitants to provide.

The needy manufacturer trusting that the ports will be opened by our arms, and thus his losses be repaired, shrieks through his famished throat '*Vivas*' to the Emperor, who salutes with the courtesy of a Bolingbroke[1] even the workhouse paupers; but in the districts which are not commercial '*on n'entend que des faussettes*,'[2] as was once before said in Italy when boys and girls were applauding Philip of Spain.

In many parts of Germany it is said that the Cossack terror is so great that prayers are put up: '*De Cossaquibus, Domine, libera nos!*' In other churches they have added the term Cossack to the original Devil as more expressive of his mischievous proceedings. It is a great pity that they should be so lawless, for they counterbalance the service which they render. I would forgive their pillage of eatables, but not of raiment, trinkets, and indeed all transferable property, although *Love* is the motive.

Oct. 16th, Rotha.

We marched at three o'clock this morning. I accompanied Prince Schwarzenberg. The soldiers rent the air with voluntary cheers as he

---

[1] Henry, Viscount Bolingbroke (1678–1751), orator, statesman and writer, who was Secretary for War and Foreign Secretary under Queen Anne. He was admired for his charm of manner and personal grace.

[2] This should be *fossettes*, literally little holes made by children playing marbles. 'The clink of marbles.'

passed. This compliment was usual to the Grand Duke Charles, but it was the first time that Schwarzenberg had been honoured by it.

Oct. 20th, Leipsic.

On the morning of the 19th the Allied army advanced. The disposition of attack as follows.

Giulai guarded the route of Weissenfels and had his post at Mark Ranstedt. Merfeldt's corps commanded by Prince Lewis Lichtenstein was charged with the attack on Connewitz and Delitszch. Colloredo's column moved upon the Elster. Wittgenstein and the Prussians upon Leipsic by the route of Probstheyda. Kleinau upon the right by the villages of Holzhausen and Zukelhausen. Beningsen upon the right of Kleinau in the direction of Leipsic via Stetenitz, and Platow connected the right of Beningsen with the Swedish Prince's moving from Taucha, and which was in connection with Blücher.

The enemy fell back with some loss to the village of Probstheyda and Stetenitz, but there they defended their line with the right thrown on Connewitz, from which they could not be dislodged. Delitszch, after being lost three times, was gained by the Austrians in a fourth assault. Colloredo was kept in check by a superior force. The Russians and Prussians lost an infinity of men against Probstheyda by unskilful management, but *not* the fault of the Prince-Marshal. Kleinau and Beningsen were unable to force Stetenitz. Platow took two regiments of Würtemberg cavalry and about a thousand infantry prisoners: and three thousand Saxons, including seven hundred cavalry with fifteen guns, joined the Allies during the action; but not without losing many men in the passage, from the enemy's grape which was profusely thrown at them. The action ceased with night.

The Allies, exclusively of Beningsen and the Crown Prince, had to lament the loss of at least twenty-five thousand men at the lowest computation. The enemy had suffered largely, but not to the same extent. They had, however, lost three guns in front of Probstheyda, and had so many horses killed that they were obliged to blow up several parks of ammunition-waggons and bury about twenty guns which were found this morning. During the day Giulai had reported that the enemy were debouching on the Weissenfels and Merseburg route with such force as to oblige his flank movement upon Merfeldt's corps. The enemy's retreat was therefore opened, and this morning at daybreak the army advanced against Leipsic; but about ten o'clock a great portion was sent on the route to Pegau that the enemy's retreat on the Saal might be checked. The remainder approached the Faubourg, and, after some cannonade, a flag of truce was sent by the King[1] proposing to surrender the town if the troops in it were allowed to retire. This was refused and the King given to understand that there was no treaty to be made with him since, as the Emperor loudly declared, he had broken his word, having signed a treaty with Austria which three days afterwards he violated. The attack continued and, notwithstanding an obstinate defence, the Allies forced the suburbs. A momentary confusion ensued, as some cuirassiers to effect their retreat had to pass through the advanced parties of the Russians; but order was quickly re-established.

When the city gates were opened and the marketplace reached, the King was found in one of the houses, and all his guards with his Baden troops assembled under arms. They had refused to fire upon the Allies. Vast numbers of Polish officers and other officers also streamed out of the houses in which they had concealed themselves. On the other side of the town the enemy still fired from the houses of the suburbs, and an open space round the wall was full of abandoned cannon, carriages, tumbrils, horses, men and women, prisoners, wounded and dead. The retreat of Moscow did not present a scene of greater confusion and ruin.

The distress of the enemy had been rendered greater by the road out of the town being very narrow, and on the right of it ran the Pleisse with steep boarded banks. In the stream many horses and cattle were plunging, and many bodies were floating. Here also it is said that Poniatowski perished, suffocated rather than drowned. After some time the enemy who escaped fell back behind the Elster and burnt the bridges, so that they have remained all the day unmolested since this operation. But they keep firing cannon upon the Allies debouching.

Fortunately the Swedes and Prussians only, supported by Beningsen, will pursue the enemy; for the novelty of the dress causes great embarrassment. The rest of the Allies will take flanking routes. It is impossible at the present moment to state the extent of the enemy's loss, but it exceeds a hundred guns, five hundred ammunition-waggons, and five thousand prisoners, exclusive of former wounded. Lauriston and several generals are taken already, and it is to be presumed that many persons of note are still concealed.

Buonaparte himself left the city at ten in the morning.

To the credit of the Allies it must be stated that they were guilty of very few excesses, and none in the city itself. They are entitled too

[1] King Friedrich August IV of Saxony.

to much admiration for their humanity. Very few of the enemy were put to the bayonet.

As I was one of the first who entered I immediately went up to the King and assured him that protection was ordered to the inhabitants and I gave a Russian company as a guard for himself, his equipages, &c. He seemed much affected, and said: "This misfortune was not to be foreseen."

Having followed the enemy to the Elster and aided the general dispositions, particularly for the re-establishment of order, which was very difficult, I re-entered the city as I had entered it amidst "*Vivats*," while handkerchiefs waved over my head, and garlands fell on it. *C'était un brave moment.*

On returning into the town and while I had five very pretty French women clinging to me, and four officers of rank, a horse, and a superb mule which I took from a mounted infantryman, in my train for protection—I met the Emperor, the King, Crown Prince, &c., and announced the capture of the artillery, which was a much greeted intelligence. Some time afterwards Blücher joined this distinguished assemblage.

When the Sovereigns had paraded through the streets and had retired, the Emperor Francis came into the town and I accompanied him to show the spoils. At the same time I made use of the opportunity to speak to him and Metternich on more important matters. The principal subject was Dantsic. Very much is concerned in the occupation of that fortress. The fate of Europe depends much upon its falling into Prussian hands *by convention* at this time; since the opportunity is offered *now* but cannot return.

The Emperor greatly approved and never could a sovereign greet a subject with more cordiality.

Wittgenstein instantly seized my idea. As the Emperor passed, the King of Saxony stood at his window. The Emperor felt for his situation and much commended my attentions.

The enemy is now in full march for the Saal; but it is probable that Giulai's and Merfeldt's corps will distress him before he passes, although Weissenfels is only six German miles from Leipsic.

Buonaparte's pressure here has tarnished his military credit,[1] but previously he had acquired and not lost reputation. Indeed I should rather say that he baffled us in both days' previous combats. He certainly moreover proved that if we had entered Saxony without

[1] "It was not then known that he had ordered three bridges to be constructed." Note by Sir R. W. in after years.

Beningsen and the passage of the Elbe by Blücher we should have been annihilated.

Schwarzenberg has the merit of having saved the army intrusted to his command. No doubt our success will be greatly exaggerated; and again we shall be at the Rhine in a fortnight *per courier*, but much is yet to be done. We may achieve great advantages, but yet we may be unable to make great progress. Much will depend on the ability of the enemy to retire from Dresden and join Davoust at Magdeburg, and the number of men actually on march from France under Kellerman. After our reduction of numbers we cannot cope with any very considerable reinforcement, except on the defensive.

Had the enemy not wanted provisions, I even doubt whether he would now have retired so precipitately; but for eight days there has not been a bit of white bread in Leipsic and the troops lived upon the charitable donations of the inhabitants.

When I calculate all the political and military disadvantages of a coalition such as ours—the want of zeal to continue the war in the Russian army—the inability of Prussia to repair her losses—and the certainty of Buonaparte being able to acquire great strength before the spring, I have no hesitation in giving my voice for peace on the terms which Buonaparte offers.

If we are now too elated and direct our view to encroachment on the natural boundaries of France, or to change of dynasty by compulsion, we may find that extravagant pretensions diminish our power of enforcing them. I wish to secure the future while the force of Europe is concentrated. Opinion in France will achieve then what remains to be done.

By present arrangement we can make France herself useful to the views which statesmen ought to entertain. By the extinction of the French power we should find victory a misfortune, since the proper balance could not be secured and the variety of interests at issue would assuredly produce new wars, prematurely for Prussian and Austrian interests.

I am an anti-Buonapartist and a soldier, but not a *grenadier politicien* —*un homme d'état enragé*, sacrificing general interests to personal passions.

21st—During the night there was a cry of "Fire!" and I went to assist, as it was in the neighbourhood of an abandoned French park of powder-waggons, &c. It burnt several hours before it was got under.

This morning the Emperor of Russia sent for me.

Mistaking something I had said yesterday he answered rather sharply at the time. On my entering this morning he expressed his distress, declaring that it had been on his conscience ever since, and that he could not feel comfortable until I declared that I bore no pained recollection towards him on that account.

On my saying what I really felt on the occasion he kissed me again and again, and certainly showed a very good heart, as well as an amiable manner.

I know very few men indeed in the world who would have taken such pains, and so liberally acknowledged error.

The discovery of men, booty, &c., continues, as I anticipated, and to General Lauriston we may add General Regnier; but unfortunately his maps have all been torn or destroyed by the Cossacks, which is a very great loss, as many were manuscripts.

I find that Buonaparte told the King he could do no more for him than send back his troops—which he did. An English merchant tells me he quitted the town about half an hour before I got in, and passed through with a very cheerful countenance.

9 o'clock P.M.—Blücher lost in the corps of Yorck alone on the 17th of October eight thousand men.

It will now be undeniable that the position of Buonaparte was most advantageously chosen. In it he resisted all; in it he wounded all; and he was enabled eventually to secure his retreat with the sacrifice of a rearguard.

The news from Dresden is that Tolstoy has been obliged to raise the blockade and retire upon the Töplitz route. St. Cyr might thus pass rapidly by Freyburg and gain Coburg, whence he could reach the Thuringer-wald, doing much mischief in the line of march; but I think he will prefer the right bank of the Elbe.

Oct. 22nd, Zeitz.

Yesterday the Emperor Alexander went to the Queen of Saxony who wept very much; but I am told that she was more satisfied before the Emperor left her. I hear that the King will be re-established, but I suppose he must pay *garnish*.

Prince Poniatowski's death is universally lamented: he deserved a better fate. His conduct of the Polish contingent, and their corresponding conduct, has been splendidly distinguished.

I fear the 'Polar Star' has sunk to rise no more; but England could make a satisfactory arrangement if she were inclined to interfere on the subject.

The Crown Prince was still in Leipsic when I went away, dressed like an opera-master. Stewart is outrageous with him, and has omitted all compliment in his despatches. He had, indeed, introduced some strong animadversions, but these he has erased. Stewart decidedly says that he not only did nothing but wilfully avoided doing anything, although he might, by co-operating with Blücher, have crushed a great portion of the enemy's forces; and yet for such a fellow we are to pay one hundred thousand pounds a-month, and sacrifice our best interests and another nation whose enmity will be eternal. I would rather see more than I choose to write than Norway ceded to Sweden.

I omitted to note that, after passing through the city, I went on with some Swedes against the enemy. One party covered the retreat of others, and were lodged in several houses beyond the river Pleisse. These fellows fired sharply and all the Swedes ran away as hard as they could; I was obliged to go back into the town and take a Russian company to dislodge the enemy. They did the business in the most masterly as well as intrepid style. I am sure that the Swedes are a brave people, but they do not appear to me well organized. They seem rather like armed peasants than the martial compatriots of Charles XII.[1]

The town in which I now am has paid dearly for its deliverance. It has been thrice plundered; but most efficaciously by the Cossacks, who have dispatched from hence waggonloads of cotton goods and kerseymeres to the Don. Here, as everywhere else in Germany, the first question is—"And when shall we have English goods?" and "Do you know Mr. Humphrey or Mr. Goodison?" &c.; for they all suppose that we are in intimate union with the traders. Had Buonaparte not adopted his continental system he might have ruled over very willing subjects in Germany.

I have just been suffering martyrdom. The daughter of the house imagines that she has a melodious voice. Unasked—she began to play a guitar, and then chant, by way of *amusing* me, a death-song of Schiller's[2] comprising at least forty stanzas. Without giving herself time to breathe, as soon as she had concluded, she rushed into a funeral-hymn on the Queen of Prussia's interment and then galloped into a la-la-la-lara ditty which had not ended when I quitted the room, although I had waited patiently twenty minutes for its termination.

Oct. 24th, Weimar.

Yesterday the Marshal had the returns of the Austrian expenditure of shot in the two days' battle, by which it appears that fifty-six

[1] King Charles XII of Sweden (1682–1718) was defeated by Peter the Great at the great battle of Pultawa in 1709, and later fell in action at Friedrichshall.
[2] Friedrich Schiller (1759–1805), German poet and dramatist.

thousand cannon balls and seven thousand shells were fired from the three hundred and twenty Austrian guns engaged. Altogether, including the enemy's cannon, one thousand six hundred guns were in action. The rattle may therefore be calculated, but the thunder can scarcely be conceived.

The Duke of Weimar[1] gave us a grand fête this day. The entertainment was magnificent and the whole establishment upon a splendid scale. In the evening I went with the Marshal to the theatre, but we only remained during one act. The building and decoration are in very good taste, and the performance respectable; but affairs do not admit of protracted amusements.

I have just sent the King of Prussia my noble mule, as he has a set and wants a recruit.

25th—The enemy have fallen back behind Erfürth, but the intention to abandon it to the defence of the garrison is not fixed, although the Bavarians and Austrians, sixty-one thousand strong of which twenty-four thousand are Austrians, under General Fresnel, have reached Würzburg this day by a most extraordinarily rapid march, as they only left Braunau on the 17th. Würzburg is strong, but Wrede proposes to push on to Frankfort. We move tomorrow to Eisleben on the left of the Erfürth road.

The Emperor of Austria has peremptorily demanded the Saxon contingent to be put under his orders. He said, *de haute voix*, that he was "resolved to have the Saxon troops. They came over to him, and he was their protector, as well as the friend of the Allies." That "Prussia's cause was his and his cause Prussia's; so that she could not object, and no one else had any interest in the matter." The Emperor Alexander was obliged to admit the right of his claim. '*Red Breeches*,'[2] I am glad to find, feels his value and will keep his own; for much as I like the Russians I do not wish to see them masters in Germany. "Every man to his own, and God for us all," but I am against cosmopolite appetites *et l'appetit vient en mangeant*—so that no limits are at last respected.

On going to dine with the Duke of Weimar today I found the Emperor Francis and the Grand Duchess together, and without any attendants, so I had nearly half an hour's conversation with them. In the course of it the Emperor said "he came to me by attachment and I will take care to keep him."

This remark I note, as it assumes Lord Aberdeen's wish; but

[1] Karl August (1775–1828) the friend and patron of Goethe who was invited in 1775 by the Grand Duke to make his home at Weimar. The Duke had commanded a corps in the 1806 campaign.
[2] The Emperor Francis's nickname.

without that remark I was well assured that no difficulty would arise in that quarter: on the contrary, that there would be the greatest *empressement*.

I suppose that Lord Aberdeen will arrange the matter somehow or other. I have written to him—"that I wave all personal feeling in the matter; that I am ready to go to England, but am sure that my presence at this important crisis is of advantage to the public interests; that no one but myself can be *au fait* of what is passing, and no other person instantly, if ever, enjoy that confidence which I have from all."

Nothing is done militarily or politically that I am not told instanter; nothing arrives that I do not see; nothing is discussed that I do not hear. There never was an ambassador more valuably aided.

I mention these facts as public features, not with any petty ostentatious feelings.

I should hope Lord B.[1] would be reasonable. Italy must be as good to him who has no immediate connection with the German army.

Lord Cathcart would not now object to my transfer. He knows that I am resolved on returning home otherwise. This is not his wish, and he will rather be inclined to arrange *à l'aimable*.

Oct. 27th, Gotha.

During the night of the 26th Lord Aberdeen arrived with Morier, and could get no other quarters than the room in which I and Charles were sleeping, as the town was overflowing full.

The next morning we went to Schwarzenberg together and had a long conference. Schwarzenberg confirmed all that I have written about the difficulties of his command; the hazards which hourly endangered his affairs; and the necessity for peace so soon as it could be made with reasonable chance of security. He particularly lamented the Russian arrangement with the Saxons, or rather their derangement; for all the Saxons have refused to serve if their King is made prisoner, or if they are detached from Austria to the Crown Prince. I strongly urged also the dissatisfaction that a war of vengeance and premature partition would excite in England; and reminded Aberdeen and Schwarzenberg of the impression which the elevation of the Austrian flag at Valenciennes and the Dunkirk expedition had still left on our country.[2]

[1] John Fane, Baron Burghersh, afterwards 11th Earl of Westmorland (1784–1859), had in 1811 married Priscilla, one of Wellington's nieces. He was in 1813 appointed Military Commissioner to the H.Q. of the Austrian Army in Germany, and in the following year Minister Plenipotentiary to the Court of Tuscany.
[2] In the summer of 1793.

I came here this day to track the enemy and see the town: the dead and dying sick were numerous on the route, but there was no other vestige of distress.

I called on the Duke, a man of about forty years of age. He was dressed in the ancient style of German princes, his ancestors, according to the pictures ranged in his spacious galleries. He seems, however, a sensible man, and bears a very good character with his people, who were living comfortable and happy until war devastated their tenements and lands. He did not conceal from me that personally he thought Buonaparte a most interesting and great man, and greater in misfortune than in success. He had with him, on passage through here, much conversation, on which it appears that Buonaparte showed that he did not feel humbled or apparently grieved at what had occurred.

I was taken, bespattered as I was, into the grand dining-hall, where I found the Duchess and Court in full gala dresses at table. The animal appetite would have preferred a household second dinner to the remains of the state banquet; but the Duchess was particularly amiable, and the presence of an Englishman really did diffuse here a very general satisfaction.[1]

After dinner I went through the palace, which is a very fine building, the rooms splendidly furnished, and the whole establishment noble.

I hope, for the sake of his friends, that the minister Stein will not come here; I am sure his fingers will itch when he sees all the glitter of this ducal property

I omitted to make a memorandum of a serious loss which occurred to me in Weimar. I had taken the chain and seals off the repeater which I sent to Jemima, and absenting myself for half an hour from my room the whole disappeared. The daily inconvenience that I shall experience from the loss of my seals will be very great. I have advertised them through the armies, but I fear without any prospect of success.

This, added to a very cold dark night's ride to our first quarters from Weimar, and reflections arising from a letter of Lord Castlereagh to Lord Aberdeen, rendered the gaiety of Gotha and the extraordinary appearance of the sun on Sunday very necessary to restore me to good humour.

The 27th of October is a memorable day in this year, for it passed

[1] In a letter to Lord Aberdeen, Wilson wrote: "The reigning Prince looks mad and dresses like the oddities in his galleries, but in talk is a sensible and shrewd person. The Duchess is a *bonny lass*, and a young Princess a ripening beauty."

without rain; indeed, the weather seems to be changing altogether
—a heavy frost, and winter setting in. Snow has already appeared,
and there is fresh ice every night.

I have mentioned Lord Castlereagh's letter. The paragraph relating to me commences by promising to write again to Lord Aberdeen by the next messenger, but continues—"I have no objection
to give you W. if you wish it, but it must be after B. is well fixed.[1]
I promised B. that he should go to Schwarzenberg's army, and it
would not be fair to change his destination unless he approves. I
foresee great difficulties unless he will voluntarily go to the South,
but W. and he must not have any connexion together or there will
be a *blow up*."

It is thus evident that B., with the rank of Lieutenant-Colonel
and no service, has had a superior military consideration to myself
in the Foreign Office and that all my claims are but secondary to
his pretensions: all the wishes of Lord Aberdeen, the Emperor,
Count Metternich and Schwarzenberg—as they have *officially*
communicated them to Lord C., but subservient to his pleasure.

Oh, Justice! thou art without respect *dans les bureaux des gouvernements*.

B. had the appointment to Schwarzenberg's army because it was
thought the best; but here, with his rank and forced presence, he
must play a minor part. It is different with me who have the consideration of a General officer, fellowship of long services, bond of
distinction and the established confidence of the Sovereign, the
minister and the chiefs. From me nothing is withheld connected
with public interests—from him everything will be withheld. From
me all opinions will be cordially accepted and attentively weighed
—from him no suggestion will come with any weight, or inspire any
kind feelings towards him from superiors.

At this important epoch it is of the utmost consequence that
Aberdeen should be daily informed of passing events, projects in
contemplation, &c.; that he should be able to work with a person
conversant in all matters interesting to him, and who possesses the
breast-key of the magnates. He also considers my comments of
value, since they embrace the subjects in a way that affords him the
full view. With a stranger, and that stranger a comparative subaltern officer, he is deprived of these aids. Were the war about to
commence instead of closing, knowing what I do of the *state of Italy*,
the great springs already in action there, and the intentions of
Government, I should prefer the appointment; with the proviso

[1] Lord Burghersh had been accredited to the Austrian Army as military commissioner,
and was placed at Schwarzenberg's headquarters.

that I should reap the harvest if I toiled successfully in the cultivation of the field.

I foresee important responsibility political and military, eminent consideration, extensive intercourse, and most advantageous ramifications of action. Independence to a great degree, and numerous opportunities for brilliant service are inseparable from the station: but how could I expect to keep the post when the Government entertained the same views of its value?

Lord Aberdeen insists on my staying with Schwarzenberg and, after the Emperor's recorded desire, he thinks himself authorized to keep me. We shall see the issue. At all events, I rejoice in the assurance of my discharge from Cathcart with whom I may then live on good terms and who will begin to acknowledge the good service I have rendered under his orders.

While at Gotha I heard more anecdotes about the Crown Prince, who is now daily becoming more generally unpopular. Pozzo di Borgo, indeed, says that his soldiery only await the moment to get rid of him altogether. It is impossible that they should not feel ashamed of him, for he is ridiculous to the highest degree. He, however, offends at the same time by his affectation. In the field he ordered Löwenheim[1] to go *ventre à terre* with some order. The Count said that he had already two horses killed and he found that his third was quite knocked up. "*Allez à pied!*" was the reply. In one of his speeches before Leipsic, he said: "The Swedes are now about to have the glory of fighting under the eyes of their Prince!" and then turning to them, he concluded with the climax, "*Allez vous faire tuer—vous faire tuer—tous!*"

Stewart, however, has greatly shocked some Swedes by answering to an observation that prayers were put up in the churches for the Crown Prince's safety: "*N'ayez pas peur pour lui. Il se conservira.*"

Speaking of Jerome[2] the other day the Crown Prince said: "Oh! he must have a kingdom: he is my friend!" And seeing some Swedes leading some French wounded, he exclaimed: "*Vous voyez quelle sympathie! quel instinct!*" These words have startled the Norwegian *disposers*. On the whole, all despise him, and some fear him.

Oct. 28th, Tambach.

On arriving here I was told by the Marshal that Metternich was made a Prince and certainly he deserves the highest distinction for

---

[1] Count Gustav Lowenhjelm, Adjutant-General at the H.Q. of the United Army of the North of Germany, under Bernadotte.

[2] Jerome Bonaparte had been King of Westphalia, 1807–13.

the ability with which he has conducted the march of Austria, so as to preserve the political ascendency which circumstances thrust upon her.

I have had the sad misfortune to lose my superb Turkish sword. Allen was charged with the care of the carriage. Like a good-for-nothing fellow, as he has frequently proved himself in the care of my property, he quitted the carriage and in the interim my sword was lost. I have dismissed him from my service and he may now find his own way—he has passport and money, but no blessing from me. I am grieved beyond measure, but I endeavour to act like a philosopher though I cannot feel like one.

Oct. 29th, Schmalkalden.

We arrived here this forenoon. The ground was covered with snow, which rendered the celebrated wild Thuringia Forest more bleak in appearance than ever I anticipated. This town is remarkable for the Protestant league against Charles V.[1] It belonged to Hesse, but now to Westphalia. It is built in the most antique fashion.

We had intelligence, *en route*, of Würtemberg having joined Bavaria and I saw a Würtemberg officer who was allowed to leave the French army with a thousand men without any impediment being opposed by Buonaparte.

This is a further proof of Buonaparte's desire to make peace and his willingness to sacrifice the Rhine Confederation Protectorship.

Buonaparte seems to be taking the direction of Frankfort, in which case Wrede will fight him; but he may still turn on Wetzlar.

I understand that Buonaparte's bulletins of the Leipsic battles are here, but I have not yet seen them. He may certainly say that he baffled us the first day, held us in check the second and lost his rearguard the third day by the misconduct of his own people in cutting the bridges too soon. He may truly say all this and add from great encomiums on the bravery of his troops, without detracting the able dispositions of Schwarzenberg and the courage of the Allies.

We shall march on without any rest-day to Frankfort. The army will then repose if the enemy permits. In two more days we shall quit the bad cross-roads; but the bad weather will not leave us.

30th—The Emperor, Lord Aberdeen, &c., came to us yesterday. The Marshal, Metternich, &c., go over to the Emperor of Russia to settle various matters of business.

The wish for peace increases with all reasonable persons.

---

[1] The Hapsburg Emperor Charles V (1500–58). A league of Protestant princes was formed in 1538 to protect their religion and territories; it dissolved after the Emperor's victory at Nuïhlberg in 1547 in the Schmalkaldisch War.

Nov. 1st, Fulda.

We arrived here after passing over a route packed by dying and dead Frenchmen and horses. The hospitals have the Siberian panic and remain untenanted. Now the most emaciated sick crawl on the highway to the rest of death. This is one of the many evils of the uncivilized system of war which has characterised modern times.

Blücher sent a despatch here noting his intention to turn off our road, which is a great benefit to us, as he leaves famine as his legacy; but the most memorable paragraph is: "The Crown Prince is advancing to Cassel *under the protection* of General St. Priest, who entered on the 30th."

This is an old town, much attached to the House of Orange, but poverty-struck by the war, pillaged by the passing enemy and replete with misery. In one hospital we found three hundred and fifty dying and one hundred and twenty dead.

I learnt this day that Stewart had received the Order of the Sword from the Crown Prince.[1] The Crown Prince has here shown himself skilful: "*Il a préféré ses intérêts à ses passions.*"

The Emperors of Germany receive their crowns at Frankfort. I am there to be decorated with my Theresan Collar, and I shall be as proud of it as any prince has ever been of his insignia. In England this feeling might create a philosophical sneer, but through continental Europe this badge is justly appreciated. To reconcile, however, the English philosophers I shall add that it is not only ornamental: it cannot fail also of being useful.

2nd—The messenger from General Fresnel arrived as we were about to march on Schluctern. He has postponed our journey two hours. The tidings he brings are most important, and on the whole very unfavourable. The Allied army has certainly been forced and very much shattered. Fresnel's words were "our loss is *sehr empfindlich*," which signifies sensible as well as considerable and I understand that the loss of officers is extraordinarily severe. I am sure from the details I have gathered that if Buonaparte estimates the loss at twenty thousand he will be within bounds.

The death of Wrede[2] will be a fatal blow to us. He was the life and soul of the alliance. Mongelas[3] will now again have the supremacy and the military exertions of Bavaria will languish. Fortune

[1] A Swedish military order, presented by Bernadotte in recognition of Sir Charles's conduct at Leipzig.
[2] Karl Philipp Wrede (1767–1838), later Bavarian representative at the Congress of Vienna, had been defeated by Napoleon at Hanau. He was wounded, but not killed.
[3] Count Mongelas, Bavarian *Ministerpräsident.*

has not yet deserted Buonaparte and, I repeat, he merits her favours more than ever.

After all his losses it appears that he has still eighty thousand men under arms and Kellerman writes that "between thirty and forty thousand had already passed the Rhine." With Kellerman's force, the Hesse Cassel forces, &c., he cannot have less than one hundred and thirty thousand men to defend the frontier and, as I think, keep footing on this side of the Rhine in the neighbourhood of Mentz Cassel (I prefix *Hesse* and *Mentz* to prevent mistakes by similarity of names).

Davoust's, St. Cyr's troops, the Danish troops, the garrisons, &c., still engage portions of the Allied armies; and the new conscription of one hundred and twenty thousand men, without including the war conscription of one hundred and sixty thousand, will make him very respectable and in my opinion intangible at present on the Rhine: for it may well be imagined that after thirty days' incessant marches on such bad roads, and in such weather, the effective state of the pursuers is not good, especially as the country is entirely ruined through which they pass. To make these exertions with comparative impunity the men must live well and have shoes. Neither of these needs can be supplied and it only astonishes me that without them we should muster so strong and look so cheerful as we do.

Nov. 2nd, Schluctern.

We arrived here this afternoon. On the road we had passed two hundred and seventy dead horses and one hundred and seventy bodies of men—the distance three and a half German miles; and many half-dead men were not included in this hundred and seventy. I did not see one carcase wounded—the whole had perished from disease and famine. Here we found Russian and Polish misery: a scene of general desolation and exterminating poverty.

Nov. 5th, Frankfort.

On the 3rd we marched to Gelnhausen where General Hake, the Prussian general, contrived to give a general fête in the midst of poverty and desolation.

Yesterday we made a forced march, passed by Hanau where I saw with pain a monument of Wrede's incapacity as a general and entered Frankfort in triumph.

We were well received; although Buonaparte gave the inhabitants warning not to commit any follies, as he should reappear in the spring and particularly cautioned them against importations of English merchandise.

213

It was the Marshal's name-day. After dinner I rose and said—
"*Cest le jour de nom du Prince Maréchal. Je ne porte pas le toast à sa gloire, il en a assez; mais je porte le toast à la santé et au bonheur du Chef digne de l'Empereur qu'il sert et les braves qu'il commande.*"

The Marshal was loudly cheered, and I received the most affectionate thanks from the society when we rose. No man can be more, or more deservedly, beloved than the Prince. It was quite a high gratification to see the martial aspects of the grenadiers, throwing the joyful smile from their hearts into their countenances, as he passed through the streets. It was a proud welcome.

The complaints against Tchernigow in person, and all the Cossacks, increase and multiply so fast that the whole of Germany seems to have been swept already by their scourging brooms. "If the Cossacks will but pass the Rhine and destroy two or three villages, it will be worth a million of men to me," Buonaparte said, ungraciously. The Prince Marshal, however, knowing the effect not to be overrated, refuses firmly permission to the Cossacks, who are anxious to revel in the nest of the Moscow vultures.

Almost the first words Wrede said yesterday to the Marshal related to some arrangement for the removal of the Cossacks, on account of the mischief they do the cause and the army by their devastations.

5th—Yesterday the Emperor of Russia came into Frankfort. He wished to enter before the Marshal, but was disappointed; the people received him well, but with no extraordinary greeting.

Metternich gave us dinner. I happened to sit next to him, and had a very interesting conversation. He said that if the Allies would be cordial as to their real objects and put confidence in him he would engage to make a satisfactory peace or deprive Buonaparte of the support of France, which could alone enable him to make the necessary efforts.

He spoke highly of Aberdeen, but hoped that we should, as well as Russia, state our '*ne plus ultra*' and '*sine quibus non*,' without endeavouring to extract more as negotiations proceeded to the hazard of pacification and confusion of the negotiators. It is evident that he wishes to be charged himself with the full powers and I verily believe he would attain all the legitimate objects of the Allies, or throw the responsibility of further hostilities on Buonaparte.

This day the Emperor of Russia, the Prince Marshal and all the minor powers rode out to meet the Emperor Francis, who entered the city amidst the most joyous cheers, &c., of a people who evidently felt what their cries and gestures expressed. Since he gave up the sceptre it has not been 'a piping time of peace' for the inhabitants of Frankfort. They have paid pounds where they only paid pence and, what was worse, they were never sure of what remained.

Te Deum followed his entry and we froze for two hours in a cold church. The troops then filed by the Sovereigns, and this ceremony was almost as chilling. We then went to dine with Mr. Bethmann,[1] who gave *grande fête*. Afterwards we passed to the opera, where '*Titus*'[2] was performed before the Emperors and an overflowing house by some very able actors.

I should swell my diary into an encyclopædia if I were to note all that interested the eyes and ears in these eventful days, but I must not be too concise, as I wish to give a real *tableau* of the state of things according to the most accurate observations.

It appears that Buonaparte said, on passing, that "the Continental system was a chimæra" and the merchants of Frankfort consider that system at an end, whatever warlike changes may occur.

Mr. Müller, the great banker, on being asked by me whether he thought Buonaparte had the means to complete his conscription, informed me that he had been about a month since in France, and that the men were to be had and would be produced; but that great discontent prevailed at this never-ending war and that the peasants began to group together and, in defiance of Savary's espionage, express their ill-will and dislike of Buonaparte, to whose name they generally applied some disrespectful term. He further declared to me that when he was in France, an order was given for some prayers to be recited for Buonaparte, and that in the village where he was all the people quitted the church after the usual prayers and left the priest and his clerks to sing the appendix.

These are strong and expressive traits; but still Mr. Müller thought that France had great power.

All the persons here assure me that above seventy thousand effective men under arms passed through Frankfort with Buonaparte; General Fresnel, who commanded under Wrede, this day said publicly at table in answer to a question from me, that Buonaparte had not less than eighty thousand effective men after he quitted Hanau; and that with the preceding stragglers, &c., he would have a hundred and twenty thousand men in a fortnight under arms, of the original Leipsic force. This *calcul* tallies with mine and I am sure it is accurate.

[1] Simon Moritz Bethmann, a rich Frankfort banker in whose house Napoleon stopped for two days. He seems to have been a sort of agent of Russia, and his lavish entertainments put him and his wife in temporary vogue.
[2] Mozart's opera was first performed in 1791.

I had news from Brinken, who passed through here. He told Mr. Bethmann that he saw Buonaparte and was well treated by him, until he said that he was my aide-de-camp, when Buonaparte said: "Oh! if you are aide-de-camp to an English general you must be a spy," and ordered him immediately into France. His treatment from that moment became harsh.

8th—Yesterday morning Lord Burghersh came here. We dined together, with Aberdeen. I was always resolved not to make mine a personal affair with him and he presented himself in the same disposition, so we met and parted good friends.

This day Lord Aberdeen, having received another application from Prince Schwarzenberg, spoke to Lord B. on the subject of his appointment and in addition to the Emperor's, Metternich's and Schwarzenberg's opinions, expressed his own conviction that my removal would be prejudicial to the public service; he begged him to go to Italy, notwithstanding that Lord Castlereagh had appointed him to reside with the Commander of the Austrian army.

B. replied that he had no idea of being thrown into a secondary position—that he had the highest post and was resolved to keep it. At the same time he hoped I should not conceive that he acted with any ill-will towards me: he disclaimed all such feeling. Lord Aberdeen in vain urged the delicacy of forcing himself *malgré le souverain*, &c., and in spite of the public interest, but B. was inexorable.

On Aberdeen's mentioning his conversation to me, he said that if I could not be placed here and would not go to Italy—which he could not recommend, as I had been superseded by a junior officer —he would make it a *sine quâ non* with Government that Burghersh should not remain at headquarters so long as the Emperor, and himself consequently, were with the army; for Burghersh has instructions not to be in any way under his control.

I endeavoured calmly to judge what best became myself and what my friends would most approve. I have desired Aberdeen, therefore, to request Lord Burghersh to await another letter from Lord Castlereagh, which Lord Castlereagh notified his intention of sending. That letter will give an ultimatum which may settle the question *à l'aimable*: if not, the very arrival of a new courier will enable me to find a pretext for withdrawing to England without the unpleasant attraction of public observation to the real cause.

I have no shame to apprehend; but I cannot, as an Englishman, wish to excite an interest to the prejudice of a British Government in a private matter. I do not wish to become the object of such conversation. I have run my course without a spot in my character.

I shall present myself to my country free from reproach and loaded with proofs of approbation. I shall return no Government debtor: I shall carry with me testimonies that I have more claims on them than they on me; and their own friends—their most intimate friends —shall sign my certificates of unrequited labour.

Certainly I have been most harshly and undeservedly treated— most offensively slighted. The appointment of a junior officer is an insult as well as an injury. Government cannot plead ignorance of my wish. I will, however, keep on the high ground which now supports me, and not lose my footing by any rash and unadvised step. I have Aberdeen as my counsellor, who will regard my honour as well as my interests in all his opinions.

We have no letters later than the 12th of October; so there must be a courier in a few days, and then we shall come to issue.

In the evening we went to Bethmann's house and had an agreeable soirée. Metternich was there. Madame Bethmann is a Frankfort beauty, but she is not much of a Venus: although *on dit* that the Emperor of Russia has pronounced her to be the goddess.

George Jackson's diary provides further details of the ball.

As to women, I never saw at any *réunion* less beauty or more vulgarity. . . . The first in *rank* as well as beauty was the banker's wife, Madame Bethman, her pretensions to either one or the other being founded only on the poverty of all around her in both those qualities. Even a town-hall at Hull could hardly show a collection of women with less distinction in their appearance and manners. . . . There was a great crowd, but very little dancing. Alexander, and afterwards the King, led out Madame Bethman, whose eyes—the best part of her face—then sparkled almost as brightly as the diamond stars of her illustrious *cavaliers*. She displayed some fine diamonds herself, and was certainly most superbly dressed (ii, 354–5).

This day we dined with Cathcart. Tomorrow we attack Hochheim, where the enemy have an advanced guard, which is not very strong but it may be supported by his troops at Cassel.

10th—Yesterday I accompanied the Marshal in his droska to the ground near Hochheim: we there mounted. As the action advanced I could not refrain from putting myself at the head of his troops with another general, and entering the town on foot through the palisades.

I was prompted to do so from a military motive, as our presence restrained the firing and the confusion which it would have occasioned when crossing our own columns piercing by other points: and again I was anxious to take an honourable farewell of my brave comrades, to show them that I embraced their fortunes to the last with undiminished zeal.

Altogether it was a fine spectacle and I really could have cried, as the men cheered on our return from a variety of highly-excited feelings.

We came back as we went and, after a journey of more than forty miles and so much exercise, sat down to dine with hunters' appetites.

This morning I gave my report to Lord Cathcart, who promised, for the first time in his life, to send it to England.[1]

About midday we had a parade. The Russian guards entered: they looked as well and turned out as complete as if Frankfort had been St. Petersburg. The Prussian guards bore them company and have much improved by the association. They had marched from Aschaffenburg to be looked at, and were marching back again as we have more troops here than we can feed.

Aberdeen, Metternich and Schwarzenberg have all expressed pain at my expected departure. Metternich will not hear of it and Schwarzenberg is equally vehement in protest. Independently of personal feeling they represent it to be most mischievous to the general interests and prejudicial to Austria and England; for I have a confidence with a consideration that no one else can enjoy, since there cannot be similar opportunities to found it.

This is their language and far weaker, indeed, than theirs, as Aberdeen will certify. Metternich even said that I possessed the military good opinion of Prince Schwarzenberg so much that he thought, as an officer, my presence was of the greatest value to him.

Extracts from two letters addressed by Lord Aberdeen to Lord Castlereagh are quoted in support of this claim:

Nov. 11th, 1813.

Schwarzenberg and Metternich have frequently spoken to me on the subject [of Sir Robert Wilson's removal]. The first has written to me in the most pressing manner; the latter has told me that he had it in command from the Emperor to express his sense of the

[1] In an accompanying note to Lord Castlereagh, Lord Cathcart wrote: "It has been the constant practice of the Major-General, throughout this and the last campaign, to accompany every attack of consequence that has taken place within his reach, and on this occasion he was with one of the storming parties. In adverting to this circumstance, it is but justice to this officer to state that the zeal, activity and intrepedity which he has displayed on every occasion have conciliated for him the esteem of all officers of every rank and nation who have been witnesses of them, and have certainly done great credit to His Majesty's service."

great services of Wilson and to state his wishes that he should continue with the army. Schwarzenberg told me that he would as soon part with Radetsky, the Quartermaster-general; that Wilson was admitted to all their councils; that they had the most entire confidence in his zeal and talents. His services in the field have been most conspicuous. On the 16th at Leipsic—which day was saved by the brilliant conduct of the Austrian cavalry under Nostitz—Schwarzenberg declares the success to be chiefly owing to the intelligence and able dispositions of Wilson. In short, to enumerate his military services would be endless. Great as they are, however, they fall short, in Schwarzenberg's estimation, of those which he has rendered out of the field. From his intimate knowledge of the Russian and Prussian armies and the great respect invariably shown him by the Emperor of Russia and the King of Prussia, he is able to do a thousand things which no one else could do. He was the means of making up a difference between the King and Schwarzenberg which was of the utmost importance. In short, I cannot possibly be deceived; I hear it from morning to night, from all nations; and I am perfectly persuaded there is no man in existence who unites in the fourth part of the degree, the love and admiration of the three armies. What Stewart is with the Prussians, Wilson is with all.

Again:

Nov. 17th, 1813.

The Emperor of Russia has flatly declared that he will take on himself the responsibility of *making* him [Wilson] stay; and that he will write to the Prince Regent accordingly. The King has been equally kind; and old Blücher has pressed him to come and share his quarters for the rest of the campaign, where he shall be treated as his son. But in the Austrian army, from the first to the last, the feeling is the same, and as strongly expressed. Schwarzenberg more than once in speaking of it [Wilson's removal] has absolutely cried with vexation: a pretty good proof that he was in earnest. He says, that in the disagreeable sort of command which he has over Russians and Prussians, if it were not for Wilson there are many things which he should never venture to propose. In the field it has frequently happened that he has sent Wilson to *persuade* Russian officers—nay! even the Emperor himself—to do what he would not otherwise have thought of.

Aberdeen agrees with me that I cannot remain or go to Italy without sacrificing my own consideration, Burghersh being with

Schwarzenberg ex-officio. I should be acting as a make-shift public servant: one who would bear all insults and all injuries, and be thankful for the bread of humiliation.

Metternich told me at dinner this day, that I should not go—that he would charge himself with the arrangement; but, although most capable to do all possible things, I suspect this undertaking is above his power.

Nov. 11th—The days pass as if it were the 'piping time of peace.' Courts, galas, parades, banquets, &c. &c., have succeeded the iron age. Last night there was a grand ball. All the Sovereigns were present, and a sufficiency of *beauté bourgeoise* to ornament the scene.

The theatre and stage formed the *salle*, and the boxes might have afforded a contemplative seat for a philosopher, but I did not see one at this interesting post.

I could make some remarks on the new congregated chiefs, but discretion buries them as they rise. Every *preux chevalier* [valiant knight] will however image them and feel as I have done.

To investigate motives of action would be unprofitable at this season.

Although the note of warlike preparation is not heard in Frankfort, still Mars is in the field. The columns are marching to their given stations, and the maxim is in force: '*Si vis pacem para bellum.*'[1]

My proposed departure for Italy has excited an extraordinary sensation. Monarchs, ministers, generals all combine to form a phalanx of support; and the Government of England will learn at least that an individual, without their favour, may acquire by loyalty of conduct to his country a consideration that is not to be overborne by the oppression of power.

I cannot write what has been said on the subject by the Emperor, the King and others, but they all tell their ministers in England to hold the same discourse; and Aberdeen will be the recorder of the aggregate as well as of much valuable detail. Nor is it a feature of minor credit that I have obtained the friendship, and from public motives command the zeal, of this personage in my cause. I may not be reinstated in my post, but I tower above the humiliation proposed.

17th, evening—I went to the Emperor at six o'clock. I shall not enter into all the details of our conversation, but note these words: "In Russia you rendered me the greatest and most essential service. You told me the real truth. I owed to you, and to you alone, a knowledge of what was passing. On my arrival at Wilna I verified all that you had written. I found all exact as to fact and accurate

[1] "If you desire peace, prepare for war."

as to opinion. I never but once imagined that I had any occasion to feel displeased with you. I was told that you under-stated the numbers of my army and thus would weaken the confidence of England in my power. I soon found out that I had not been well informed. Your zeal and the gallant efforts that you made proved still more my error. You have continued without intermission to augment your claims on my esteem and protection. I regard you as my friend—as one whose good services I shall never forget. I shall immediately dictate a letter to Count Lieven,[1] in which I shall desire him to express these sentiments to the Prince Regent and solicit that you may be at the headquarters of the Allies as heretofore. Indeed I shall take upon myself to prevent your departure for Italy."

Some conversation then passed with reference to a certain person, and also to another person who has been writing to England for my removal from the Russian headquarters, as I discovered by accident.

His charge against me was that I approved the armistice and recommended peace, if Austria did not join.

As he is a Prussian subject, I mentioned the matter to the King, who said: "To the armistice I owe my throne, but with regard to that said person he is a mischievous meddling being who requires constant surveillance." The King then proceeded, and told me that he should make his minister express his sentiments, without committing names according to my request.

Of this aforesaid person the Emperor said: "He is a man with a wild, heated imagination, and most intemperate. He has two or three times nearly ruined our affairs with the Crown Prince. He was an agent of the Hanoverian interest. His connection with Count Münster,[2] as proved by the letter containing the accusation against you, shows that this agency exists. He requires watching, and it is most fortunate that he has a Sovereign with judgment and circumspection enough to weigh well his character and observe his conduct."

Of the same person the Prince Schwarzenberg told me he had every reason to be *méfiant*; that it had been long evident to him that he was influenced by some policy foreign to the common interests. General Radetsky said to me, before the subject of this charge was mentioned to him: "I have received such and such a plan, and have had such and such conversation, but I have told the Prince that this

---

[1] Lieven was Russian Ambassador in London from 1812 to 1834.
[2] Ernst Friedrich Herbert, Count von Münster, was Hanoverian Minister in London. He later represented Hanover at the Congress of Vienna.

man is not counselling by his head but by the necessities of his purse. He is, I am sure, a *mauvais sujet* in some foreign pay."

I now name my accuser—Gneisenau,[1] an able officer, but such a man as I have described him, and who wrote to Count Münster a note in the sense I have stated, because he knew me to be a loyal friend to the Allies and an uncorruptible public servant.

There is no excuse for Government in giving credit to such a mercenary on his *ipse dixit*. No man is safe if such agents are respected as authority for condemnation.

I note these heads that my defence may remain on record, if the accusation be made public at home hereafter as a defence for Government; but I request that the matter may not be brought into notice through my information, as I am under promise to forbear and preserve silence. When I can notice the transaction I shall do so with astounding *éclat*.

I must not omit that when the Emperor spoke of the armistice, he said: "Your Government is always several months in arrear. It writes now as it might have been excused for writing on the first news of the armistice, but not at a time when we owe to that armistice all the success that we have obtained."

There is no answer yet from France, and the plan of campaign is not yet settled, but it will be in a day or two.

Count Bellegarde,[2] who is going to Italy as Commander-in-chief, will be here in a few days, and then, I think, notwithstanding the Emperor's veto, I shall make an excursion there for a short time.

24th—The calm of a few days appears the repose of years. Already the restless spirit murmurs at the tranquillity which has succeeded the perpetual motion of the last eighteen months.

The arrival of the King of Würtemberg produced some novelty to dissipate the thoughts of a day, and the entrance of the two Grand Duchesses yesterday enlivened the scene, but a change of locality only can satisfy the military craving of the army.

If the *Morning Post* had sent an imp here he would have found, however, much matter for his columns. Grand dinners, bon-mots, &c., afford a vast field for the journalist caterer.

The day before yesterday I should have been noted as the first in the order of the day: Metternich, Schwarzenberg, &c., being my guests.

---

[1] General August, Graf Neithardt von Gneisenau (1760–1831) was Blücher's Chief of Staff.

[2] Henri de Bellegarde (1755–1831), an Austrian marshal. Wilson had known him in 1794 and again at Verona in 1801.

November 24th, 1813

The Supplementary Despatches *of the Duke of Wellington, vol. viii,* contain an extract from a private letter written from Holland in December 1813 and forwarded to Wellington by a friend at the Irish Office.

I saw the celebrated Hettman Platow for the first time at Frankfort: he speaks no language but Russian and observed the ancient simplicity of costume so faithfully when I saw him that I should not have distinguished him from a common Cossack had I not been told who he was. I was walking at the time with Sir Robert Wilson, whom he stopped to tell him, through an interpreter, that it was evident he (Sir Robert) no longer loved him, and he wished to know the reason why. . . . On the 7th instant, the day previous to my departure from Frankfort, I was in company with General Wrede, who you will recollect received a ball in his abdomen at the battle of Hanau. He is perfectly recovered, and told me that having determined to get on horseback contrary to the advice of his surgeon, the effort which he made to get into the saddle forced the ball into a position where it does not give him the least pain.

You will have great pleasure in hearing that although the flower of chivalry may be said to be collected together from all parts of Europe, the few English officers who are with the armies decidedly bear away the palm of superior courage and enterprise. The Honourable Sir C. Stewart and Sir R. Wilson, with their aides-de-camp, are always at the post of danger, and seem to have no other object in view than to go in quest of death wherever it is most likely to be found. This appears the more remarkable as one is now a diplomatist and the other is merely an amateur, without any official appointment, military or civil; but, as the Yorkshireman says, 'they takes deloight in foighting.' Sir Robert wear five stars and two medals, which he has received from different sovereigns; Sir Charles wears a constellation (pp. 562–3).

Dec. 3rd—This morning was the fête of one of the foot-guard regiments, on which occasion there is always a gala. At the parade the Emperor came up to me, took me by the hand, and asked why I did not wear the new medal for the campaign of 1812.[1] I replied that 'I awaited his orders to be nationalized.' He answered that no one deserved the medal better and said other flattering words, which, as relating to that campaign, was most interesting to me.

Before dinner the Emperor again spoke to me on the subject of

[1] Lady Burghersh wrote: "They are very pretty—silver medals hung to light blue ribbon."

the Moscow medal, and desired General Arakchiew[1] to send me one, who immediately asked me to accept his. But the Grand Duke, over-hearing the Emperor, desired me to '*chasser*' all others and wear his own, as he 'did not care for the Tory frowns.' I answered that certainly by this distinction he 'added *valoir* to the Whigs.' This joke about Whigs and Tories is always on the tapis whenever he sees me or speaks of me; and, indeed, he always asks as his first question of every Englishman, 'Are you a Whig or a Tory?' Some one had told him that Whigs were Jacobins and this greatly tickled his fancy; so much so that he made the Emperor once join in his badinage against me on the subject. I have at last made him understand that the *outs* are always the Jacobins; and I am sure he would gladly hear of a change of administration, that he might hail Lord Cathcart in his new character.

I should not be surprised, however, if his wit were some day repeated in England as serious proof of my being *partout* recognised by my language as an *élève* of Bernadotte's school.

The banquet was really magnificent.[2] The Grand Duchesses and Prince Louis of Würtemberg were present, with all the Sovereigns, Princes, &c. Of the English, Lord Cathcart and myself only were guests.

At length we have received papers to the 12th of November.

John Bull is always honest John, but not wiser than before. Experience has the least influence on him of any of the moral powers of direction. I am sorry to observe, however, more bad language, more filth than usual passing between the antagonistic parties.

The contest whether Buonaparte is to be killed, and if killed, *eaten*, &c. &c. &c., amuses us much here. We all wish either or both events, but we recollect that the direction of Mrs. Glasse[3] is 'first to catch him.'

Much is done; more may be done; but we shall all be *undone* if we do not investigate causes as well as effects.

If I were member of a Government, I would grapple to my friendship with hooks of steel that man who could tell me and would tell me only truth; but I remember what old Lord Lansdowne always said to me when he spoke about public life—"Never give a minister counsel and above all avoid unpleasing information.

---

[1] Count Alexei Andreivich Arakchiew had been War Minister till 1810.

[2] In a letter to his brother Edward, Wilson wrote: "It is necessary that I should feast myself into a little more *embonpoint*, for otherwise I shall not have sufficient carcase to suspend my tackling upon."

[3] Hannah Glasse, whose books *The Art of Cookery made Plain and Easy* and *The Servant's Directory, or Housekeeper's Companion* appeared in 1747 and 1770.

When you write it, you sign your sentence of excommunication. Agreeable fiction will never be cited against you except as patriotic and laughable errors of zeal. Unsatisfactory predictions when verified will only create or aggravate ill-will and accelerate its effects."

8th—I discovered that both Lord Cathcart and Sir C. Stewart deem me too friendly to Austria and think that I have too much influence with Aberdeen; they therefore seek to remove me. Cathcart offered me to go to the Elbe or Italy, but under most confined instructions and *his* orders. Stewart thinks I might do political mischief with Bellegarde and he wishes me to remain with the Russian advanced guard, as I was serving previously to the Austrian campaign.

The Emperors, &c., wish me to gain time, and with time I am assured the position I coveted; but a letter from Lord Castlereagh to Aberdeen, dated the 30th, evidently supposes that I have accepted the Italian service and explains to Aberdeen that private arrangements prevented any alteration of Burghersh's appointment.

Stewart, indeed, told me that it was a very old political engagement, almost coeval with Castlereagh's own appointment; he is very angry at the measures which have been taken to show the inconvenience resulting to the service from its maintenance to my exclusion, as it embarrasses his brother.

The Austrian Emperor, Metternich, and Schwarzenberg, Duca, Radetsky, &c., &c., are very seriously displeased at a transaction which they think proves ill-will to them, as I was their friend and a common friend. The same feelings prevail in other high quarters, but it is impossible for me to resist power under the action of political and personal jealousies; I see no alternative but to accept the Italian service and linger on the Continent in the hope of a more favourable gale to conduct my vessel where I would moor her. I fear from a paragraph in Jemima's letter of the 22nd of November that if I resigned and went to England I should be shipped off to some remote settlement.

Patience and suffering must, in the long-run, make my public claims more conspicuous. Cathcart's plaudits, so long withheld, have more importance than if they had been noted in detail; but I suppose I am the first instance where the services of two years have been suffered to aggregate in silence.

I hear that Cathcart is to be made an Earl and Stewart a Peer! He deserves it most, I think, for converting the Hanau defeat into a victory with a loss of thirty thousand men to the enemy. These are services of magnitude rendered to a Government and they merit adequate recompense. Cathcart has been the attendant upon a successful Emperor and I think his elevation not unsuitable.

I have just seen another note of Lord Castlereagh's which observes that "if I have the confidence of all other Governments, &c., I want that of my own." There is no harm in that remark. I expect and seek no intimate connection: I would have none that even appeared to be a party tie. I require only justice, and that good or ill should be meted out to me according to my merits or demerits as a public servant.

Bellegarde goes tomorrow. He has given me a most cordial invitation, and I think we should be good friends.

Dec. 17th, Freyburg.

On the evening of Saturday the 12th, General Merfeldt and I left Frankfort. We slept at Darmstadt—a most excellent town. On the 13th we proceeded to Mannheim, the best-built city in Germany; all the streets at right-angles. The enemy's posts were on the opposite banks of the Rhine.

It is here, perhaps, that the European olive-branch may be planted; in which case the parties should subscribe to the rebuilding of the palace which was burnt during the siege.

The next day we passed through Carlsruhe, which is now the chief residence of the Grand Duke. Here were assembled the King and Queen of Bavaria, the deposed Queen of Sweden, and the adopted daughter of Buonaparte as Grand Duchess—Stephanie-Pagani. Notwithstanding the beauty of the ladies and the interest of the group, I did not think it the moment to pay my court. I was assured a most cordial reception, from various reasons, and particularly from the favourable impression which I know remains of Louisa and her family; but I had more potent considerations which determined me to defer the interview. Hereafter I shall be very desirous of having that interview with a part of this family. I should have thought that the Emperor Alexander would rather have declined a residence in this quarter, but he will remain here for a few days.

After a short rest at Carlsruhe, to look at the palace, &c., we went on to Eppenheim. The next day we passed Turenne's Pyramid near Katzbach, and the village of Ettlingen whence the Duc D'Enghien was carried off to be murdered at Paris.

Yesterday morning we reached Freyburg, after a journey through one of the finest countries I ever saw, and which presented all the characteristics of a Government well administered for the mutual interests of Sovereign and people.

The Emperor Francis had arrived the day before us, and had been received by the inhabitants of this town—which had long been the property of his House—with a joy that, if possible, exceeded all preceding greetings.

Schwarzenberg, &c., have already been here several days and our meeting was a most sincere pleasure to me, and, I believe, to all, since my absence had excited an apprehension that I had been detained altogether by Cathcart.

The news of the day is that the Rhine is to be passed near Basle on the 20th, when the siege of Huningen,[1] where the French have a garrison of five thousand men, is to be formed. Giulai's corps is to undertake the siege, and the main army is to cover it by advancing into France to the River Doubs.

It is pretended that the Swiss will not oppose the passage; that the enemy are very weak and only preparing the formation of an army at Beauvais; that there is nothing to fear on the side of Kehl, &c.; and that even the French will join the Allied standard. I state what I hear, not what I believe or calculate.

The Allies will muster about a hundred and forty thousand men for the operation if the Russians acquiesce in the movement.

Dec. 22nd, Basle.

I quitted Freyburg this morning. Our time had passed interestingly: every night Stadion received, and all the political and military chieftains assembled.

Wine is said to unlock the heart, but I thought that a pipe on this occasion answered better. I am sure that it will pick the most diplomatic German Bramah.[2]

I had promised Cathcart to come direct to Basle, without visiting Schwarzenberg, whose headquarters were on the left of the route at Löerach. Burghersh's unhandsome remonstrances against even my appearance in Schwarzenberg's presence induced my commander, for the sake of keeping the peace, to urge this request.

On coming near Basle I was told that I must pass through Löerach, as the guns of Huningen played at half-grape distance on the regular chaussée: but I preferred keeping my word. I confess that the passage was nervous—more so than when running the Glogau gauntlet, as the distance was less and our horses were knocked up. I calculated on leaving my carriage at least as a target, but, fortun-

---

[1] A town on the Rhine north of Basle.
[2] A reference to the Yorkshire engineer and inventor, Joseph Bramah (1748–1841) who had patented a lock as well as a hydraulic press.

ately, the enemy neither fired musketry nor cannon against us, although they had before swept everything in motion from the road and although they had a good quarter of an hour's command of our track.

The people here would scarcely believe that we had passed as we pretended and the incident has augmented the number of pre-destinarians.

Basle seemed to frown on us all as unwelcome guests, and I understand that when the troops entered there was no sign of good will.

I have already spoken with several well-informed men of various classes, and they all declare that they feel ashamed of the situation in which they are placed by the variance of their conduct with the decree of the Diet.

The whole population publicly express their consciousness of a sale having been made of their Swiss neutrality by the Berne deputies; and they already denounce the presumed traitors, among whom they name Count Salis (but I believe there they are wrong, for his motives were not avaricious) and they boast that they did not dare to pass through Basle in the daytime.

From what I hear and see, I think it not impossible that there will be even yet an insurrection in Switzerland; but I am sure that, if we retire, woe will betide us and our agents in retreat.

Unfortunately, the Cossacks began last night to pillage and three houses in the Basle district were sacked. A few repetitions, and Buonaparte need not employ a Frenchman against this army.

I presume that the siege of Huningen will begin in a few days. I passed the 18-pounders and the mortars four miles from this place. It is, however, hoped that a golden shower may beat down all the bars to our entrance before iron shot is hurled at them.

Huningen is yet a virgin fortress. Vauban[1] built it and the site is excellent, but the works have been neglected. If the garrison, however, do their duty, it will be difficult for our 18-pounders to make any impression. I should hope more from escalade.

Basle is an ugly old town, but I am lodged in one of the best houses with fire-places, and nothing but the pleasure of riding *en maître* in France would console me for relinquishing them during the month of January.

I still feel the icy paw of last year's winter in the ankle injured by the droska summerset and the Lützen impression has made the bone of my left leg quite a barometer.

---

[1] Sébastien de Vauban (1633–1707), the great French military engineer, who built or strengthened numerous fortresses as well as conducting forty sieges.

December 25th, 1813

25th—The day before yesterday I went to dine with the Marshal, and yesterday reconnoitred the fortress of Huningen very close and with usual good fortune. The Marshal came to dine with me, but, just as we were sitting down, the enemy made a sortie. It was, however, of small importance: I had in the morning predicted the intention and warned the posts which I thought required better arrangement.

In the evening I received instructions from England which appointed me military resident at the Italian army to correspond direct with the British Government; and only to keep the Ambassador of Austria informed but not to be under his control. This is a clause of no consequence while Aberdeen remains, as we are on terms that require no such powers of independence.

Lord Castlereagh also notes that my income will be suitably augmented by a bât and forage allowance to meet the exigency of extraordinary expenses. On the whole, neither the spirit nor the letter of the instructions is liable to objection; but I thought it right to record the feelings of regret which attend my removal from the Allied army. I hope that I have done so with temper and success.

I shall send Charles tomorrow to Lord Aberdeen to learn where I shall present myself, as the headquarters of the Emperors may be moving and I have no wish to wander about—losing time when interesting operations are before me.

I went this day to communicate the instructions to Prince Schwarzenberg, and he has settled to come and dine with me the day after tomorrow, when he will bring me the letters which his friendship will dictate and note the line of march which I must take and the one by which I must send my horses, &c.

I do not dwell on the regret my departure occasions: it is sincere and most flattering.

I presume that I shall leave this on the 28th and be fairly on my road about the 2nd of January. The leave-taking at the Imperial headquarters is a ceremony full of pain which I would avoid if possible, but I cannot do so.

I shall endeavour to keep myself in the thoughts of all, though separated without the prospect of reunion in the course of this war, and finish my Continental career with the approbation of sovereigns, chiefs and soldiery abroad.

The movements of the enemy on the side of Strasburg have induced the Prince-Marshal to forbear from entering Switzerland in person. It appears that an attempt is probably in progress for the relief of Huningen, which is to be besieged in three or four days.

Three thousand horse have already fallen in with Colonel Scheubler's cavalry detachment, wounded him and many other officers, and put their whole party to flight. This occurred yesterday near Colmar. Wrede also, who has forty thousand men to besiege and cover the siege of Huningen, had detached ten thousand to Belfort: these are recalled. If the enemy can muster an equal force to Wrede's before the Russian reserve is up to support him, I speculate upon Wrede's being beaten: for although a most gallant, he is a most unskilful, officer. I do not feel confidence in any of his dispositions, nor much in the military conduct of the Bavarians. The Commandant of Huningen has made several gallant sorties, in which he has worsted them; and if his stores are not deficient or his aids perfidious, he will make a memorable defence should they be the only assailants. The Commandant has begun like a chief determined to do his duty. Although an enemy, he is entitled to this encomium.

The instructions from England prevent my going on the expedition as I proposed; but I had intended to attempt the destruction of a manufactory of arms near Strasburg and to gain the high road on which I might have reason to believe that Buonaparte would be travelling. I have, however, taken several rides in Alsace, and the country presents no features of distress. The towns and villages are partially such as would honour any district in England and in none is there any appearance of decay. The land is universally cultivated, and there seems no want of husbandmen or deficiency of children from infancy to manhood.

I do not believe that the damsels have suffered any privations from the war.

It is true that I have not been over a considerable tract of country, but I have seen enough to enable me to judge of the accuracy of what I have heard from others, and it is quite at variance with British general opinions as to the state of the French empire.

Dec. 30th, Freyburg.

Last night the bombardment of Huningen commenced; about fifty guns opened their fire. I went into the trenches (the first parallel) and remained until near three o'clock this morning, being ashamed to leave them, although I was very much vexed at seeing them so ill-constructed as to present scarcely any defence. The town was fired, but about the time I went away our guns relaxed their fire, and in a short time the cannonade was very partial. The principal batteries of the besiegers (all Bavarians) were on the right bank of the Rhine, whence they never can make any serious impression; and through the whole plan I never saw more unskilful arrangements. Huningen will never be taken by such means as are now used, since gold will not combine and science is wanting. The whole operation is Bavarian, no other interference has been allowed hitherto.

The return was not very easy on an unruly horse through a cross-fire of apparently *singing and skipping Moons*; but notwithstanding that my steed, like the Russians at Borodino, was "unable to stay and unwilling to go," I at last got him with myself disentangled and at daybreak I set off for Freyburg to pay my last devoirs and receive farewell honours.

I found Aberdeen who, as usual, imparted pleasure by his society, though he could not impart comfort. It appears that Lord Castlereagh considers the application that has been made for my stay as an unwarrantable interference, and that these proofs of esteem here are additional causes for my removal.

There was a grand ball given to the Sovereigns, but having read my letters and seen the papers announcing poor Bosville's[1] death— and a great blank in the future comforts of my London residence by the loss of a friend whom I sincerely valued, whose real worth I know to have been great—and with whom I had such habitude of intercourse—I had no heart for public amusement. In the evening I went to Stadion's and rejoined the circle of the *élite*. My announced early departure was received with regret.

The cold weather has been rather favourable than otherwise to the troops; but sickness is still prevalent, as most of them are very young.

When in the trenches the night before last, I found that the men had been forty-eight hours on duty in them without fires or warm food during the whole of that time, notwithstanding severe frost and dense cold fogs. With such service it is impossible but that at last there must be a considerable sick-list.

I was sorry to find on my arrival here that the Crown Prince had refused to accept the terms agreed to by Denmark; that Russia had again supported the claim to Norway; and that the Austrian Government in despair had abandoned the subject. Norway loses us the Low Countries and probably Holland.

Every day increases the political difficulties of our edifice. The Swedes, the Swiss, the Saxons, and Poland, are all intricate embarrassments; and the King of Würtemberg has augmented the chaos by carrying on, it is said, a correspondence with the enemy. His ill-will had long been expressed.

---

[1] Wilson's sister Frances had married, first, Colonel Bosville of the Coldstream Guards, who was killed in 1793. The Bosville referred to was his brother.

1814

Jan. 2nd, 1814—Yesterday morning I went to see the Russian grenadiers pass with sixty cannon. When it is recollected whence they have come, what they have done, and where they are, the order and condition of men and horses is quite marvellous.

The Emperor of Austria gave a dinner to the Emperor of Russia. I had in the morning been with Aberdeen to be presented as accredited to the Italian army and had a long conversation on the subject of peace and war, &c. The Emperor spoke with much good sense; saw the difficulties of protracted contest, but the necessity of such a peace only as would assure some time of repose and make the future chances of war equal at the outset. He said that Buonaparte having agreed to the basis, and proclaimed to France that he had done so, could not retreat; but that preliminaries of peace might be signed by the negotiators in three days if they chose to avoid forms which are by no means requisite.

I could not help observing that Buonaparte was *ab origine* and emphatically a military chief, and that if the term of pacification was protracted until he found himself again at the head of an effective army it was to be apprehended that warlike feelings would prevail over political considerations.

The Emperor perfectly agreed and said: "The sight of an army is a temptation that Buonaparte never can resist."

We had but a small party at dinner. In the evening I went to the Emperor of Russia to take leave: the Grand Duke was present. The Emperor would not believe that I was ordered away and expressed much dissatisfaction, until I told him that my instructions were dated the 10th, and his letter did not reach England until the 13th— which Balachiew told me. He felt confident that I should be recalled, and asked me to return if he sent for me, which of course I promised to do. He then added: "You have always proved yourself my friend. You have in the field shown the ardour of your regard; and you have in your communications always told me truth. You have maintained the credit of your country, and at all times proved how much you have respected its interests." He then, as is usual in like cases, kissed me several times, and so did the Grand Duke afterwards; but the Emperor did not choose that his brother should give the last greeting, and so repeated his salutations.[1]

I had scarcely got to Aberdeen's, who, of course, feels much interest in all these *soutiens* of his representations, when I received the Grand Cross of the Order of St. Anne from the Emperor, and had an *avis* that the letter[2] would be transmitted in the morning.

I put on the star[3] in compliment and went to the ball given by Lord Cathcart (strange to record). I then made my bow to the Emperor and expressed my acknowledgments.

The Emperor of Austria during the evening engaged me again in a long conversation, which ended by the observation: "I have a consolation in thinking that you will not make a long sacrifice, for the war must speedily end; and I beg you to come to Vienna on your way home, although even then I hope your absence will be short. The oftener you come to the continent the better."

He then hinted that he should send in the morning some public proof of his regard.

I mention these speeches not from any silly feeling, but to show that I have preserved the good-will of the chiefs under whom I have been serving, and to offer some consolation for the hostile measures of my own Government.

I know in general that phrases are not sincere, but such phrases, accompanied by acts, after a knowledge of my position at home, certainly evince sincerity and substantial *bienveillance*. Government may consider these favours, &c., as an additional evidence of my being '*un enfant gâté*,' but all here know that I have not acquired them without connecting the honour of my country. I owe nothing to a crooking knee or a false tongue—nothing to any conduct which can stain hereafter.

5th—Metternich not having returned, I was obliged to remain the day in a species of incognito as far as concerned the Sovereigns, since I had avoided all further interviews, dinners, &c., by announcing my early departure; but the Chancellor Hardenburg required me to dine with him, and I complied in order that he might see that,

[1] Wilson met the Emperor again in July 1814 and wrote: "The best personal friend could not have been more affectionate in his welcome, or more gracious in his references to the past. He took me afterwards by the hand, led me to the Empress, and told her to regard me as his faithful companion of arms."

[2] The Emperor Alexander said he wished to give yet another proof of his satisfaction with Wilson's conduct, his zeal and his outstanding valour. "The fine men with whom you have so often fought will miss you. As for myself, I shall always remember your courage and your tireless activity."

[3] Colonel Neil Campbell wrote: "The badge is worn round the neck, suspended by a red ribbon with yellow edges. It is supposed to be in diamonds and precious stones, which, however, are only imitation; and there is a cross in the centre, set in gold."

although I had much cause to complain of a Prussian general's conduct, I did not extend any ill-will. I gave the Chancellor a letter for the King, in which I alluded again to the representations of General Gneisenau as the principal cause of a failure in the attempt to alter my destination, but added that this inconsiderate accusation did but augment my ambition to promote the general interests, and particularly to prove that my attachment, &c., to him was invariable.

We assembled at Stadion's and Metternich arrived, but too late to transact a business in hand, yet I would not remain any longer; so, obtaining my letters of accreditation, &c., I set off at one o'clock in the morning. I had withdrawn from Stadion's without bidding the last farewell—I could not; but it was otherwise with Aberdeen, who accompanied me home. Lord Castlereagh will find, I think, when he arrives at headquarters, that he will not be able to dislodge me from that regard.

We passed Huningen very much dependent on French forbearance—which we found and at this I confess myself surprised after our nocturnal bombardments.

6th—This morning, as the firing increased, I went into the trenches; but I found that we were only endeavouring from the opposite bank to destroy some boats and that we had made no progress in the works. I wished to reconnoitre along the bank of the river as there are some who pretend that the place is vulnerable on the water-line. My stars, &c., however, were too refulgent, and I was obliged to get back again into the trenches to the regret of the enemy, who wished to mount me to Paradise either on great or small shot.

On my return I took post and went to Altkirch, where I dined and took leave of Schwarzenberg, Radetsky, and others: each giving me a cordon of Maria Theresa and a farewell that is indelibly stamped on my memory.

Circumstances have made my removal more sensibly felt and rendered the arrangements of the British Government more unpopular. There is an expression in Schwarzenberg's letter to Bellegarde which I cannot help recording: "*Vous trouverez en lui un Anglais assez fier pour croire que sa patrie s'étend sur l'Europe entière, et que le bonheur insulaire ne doit pas être l'unique bon action de vrai patriote Anglais.*"

THE END

BIBLIOGRAPHY

Annual Register, or a View of the History, Politics, and Literature for the Year 1816 (1817).

Burghersh, Lord: *Memoir of the Operations of the Allied Armies under Prince Schwarzenberg and Marshal Blücher during the latter end of 1813–14.*

Campbell, Major-General Sir Neil: *Napoleon at Fontainebleau and Elba. Being a Journal of Occurrences in 1814–1815 with notes of Conversations.* With a Memoir by his Nephew, A. N. C. Maclachlan (1869).

Cathcart, Colonel the Hon. George: *Commentaries on the War in Russia and Germany in 1812 and 1813* (1850).

Dundonald, Thomas, 10th Earl of: *The Autobiography of a Seaman* [Admiral Lord Cochrane] (2 vols., 1860).

Jackson: *The Bath Archives. A Further Selection from the Diaries and Letters of Sir George Jackson, K.C.H., from 1809 to 1816* (2 vols., 1873).

Lavallette: *Mémoires et Souvenirs du Comte Lavallette* (Paris, 1905).

Londonderry, Lieut.-General Charles William Vane, Marquess of: *Narrative of the War in Germany and France in 1813 and 1814* (1830).

Public Characters of 1807 (1807).

Royal Military Chronicle or British Officer's Monthly Register and Mentor (vol. 3, 1811, vol. 5, 1812).

Stanhope: *Memoirs of Anna Maria Wilhelmina Pickering, together with Extracts from the Journals of her Father John Spencer Stanhope, F.R.S., describing his Travels and Imprisonments under Napoleon* (1903).

Warre, Lieut.-Gen. Sir William: *Letters from the Peninsula, 1808–1812.* Edited by his Nephew, the Rev. Edmond Warre (1909).

Wellington: *Supplementary Despatches, Correspondence and Memoranda of Field Marshal Arthur Duke of Wellington* (vol. 8, 1861).

Werry: *Personal Memoirs and Letters of Francis Peter Werry*, Attaché to the British Embassies at St. Petersburgh and Vienna in 1812–1815. Edited by his Daughter (1861).

Wilson, Sir Robert: *Brief Remarks on the Character and Composition of the Russian Army, and a Sketch of the Campaigns in Poland in the Years 1806 and 1807* (1810).

Wilson, Lieut.-Colonel Sir Robert: *History of the British Expedition to Egypt* (1802).

Wilson: *Life of General Sir Robert Wilson, from Autobiographical Memoirs, Journals, Narratives, Correspondence, &c.* Edited by his Nephew and Son-in-Law, the Rev. Herbert Randolph (2 vols., 1862).

Wilson, General Sir Robert: *Narrative of Events during the Invasion of Russia by Napoleon Bonaparte, and the Retreat of the French Army, 1812.* Edited by his Nephew and Son-in-Law, the Rev. Herbert Randolph (1860).

PERSONAL INDEX

Aberdeen, George Hamilton Gordon, Earl of, 14, 181–2, 192, 206–11, 216, 218–20, 225, 229, 231–4
Abercromby, General Sir Ralph, 5
Adair, Mrs. Angélique Gabrielle, 98
Adair, Mr., later Sir Robert, 98
Alexander the Great, 49
Alexander I, Emperor of all the Russias, 11, 16–18, 20, 30, 35–39, 42, 53, 55, 70, 72, 75, 91, 94, 95, 97, 98, 101–2, 114, 117–19, 129, 132, 139–44, 147, 152, 155–6, 162–3, 165–6, 169–71, 173–4, 176–7, 179, 181, 185, 187, 190–4, 203–4, 211, 217, 219–24, 226, 232–3
Allen, Wilson's orderly, 23, 50, 119, 126, 182–4, 211
Alopeus, David, Baron d', 122
Amande, General, 56–7
Amelia, Princess, 38–9
Angoulême, Louis Antoine de Bourbon, Duke of, 149, 150
Arakchiew, Alexei Andreiwich, Count, 224
Arnsted, Baron, 107–8
Artois, Louis Charles Philippe, Count of, 149, 150
Augerausky, General Count, 81, 142
Augereau, General Jean-Pierre, 76, 85

Bagawouth, General, 61
Bagration, General Prince Peter Ivanovich, 29, 35, 43, 50, 120
Baird, Lt.-Gen. Sir David, 6
Baltier, General, 62
Barclay de Tolly, General Prince Michael, 16, 29–31, 34, 35, 52, 97, 137, 144, 151–2, 155, 169, 173, 178
Beauharnais, Prince Eugène de, 17, 19, 20, 64, 69, 80
Bellegarde, Marshal Count Henri de, 14, 222, 225–6, 234
Bellingham, John, 36
Bennigsen, General Count Levin August Theophil, 18, 28, 31–33, 36, 42, 54, 59–61, 65, 67, 73–75, 81, 82, 97, 151, 187, 191, 193, 200, 203
Bentinck, Lt.-Gen. Lord William Cavendish, 19
Beresford, Lt.-Gen. (Marshal) Sir William Carr, 7
Bernadotte, Charles-Jean, Marshal of France, later King Charles XIV of Sweden, 17, 18, 113, 151, 158–9, 172, 184, 187, 191–2, 197, 200–2, 204, 210, 212, 221, 224, 231

Berthier, Alexandre, Marshal of France, 185, 195, 199
Bethmann, Madame Louise Friederike, 215, 217
Bethmann, Mr. Simon Moritz, 215–17
Bidwell, John, 154
Biron, Prince, 156
Birt, Mr., 35
Blücher, General Gebhard Leberecht von, 18–20, 126, 140, 172, 176–7, 184, 187, 196–8, 200, 202–5, 222
Bolingbroke, Henry, Viscount, 199
Bonaparte, François-Charles-Joseph, Roi de Rome, 195
Bonaparte, Jerome, King of Westphalia, 114, 210
Bonaparte, Joseph, King of Spain, 159
Bonaparte, Lucien, 35
Bonaparte, Napoleon. See Napoleon I.
Borasdin, General Mikhail, 150
Bosville, Colonel, 88, 91, 231
Bowles, Captain William, 39
Bramah, Mr. Joseph, 227
Brandenburg, Countess of, 155
Brinken, Baron, 33, 40, 66, 69, 70, 91, 115, 132, 153, 178, 184, 192, 216
Bruce, Michael, 7
Bubna-Littiz, General Baron Ferdinand, 118, 146
Budberg, Baron, 108
Bülow von Dennewitz, General Count Friedrich Wilhelm, 17–19
Burghersh, Lt.-Col. John Fane, Baron, later Earl of Westmorland, 207, 209, 216, 217, 219, 225, 227
Burghersh, Priscilla, Lady, 207, 223
Byron, George Gordon, Baron, 127

Campbell, Col., later General Sir Neil, 128, 132, 139, 144
Camus, General, 84
Canning, George, 6
Canute, King, 65
Caroline, Queen, 9
Cassewitch, General, 67, 82
Castlereagh, Robert Stewart, Viscount, 10, 11, 20, 91, 135, 143, 208–9, 216, 218, 225–6, 229, 231, 234
Cathcart, Frederick, 39
Cathcart, George, later Lt.-Gen. Sir George, 39, 154
Cathcart, Lt.-Gen. William Schaw, Viscount, later Earl, 14, 37, 39, 40, 51, 55, 62, 63, 65, 66, 70, 91, 108–9, 115–17,

Cathcart, Lt.-Gen.—*contd.*
  128–9, 131, 143, 146–7, 151, 155, 158,
  160, 170, 179, 182, 190, 197, 207, 210,
  217–18, 224–7, 233
Catherine II, the Great, Empress of
  Russia, 28
Caulaincourt, Armand de, Duke of
  Vicenza, 72
Charles V, Emperor, 211
Charles XII, King of Sweden, 205
Charles, Captain, 100–3, 106, 119, 126,
  131–3, 153, 161, 167, 178, 192, 207,
  229
Charlotte, Princess, 76, 161
Charnhotzh, General, 132
Chasteler de Courcelles, Johann Gabriel,
  Marquis du, 182
Chevers, Colonel, 67
Cibber, Colley, 125
Clarke, Dr. Edward Daniel, 49, 96
Clarke, General Henri-Jacques-Guillaume,
  61, 66
Cochrane, Admiral Thomas, Earl of
  Dundonald, 9
Colloredo-Mannsfeld, General Count
  Hieronymus, 167, 186, 200
Constantine, Grand Duke, 35, 40, 74, 91,
  97, 128–9, 152, 155, 172, 179, 187, 190,
  224, 232–3
Cooke, Colonel Henry, 158, 161, 167,
  174–5
Cumberland, Ernest Augustus, Duke of,
  9, 161, 177–8, 180–1, 183, 187
Czartorysky, Marshal Adam George, 108
Czartorysky, Princess, 67

Danskow, Princess, 81
Daun, Count Leopold Joseph von, 136
Davout, Louis Nicholas, Marshal of
  France, Prince of Eckmühl, 48, 57, 63,
  69, 80, 89, 113, 133, 198, 203, 213
Dawson, Captain George Lionel, 39, 51,
  79, 87, 91, 92, 99, 102, 132, 154, 178, 192
Dering, Captain, 167
Desgenettes, Baron René-Nicolas Dufriche,
  96, 97, 99
Dessau Anhalt, Duke of, 122
Dokhturow, General Dmitri Sergeiwich,
  32, 62, 64, 100, 106, 151
Dollond, Peter, 52
Dombrowski, General Jan Henryk, 82, 83
Dorokow, General Ivan Semenowich, 60
Duka von Kadar, Freiherr Peter, 225
D'Urban, Major-General Sir Benjamin, 7

Elliott, 61, 66
Enghien, Louis-Antoine-Henri de Bourbon-
  Condé, Duke of, 226
Ertel, General, 82, 100
Esterhazy, Prince Paul, 162, 165

Fanshaw, Captain, 55, 61, 114
Faustenberg, Princess, 157

Ferdinand, King of the Two Sicilies, 10
Ferrier, General, 48
Fontanges, Captain Amable-Hugues de, 99
Francis II, Emperor of Austria, 5, 125,
  145–6, 159, 177, 180, 188, 202, 206, 232
Frederick II, the Great, King of Prussia,
  18, 119, 121, 136
Frederick Augustus IV, King of Saxony,
  150
Frederick William IV, King of Prussia,
  16, 17, 102, 110, 113–14, 117, 130, 135,
  141, 145, 147–8, 152, 156, 161–2, 171,
  175, 180, 187, 193, 206, 219, 221
Fresnel, General Ferdinand Peter, Count
  Hennequin de, 206, 212, 215
Fulford, Roger, 161

Galitzin, General Prince, 29–31, 52, 175
Galitzin, Princess, 38
Gardiner, Lt.-Gen. William, 87
George III, King, 76, 146, 161
Giulai von Maros-Németh und Nádaska,
  General Count Franz, 200, 202, 207
Glasse, Mrs. Hannah, 224
Gloucester, William Henry, Duke of, 11,
  14, 15, 92, 139
Gneisenau, General Count August Neit-
  hardt von, 222, 234
Goethe, Johann Wolfgang von, 206
Golz, Countess, 156
Gordon, Mr. Robert, 131
Gortschakow, General Prince, 40
Gotha, Duke of, 126, 208
Grey, Charles, Earl, 8, 10, 15, 92

Hake, General Karl Georg Albrecht Ernst
  von, 213
Hamilton, William, 70, 108
Hammersley, 88
Hardenberg, Karl August, Prince von,
  179, 180, 184–5, 189, 233
Hely-Hutchinson, Captain John, 7, 8
Herod, King of the Jews, 101
Holland, Henry Edward Fox, Baron, 8
Hutchinson, General John Hely-, Baron,
  later Earl of Donoughmore, 6, 15, 61

Ilovaisky, General, 130

Jackson, Mr., later Sir George, 12, 37,
  135, 190
James, John, 138, 154, 192
Jomini, General Baron Henri, 163, 171
Joséphine de Beauharnais, ex-Empress of
  France, 69

Kamenskoi, General, 85
Kanow, General, 106
Keate, Thomas, 52
Keating, Colonel, later General, 42, 79
Kellermann, General François-Etienne,
  193, 195, 203, 213
Kinnaird, Douglas, 174
Kleinau (*correctly* Klenau), General Count
  Johann, 164–6, 184–5, 200

Personal Index

Kleist von Nollendorf, General Count Friedrich Heinrich Emil, 99, 102, 137, 140, 166, 169, 176, 185

Knoring, General, 88

Korff, General Baron Feodor Karlowich, 56, 73

Kreutzer, General, 186

Kutusow, Colonel, 26

Kutusow, Marshal Prince Mikhail Hilarionovich Golenischew, 16, 36, 40–44, 47, 48, 53–55, 58, 59, 65–68, 70, 72, 77, 78, 80, 91, 95, 101, 106, 116, 133

Labanow, Prince Alexander, 46

Lambert, General Count, 82, 83

Langeron, General Count Alexandre Arnault, 83, 84, 155

Lansdowne, Lord, 224

Lanskoi, General, 27, 85, 151

Lauriston, General Jacques-Alexandre-Bernard Law, Marquis de, 54, 55, 201, 204

Lavallette, Antoine-Marie, Count, 7, 8

Legrand, General Juste-Claude-Alexandre-Louis, 84

Lichtenstein, Prince Louis, 189

Lichtenstein, Prince Maurice, 167–8, 189

Lieven, Prince Christopher, 159, 221

Lieven, Princess Dorothea, 159

Liston, Mrs. Henrietta, 22, 23

Liston, Mr. Robert, 7, 14, 22, 23, 26, 57, 58, 97

Louis XVIII, King of France, 20

Louisa, Princess of Prussia. See Radziwil.

Lowenhjelm, Count Gustav, 210

Macdonald, Alexandre, Marshal of France, 18, 85, 136

Mack, Field-Marshal Karl von, 149

Mahmoud II, Grand Signior and Sultan, 21

Mahomet, 26

Manteuffel, Count, 27

Maria Carolina, Queen of the Two Sicilies, 10

Marie Louise, Empress of France, 17, 125, 145, 195

Markow, General, 43

Marmont, Auguste, Marshal of France, 39, 55, 77, 178

Masséna, André, Marshal of France, 64

Merfeldt, General Count Maximilian von, 186, 200, 202, 226

Merle, General, 84

Metsko, General, 165

Metternich, Count Clemens Lothar Wenzel, 14, 17, 145–6, 152, 163, 180–1, 191, 195–6, 202, 209–11, 214, 216–18, 220, 222, 225, 233–4

Meyer, General Josef, 109

Milaradowitch, General Mikhail Andreivich, 38, 43, 48, 50, 56, 58, 69, 70, 73, 76–78, 92, 106–7, 119, 126–7, 134–5, 139, 142

Mongelas, Count Maximilian von, 212

Moore, Lt.-Gen. Sir John, 6, 10

Moreau, General Jean Victor, 158–9, 162–3, 166, 168–71, 181

Morier, David, 207

Morland, 103

Mozart, Wolfgang Amadeus, 215

Müller, Mr. 215

Münster, Count Ernst Friedrich Herbert von, 221–2

Murad, Prince, 22

Murat, Joachim, Marshal of France, King of Naples, 45, 48, 51, 54–58, 60, 61, 69, 194

Napoleon I, Emperor of France, 16–20, 33, 36, 45, 47, 48, 53, 57, 59, 61, 66, 68, 78–82, 85, 86, 89, 97, 98, 100, 102, 110, 117–18, 125, 127, 129, 133, 135, 137, 140–1, 145–6, 151–2, 158, 160, 163–5, 172, 179, 183–6, 188, 191, 193–5, 197, 199, 201–4, 211–16, 226, 228, 230, 232

Nesselrode, Count Karl Vasilievich, 147

Nevsky, Alexander, 40

Ney, Michel, Marshal of France, 7, 19, 79, 80, 89, 137, 163, 199

Nithsdale, Winifred, Countess of, 8

Nostitz-Rieneck, General Count Johann von, 219

Nowosiltzow, Nicholas, 28, 111, 151

O'Donnell, Colonel, 98, 113

Oldenburg, Duke of, 14, 35, 47, 50, 54, 56, 58, 60, 65

Orsinew, Madame, 157

Ostermann-Tolstoy, General Count Alexander Ivanovitch, 53, 76, 141, 173, 176, 193

Oudinot, Nicolas Charles, Marshal of France, 18, 84

Ouwarrow, General, 53, 126

Paskewitch, General Ivan Feodorowitch, 106

Perceval, Mr. Spencer, 36

Peter I, the Great, Emperor of Russia, 205

Platow, Matvei Ivanovich, Hetman, 12, 33, 42, 47, 51, 59, 67, 76, 77, 79, 84, 129, 156, 192, 223

Poniatowsky, General Prince Josef Anton, 48, 67, 201, 204

Portarlington, John, Earl of, 39, 51, 79

Potoski, Count Alexander, 48

Potoski, Countess Alexander, 38, 108, 111

Potoski, Countess Serivan, 112

Pozzo di Borgo, Count Carlo Andrea, 117, 210

Prince Regent, later King George IV, 9, 181, 194, 219, 221

Queensberry, William Douglas, Duke of, 196

Radcliffe, Mrs. Anne, 156
Radetsky, General Josef Wenzel, 163–4, 175, 179, 188, 192, 219, 221, 225, 234
Radziwil, Princess Louisa, 111, 112, 122, 159
Radziwil, General Prince, 122
Randolph, Rev. Herbert, 13, 14
Rapp, General Jean-Baptiste, 150
Régnier, General, 89, 110, 113, 204
Richelieu, Armand du Plessis, Duke of, 21
Roedler, Colonel, 149
Roi de Rome. *See* Bonaparte, F. C. J.
Romanzow, Count, 97
Rosslyn, General James St. Clair Erskine, Earl of, 79
Rostopchin, Count Feodor Vasilievich, 38, 42, 45, 47–50
Rousseau, Jean-Jacques, 153

Sacken, General Baron Fabian von der Osten, 82, 89, 100
St. Cyr, General Laurent Gouvion, 83, 178, 204, 213
St. Priest, General Count Emmanuel de, 120, 212
Salis, Count de, 228
Savary, Anne Jean Marie René, 68, 215
Scheubler, Colonel, 230
Schiller, Friedrich, 205
Schroetter, 101
Schwarzenberg, Marshal Prince Karl Philipp, 18–20, 89, 107, 109, 148, 162, 169, 171, 174, 179, 183–9, 193–6, 198–200, 203, 207, 209, 210, 214, 216, 218–22, 225, 227, 229, 234
Scott, Sir Walter, 8
Siewers, General Count, 32
Sinclair, Sir John, 121
Sislavin, Colonel, 81
Smith, Admiral Sir Sidney, 12
Sobieski, King John III of Poland, 99, 108
Soltikow, Count, 41
Soult, Nicolas, Marshal of France, 7, 165
Stadion-Warthausen, Count Johann Philipp, 136–7, 148, 152, 181, 227, 234
Staël, Madame Germaine de, 38, 39
Stanhope, Lady Hester, 7
Stanhope, Mr. John Spencer, 153
Stein, Karl, Freiherr von, 129, 208
Stewart, Lt.-Gen. Sir Charles William, later Marquess of Londonderry, 12, 135, 137–9, 141–5, 147–8, 154, 158, 161–3, 167–8, 171, 176, 181, 184, 188–9, 191–2, 204–5, 212, 223, 225
Strogonow, General Count Paul, 38, 59
Suwarow, General Alexander, 56

Talleyrand-Périgord, Charles Maurice de, 88, 194–5
Tauenzien, General Friedrich, 149
Tchaplitz, General, 84, 85
Tchernigow, General, 214
Tchernishew, General Alexander, 18

Tchichagow, Admiral Pavel Vasilievich, 26, 51, 57, 58, 66, 68, 82–5, 97, 100–1, 115, 118
Thielmann, General Johann Adolf von, 192
Thurn and Taxis, Princess Therese Mathilde, 162
Tolstoy. *See* Ostermann-Tolstoy
Tormazow, General Count Alexander Petrovich, 46, 82, 90, 91, 99
Tyrconnel, George, Earl of, 36, 40, 42, 51, 57–60, 66, 82, 93, 94, 116

Vandamme, General Dominique-René, 17, 19, 170, 174, 177–8, 183
Vauban, Sébastien de, 228
Vernon, Mr., 137
Victor, Claude Victor Perrin, Marshal of France, 83
Virgil, 97, 119

Wallis, General Lewis Bayly, 123
Walmoden-Gimborn, General Count Ludwig Georg Theodul, 117, 124
Warden, Dr. William, 5
Warre, Major, later Lt.-Gen. Sir William, 11
Wellington, Arthur, Duke of, 8, 39, 126, 135, 159, 165, 207, 223
Weimar, Karl August, Duke of, 206
Weimar, Grand Duchess of, 206
Werry, Francis P., 70, 108, 109
Willeminew, Colonel, 150
Wilson, Edward, 15, 224
Wilson, Harry, 115
Wilson, Jemima, Lady, 9, 15, 208, 225
Winzingerode-Ohmfeld, General Ferdinand von, 113, 124–5, 130–1, 151
Witt, Colonel de, 46
Wittgenstein, General Peter von, 18, 70, 83–5, 100–2, 123–4, 128, 132, 134, 136, 142, 158, 169, 173, 177–8, 185, 196, 198, 200
Wolkonsky, Prince, 54, 55, 123
Woronzow, Count Simon, 31
Woronzow, Marshal, 31, 32, 35, 40, 41, 81, 93
Wrede, General Karl Philipp, 19, 212–13, 215, 223, 230
Würtemberg, Duke Alexander of, 32, 34, 47, 50, 54, 56, 87, 91, 92, 129, 150–1
Würtemberg, Prince Eugene of, 32
Würtemberg, Friedrich Karl Wilhelm, King of, 222, 231
Würtemberg, Prince Louis of, 224
Wyburn, Mr., later Captain, H., 27, 30, 50, 92
Wylie, Dr., later Sir James, 53, 57, 170, 174, 176

Yorck von Wartenburg, General Hans David Ludwig, 16, 17, 99, 124, 137
York and Albany, Field-Marshal Frederick Augustus, Duke of, 36, 129